ALSO BY P. E. CAQUET

The Orient, the Liberal Movement, and the Eastern Crisis of 1839–41

THE BELL OF TREASON

THE BELL OF TREASON

THE 1938 MUNICH AGREEMENT IN CZECHOSLOVAKIA

P. E. CAQUET

PROFILE BOOKS

First published in Great Britain in 2018 by
PROFILE BOOKS LTD
3 Holford Yard
Bevin Way
London WC1X 9HD
www.profilebooks.com

1 3 5 7 9 10 8 6 4 2

Typeset in Garamond by MacGuru Ltd
Printed and bound in Great Britain by Clays, Elcograf S.p.A

A CIP catalogue record for this book is available from the British Library.

ISBN 978 1 78125 710 4
eISBN 978 1 78283 287 4

FSC
www.fsc.org
MIX
Paper from
responsible sources
FSC® C018072

Contents

Acknowledgements

My thanks go first to my editors: Ed Lake, whose comments on the book have been transformative, and John Davey, who first helped me get the project going but sadly passed away before it reached completion. Special mention should be made of the staff at the foreign ministry archives, the AMZV, and the Klementinum site of the Czech national library, who have been friendly and helpful throughout. I am also indebted to Anita Herle for her remarks and insights on anthropology and ethnicity, to Daniel Hucker for his contribution to the book's military chapter, and to my colleagues Mary Laven and Brendan Simms. Jerry and Anne Toner have once again borne with me and supported this endeavour from its conception, and so has my wife Irena. Lastly, I wish to thank my friends in Prague: Tom and Hana Sherwood, Brian and Emilia Wardrop, David Linha, and Petra Tichá.

Note on place names and translation

Many of the towns and villages cited here had both a Czech and a German name at the time this history describes. This book uses Czech names, both for consistency and because these are the names that can be found today. Exceptions are made for places with an accepted and well-recognised English or international name, e.g. Prague, Carlsbad, or Marienbad.

Numerous quotes presented here in English originate in material in Czech, Slovak, French, or German. Unless otherwise noted, they are in the author's translation.

There tolls the bell of treason, the bell of treason
Whose hands have swung its rope?
Sweet France, proud Albion
The very ones we loved

František Halas, 'Zpěv úzkosti'[1]

1

In the boa's gaze

ON SATURDAY, 12 MARCH 1938, the Czechoslovak ambassador in London, Jan Masaryk, called on Lord Halifax, who had recently been appointed foreign secretary. The situation was urgent: as they met, German troops were marching through Austrian territory and towards Vienna. Hitler had finally launched the *Anschluss*, his long-planned annexation of Germany's smaller Alpine neighbour, and in the night his armies had crashed through the German–Austrian border. The European chancelleries were yet to react, and it remained unclear what ramifications the attack might have. That these involved Czechoslovakia, whether as participant in a hypothetical intervention, merely as an interested observer of what went on beyond its southern frontier, or as the target of a further German advance, was not in doubt. Masaryk was concerned that this was only a first step. His hope was to convince his interlocutor to deal with Hitler firmly and ward off any attempts against his own country.

> Halifax: 'I have learnt a lot in the last few days, but I don't want to give up all hope that one day a dialogue will be possible with the Germans.'

Masaryk: 'Once they rule Europe, then yes – until then, only an armed dialogue is possible.'
– You think so?
– I am convinced of it.
– I am new to the job. I only perceived it from a distance before, and even when I went to Berchtesgaden, I did not realise how complicated the situation was, as I do now. I understand, though, that Goering has assured Mastný [the Czechoslovak ambassador in Berlin] that they are not planning anything against Czechoslovakia. What value do you ascribe to that?
– It is momentarily true. Even the boa constrictor, when it has eaten, needs a few weeks of digestion, and today's feast is worthy of Lucullus.
– You are probably right. You said you need some gesture of moral support. I would very much like to help you, but I don't know what I can do.[1]

Halifax was a Conservative peer, Eton- and Oxford-educated, whose long political career had taken in various ministerial posts but whose only overseas stint had been as viceroy of India. He owed his elevation to the desire of his prime minister, Neville Chamberlain, to retain a more direct line of control over foreign policy. His predecessor as foreign secretary, Anthony Eden, had resigned a month before under a cloud, creating a vacancy for a less experienced and therefore more amenable candidate to the post.

Masaryk embodied his small nation's twentieth-century tribulations. The son of Tomáš Garrigue Masaryk, a founding figure of the republic, Jan had been a headstrong youth. Before the First World War, he had emigrated to the United States, leading a penniless existence. On his return he was drafted into the Habsburg armies, where he rose to the rank of lieutenant and earned a medal of valour. After the Great War, with his father now president of a new Czechoslovakia, Masaryk embarked with fresh energy on a diplomatic career. Thanks to his adventures in the US and a brief marriage to an American woman, he boasted a 'fantastic command of any and all shades of the English language; of nuance and argot and profanity and slang in either British or American idiom'.[2] Sometimes nicknamed the 'Playboy of the Western World', he could be at once charming, restless, and plain spoken. It is perhaps this last trait that was most apt to appeal to the hesitant but austere, high-Anglican British lord who was his interlocutor.[3]

Czechoslovakia's motto was 'The truth prevails', taken from the fifteenth-century religious martyr Jan Hus. 'The truth prevails, but it can be such a chore,' Masaryk liked to joke.[4] Would it prove a chore to recruit Halifax to the Czechoslovak cause? In November, still in a private capacity, he had visited Berlin and Berchtesgaden. The pretext was a hunting exhibition given in the German capital. Feted by Nazi dignitaries, the future foreign secretary had posed in front of giant pairs of antlers and revelled in the award of the nickname 'Lord Halalifax', after the hunting cry. The visit to Hitler's mountain residence had been more awkward: the Führer, who felt a strong sympathy for animals, had raged about the hunting show and the pastime itself in equal measure and sarcastically proposed to 'spare ourselves all bother and make a comradely expedition to a slaughterhouse'. Behind his back, he called his visitor 'the English Parson'. Yet Halifax had at least been able to convey, privately, the message he was sent to deliver: 'Danzig, Austria, Czechoslovakia [...] we were not necessarily concerned to stand for the status quo as today, but we were concerned to avoid such treatment of them as would be likely to cause trouble. If reasonable settlements could be reached with the free assent and good will of those primarily concerned we certainly had no desire to block.'[5] In other words, after twenty years of stability, the door to frontier revision stood open.

THE CZECHOSLOVAK REPUBLIC was born in the last days of the First World War, as the Habsburg Empire, having sued for peace, was crumbling. On 28 October 1918, a cross-party national council took control and proclaimed independence in Prague. Revolutionary takeovers followed across the country. Two days later, the same happened in Slovakia, where another group of representatives proclaimed its union with the Czechs in the small town of Turčiansky Svätý Martin. Within a month, the merged councils had established themselves as a provisional parliament and written a constitution. Abroad, a government in exile under the philosopher and politician Tomáš Masaryk and his close associate Edvard Beneš had won Allied backing. By the end of the year, the new parliament had elected Masaryk as the republic's first president.

At first the country depended on the Versailles Treaty for the legitimisation of its borders – in particular the Slovak border, which Hungary had attacked in 1919. By 1938, though, the republic had come to rely on a network of alliances. The lynchpin was a pact with France committing both parties to support the other in the event of a German attack. In 1935, Czechoslovakia had also signed a defence agreement with the Soviet Union, a condition of that treaty being that France had to honour its own obligations before the Soviets became bound to intervene.

Among its immediate neighbours, Czechoslovakia possessed poor relations with both Poland and Hungary. The Poles, though they were fellow French allies, were not benevolent. They felt that Edvard Beneš had successfully played for a better deal at Versailles, grabbing territories (especially the Silesian enclave of Teschen) that should have been theirs. Added to this crime, Czechoslovakia was guilty of hosting the liberal critics of Józef Beck, Poland's authoritarian leader. Hungary, meanwhile, considered itself to have been even more badly despoiled by the peace of Versailles. It possessed a large irredentist community in Slovakia, and it had never ceased to favour a restoration of the Habsburg Empire.

The second set of Czechoslovak alliances, known as the Little Entente, united Czechoslovakia, Yugoslavia, and Romania. Originating in 1920, this bound the three states to come to each other's aid in case of Hungarian aggression. The value of this arrangement to the Czechoslovaks was that it guarded against the emergence of a south-eastern front that would have made fighting Germany far more difficult. By 1938, the Little Entente was not as solid as it had once been: a change of ruler had recently helped Yugoslavia, under the regent Prince Paul and the right-wing premier Milan Stojadinović, mend fences with the Germans and Italians.[6] Nevertheless, it remained quite alive as a diplomatic bloc, its members conferred together regularly, and both Romania and Yugoslavia would reiterate multiple times that year their intention to intervene on the side of the Czechoslovaks in a conflict.

Czechoslovakia was otherwise united, beyond formal diplomatic ties, to Britain and France through a host of ideological, economic, and cultural bonds. The republic embraced democratic norms, practices, and values in a part of Europe from which they had well-nigh disappeared. It played an active role at the League of Nations and, even if the League had lost some of its lustre, Czechoslovakia was committed to the collective security ideals to which the French and British publics remained attached. In 1935–6, Beneš had even assumed the important role of president of the League's assembly, the debating chamber composed of the member states' delegates.

British and French companies were significant investors in the republic. 'Great Britain and France possessed by far the greatest share of direct foreign investment in Czechoslovakia, holding between them more than half of the total,' by one calculation.[7] British companies participated in the mining and metallurgy industries, in textiles, glass, and banking. French direct investment was prominent in engineering, steel, and sugar refining. Unilever produced most of the country's vegetable oils, alongside other food products.[8] Prudential and British Overseas Bank were direct investors in the Czech Union Bank, and Société Générale in the Prague Credit Bank. ICI, alongside fertiliser plants, owned the largest share in Explosia, the Czechoslovak explosives manufacturer, alongside French and other investors. The London Rothschilds owned a majority in the Vítkovice steelworks, providing them with special ties to the British defence company Vickers. Even more significantly, the French firm Schneider-Creusot held major stakes in the Ostrava-Karviná mines and steel plants and in the Škoda works, Czechoslovakia's prime armaments concern and one of the largest in Europe.[9]

The Czechoslovak army, finally, had from its inception enjoyed close ties to the French officer corps. A cadre of forty-five officers under General Maurice Pellé had swooped into Prague in 1919 with the mission to help train and organise the Czechoslovak army.[10] In the 1930s, the Czechoslovak high command had developed its own doctrine and plans, but a French military mission remained in Prague, and grand strategy was still agreed and shared with Paris. Many Czechoslovak soldiers and officers had originally transferred over from the Austrian imperial army, but a large contingent also came from the legion, the group of combatants who, as liberated war prisoners, had joined and fought on the Allied side in the First World War. Prague's Castle guard, which was manned by legionaries, still wore the uniforms of the armies in which it had fought in the Great War: 'pale blue of French *poilu*, with a floppy, dark blue beret; grey green of Italy, with a felt hat upturned at one side; khaki, and a flat-topped forage cap of Imperial Russia'.[11]

As to Germany, in the 1920s and early 30s it had actually been one of Czechoslovakia's friendlier neighbours. Under the Weimar Republic, it was a fellow democracy and it had no claims on Czechoslovakia, which had not been carved out of German territory. Ever since his rise to power, however, Hitler and the controlled Nazi press had only had harsh words. Czechoslovakia was a Soviet and a French ally and it was militarily the strongest state in central Europe. The republic, industrialised and well armed, formed an obstacle to Hitler's expansion plans. Its Little Entente stood in the way of a German drive into the southeast, with its agricultural base and Romanian oil. In November 1937, Hitler had summoned a group of his top military and foreign-policy staff and told them he planned to wage war on Austria and Czechoslovakia. Czechoslovakia was to be destroyed. The details remained to be fleshed out, but the prize was *Lebensraum*, German living space, as well as food for 'five or six million', after at least two million Czechs had been resettled to Siberia or Volhynia, a marshy area in Poland.[12]

IN A PORTRAYAL by the *Daily Express* reporter Sydney Morrell, the men in Prague had the best tailors in Europe, and the women wore silk stockings. One could buy tomato juice from America and breakfast foods from England. Behind Hradčany, the Castle area, there were modern blocks with tennis courts on which young men and women played, 'leaping figures of white'. At Barrandov, one found 'the finest open air restaurant in Europe, with a swimming pool in what was once a stone quarry', but the city was famous for its pubs, Czech and Dalmatian, Hungarian and Serbian, where gypsies played music or bands various folk songs. On Wenceslas Square, Prague's answer to the Champs Elysées, newspapers piled high surrounded the stalls. Slovak women 'in peasant dress, some of them wearing flounced skirts that came just below the knee', sat on little stools, selling embroidered blouses and hand-made dolls or 'cheeses made from sheep's milk, shaped like a swan's egg and about as large, brown from the smoke of the cottage chimney where they had been hung'. There were also banana sellers, selling a banana for a crown, among other peddlers.[13]

The founder of the surrealist movement, the French poet André Breton, had called Prague the magical capital of Europe. Contemporary photographs show Wenceslas Square filled with motorcars, bright neon signs and glass fronts shining alongside the flowery mouldings and female busts of neo-renaissance and art nouveau buildings. The Czechoslovak capital radiated, in the 1930s, the same eclectic charm as it does today. The squat but pure lines of Charles Bridge already enchanted visiting artists and tourists, even if a bus line ran across it. So did the variegated fantasy of the Old Town Square, its town hall still intact at the time, or the Hebrew clock whose hands run anti-clockwise, then still standing in an area inhabited by numerous Jews.

Prague was not the Czech lands, let alone Czechoslovakia, yet Morrell's description was apt for mixing novelty and tradition. Czechoslovakia in the interwar period was at once a central European Ruritania and one of the most advanced countries in the world. The Czech lands were a little over 50 per cent urbanised, comparable to France and even Germany. Prague counted close to one million inhabitants and Bratislava around 150,000, but Slovakia was predominantly rural.[14] In the east, Ruthenia, a small mountainous region that was a patchwork of linguistic and national identities, remained rustic and remote.

This was the era of the Czechoslovak functionalist architectural style, with its pure, flat, whitewashed façades, its sharp angles and use of glass, often in the shape of long 'ribbon' windows. The movement had inspired Bauhaus and Le Corbusier. Though the boom had affected numerous other towns, Prague's modernist showpieces included Jaromír Krejcar's Olympic department store, a glass-fronted edifice 'whose upper floors recall the decks of an ocean liner', and Josef Fuchs and Oldřich Tyl's Trade Fair Palace ('Veletřní palác'), the first building to be endowed with a multi-storey, sky-lit atrium.[15] Nationally, rates of car ownership stood somewhere between the central European and the higher western levels; on offer were the locally made Pragas and Škodas, and the sleek, air-cooled Tatra sedans.[16] More than a million Czechoslovaks possessed radio sets, and they were offered a choice of thousands of different press periodicals, alongside movies filmed at the Barrandov studios.[17]

To Hitler, meanwhile, the country was more than an economic prize or a strategic way-station, or even a neighbour bothersome for a dynamism that was antithetical to his own models – Hitler having, after all, closed down the Bauhaus school of architecture. Czechoslovakia was also an ideological antagonist that provided a haven to his political opponents and the refugees from his purges.

Kurt Grossmann was the secretary of the German League for Human Rights and an essayist, as well as being a First World War veteran. The morning after the Reichstag fire – the incident Hitler took as an excuse, shortly after taking power, for eliminating the communists and Social-Democrats – a friendly call warned him not to go by his office, in Berlin, or even to stay home for too long. Grossmann fled to a café and, an hour later and based on a random conversation with an acquaintance, he decided to head for Prague. He waited for a suitcase and 200 Reichsmarks to be brought to him, then took the noon train out. At the border, the German guards almost detained him, but his limited means seemed a guarantee of return, he had a valid passport, and there was no visa requirement for Czechoslovakia. That same afternoon, he emerged on the platform of the Masaryk train station in central Prague, his new home.[18] Grossmann was merely one of the first among many men and women who would be taking, often in hair-raising circumstances, the road out of the Reich.

In the 1930s, Czechoslovakia had acted as the first port of call for a great number of the 150,000 people who fled Hitler's terror. Though most moved on – to France, Britain, the USA, Palestine, and as far afield as Latin America – around 10,000 remained and Czechoslovakia was long their second-largest country of exile.[19] Czechoslovakia had a liberal refugee policy which included granting passports to those who had none. It did not prosecute people for crossing the border illegally, and asylum-seekers could apply for residence permits that were almost always granted (with exceptions for individuals who were deemed a security risk, often communists).[20] It was geographically close to Germany, but it was also more tolerant of political activity than other neighbouring states such as Switzerland or the Netherlands.[21]

Safe in Czechoslovakia, German exiles kept the flame of the opposition to Hitler's regime alive, maintaining resistance networks inside the Reich and informing the world at large of the nature of the Nazi regime. Since most resistance actions consisted of smuggling pamphlets and news into the Reich or helping fellow victims escape, the border was vital. The German Social-Democrats and their organisation, named the SoPaDe (for *Sozialdemokratische Partei Deutschland*), operated from Czechoslovakia until 1938. Its leaders included Hans Vogel, the party's erstwhile chairman in Germany, Otto Wels, another ex-MP and key member, and the journalist and MP Friedrich Stampfer. With its political leadership in Prague, the SoPaDe ran a network of secretariats in the provinces which, from there, extended its tendrils into the Reich.[22] During the 1936 Olympics, it produced a 'tourist guide' to the Reich showing a map of its concentration camps and prisons.[23] It also published such periodicals as *Sopade Informationen* and *Der Neue Vorwärts* – at its peak, Czechoslovakia would be hosting no fewer than sixty German publications in exile.[24]

Not all of Germany's political refugees were Social-Democrats: German emigration was quite diverse, and it also included communists, Catholics, liberals, pacifists, traditional right-wing conservatives and nationalists, and Lutheran religious protestors.[25] Kurt Grossmann tells the story of how he ran across a certain Bernhard Weiss one day, in a Prague hotel. Weiss had been a high-level police chief in Berlin and he was a political liberal, but he was also a Jew and the Nazis had always maligned him. While on a trip to Hamburg, he had by chance heard the news of his own flight, on the radio. Though he was warned not to go home, Weiss managed to outwit a platoon of brownshirts to gather a few of his belongings, in Berlin. He then took a train to Prague via Munich. On the Munich night train, though, chance had it that he was put in a compartment with none other than Ernst Röhm, the leader of the SA! (Röhm failed to recognise him ...)[26]

Former political antagonists from all sides mixed and came across each other in the German cafés of Czechoslovakia. In Prague it was chiefly the Continental, which Kafka had once patronised, and where one 'devoured newspapers, had conversations, prophesied Hitler's end, eagerly seized on the news, and met newcomers.'[27] In Brno it was the Biber, the Esplanade, or the Grand Hotel, where doctors, industrialists, and journalists also congregated. The Bavarian poet and novelist Oskar Maria Graf enthused over Brno's charm, its cottages and gardens surrounding a well-appointed town: 'There reigned a democratic urbanity in everything. [...] A considerable share of the Czech intelligentsia, the highly educated Jewish community, the very liberal and emigrant-friendly authorities, the two socialist parties and various left-wing groups – all stood together with us against the swastika-bearing menace. [...] Oh, sweet Brno of my good and lucky years, how often I yearn for you as for a piece of my true homeland.'[28]

So wide was the political spectrum spanned by German exile society that among those prophesising the end of Hitler and thundering against him was in fact a former Nazi boss, Otto Strasser. Strasser, who considered his own brand of national-socialism to be the authentic brand, ran a Black Front from Czechoslovakia, where he had landed after an undercover stint in Austria. He maintained contact with his sympathisers in Germany, published pamphlets, and later printed a newspaper entitled *Deutscher Revolution*. The press was fascinated by him, and within a few days he was on familiar terms with most Czech and German journalists. He was also friendly with 'a number of leading Czechoslovak political figures', including the leader of the German-speaking Social-Democrats, Wenzel Jaksch.[29]

Yet Strasser's activities placed him on the Gestapo's wanted list. In 1933, in Prague, two men had shown up at his flat claiming to be local police. They asked for his identification, then searched his rooms and took his revolver. Dr Otto Baumann, as he was calling himself, just managed to fool them that time. He noticed that the car waiting outside had the wrong plates: black on white numbers, not the Czechoslovak white on black. A piece of cotton soaked in chloroform had been dropped in the gutter.[30] Later, hoping to strike back at his opponents, Strasser set up a dissident radio station, complete with its own transmitter into Germany, in the riverside village of Slapy. Despite living under a false name and staying on friendly terms with law enforcement, this was another close escape. After several days of scouting, Gestapo agents raided the place at the end of January 1938. Strasser escaped once again, but his radio engineer and operator, Rudolf Formis, had no such luck and was shot dead.[31]

Not for nothing did Goebbels call the German exiles 'corpses on holiday'.[32] Perhaps the highest-profile assassination was that of the philosopher and writer Theodor Lessing, in Marienbad in 1933, but there were many others, plus numerous attempts at abduction or entrapment. The Czech police foiled a plot to eliminate the German Social-Democrat leader Otto Wels.[33] The Gestapo sent a certain Hans

Zirker to pose as a fellow Social-Democrat and assassinate Grossmann, another prominent SoPaDe member named Lorentz, and Strasser.[34] Gestapo agents sometimes masqueraded as refugees or operated under threats to relatives in Germany. The dissident organisations responded by sending their own people back across the border, or by assisting the Czechoslovak secret service in its information-gathering.[35]

Most German refugees did not partake in such glamorous or dangerous experiences. Only a minority of the exiles were journalists or party activists; most were simple, often uneducated workers, often young.[36] Though they could count on various assistance organisations, Czech, Jewish, or democratic German, their life was sometimes wrapped in 'the grey mantel of need'.[37] Heinz Kühn, a young Rhineland exile who would later become a senior West German politician, lived for a long time in a flat on the second floor of a modern rental house in the Prague suburb of Zabiehlice, sharing with seven other young refugees. He received basic pocket money and lunched at a free soup kitchen downtown. Though he was theoretically not allowed to work, he did shifts at a coal delivery firm and wrote articles for a German publication. This afforded him such small luxuries as trips to the cinema Urania, which showed films in German and was a good place to meet local German girls.[38]

Czechoslovakia was enjoying an artistic golden age. In 1935, André Breton had come to Prague to lecture to a packed audience on 'The surrealist situation of the object'. His hosts were the poet Vítězslav Nezval and the art critic Karel Teige, joined by the Paris-based painter Josef Šíma and the Czech surrealist artists Jindřich Štyrský and Toyen (Marie Čermínová).[39] Cubism had enjoyed widespread artistic popularity in Czechoslovakia and would continue to do so in the 1930s, even as surrealism and the more strictly native-born poetism flowered. In literature, this was the age of Karel Čapek – best known internationally for his invention of the robot as part of a 1920 science-fiction play entitled *Rosum's Universal Robots* – of Eduard Bass, Jozef Cíger-Hronský, and Karel Poláček. In the German language, the 1920s and 30s had witnessed the publication of Franz Kafka's novels by Max Brod, an accomplished writer in his own right. Musically, the republic had seen the last years of Leoš Janáček and the first of Bohuslav Martinů.

On the popular scene, jazz, both in imported and native versions, was taking its first steps in Czechoslovakia's theatres and clubs. Likewise the genre of the satirical revue. In late 1937, the actor–scriptwriter team of Jiří Voskovec and Jan Werich premiered a play titled *Fat Barbara*: a parody featuring a mythical dictatorial country called Yberland that was looking for an excuse to expand into the smaller, neighbouring Eidam.[40] The Liberated Theatre, originally a stage for avant-garde plays, had begun under the Voskovec–Werich impulse to produce revues mixing jazz, gags, and intellectual humour, then moved into political plays in the 1930s. Though it poked fun at political institutions and politics in general, in Nazism it found an obvious target. Its songs were often taken up by the public, played on the radio, and repeated by word of mouth, helping propagate a mood of irreverence towards the country's totalitarian neighbour.

Hitler's partisans knew what they were doing when they slashed the canvases of a contemporary art exhibition in Ústí nad Labem.[41] Czechoslovak modernity was in its own conception a manifestation of the country's democratic values. Just as the colourful and bold contemporary art of the West would come to embody, during the Cold War, its carefree diversity in opposition to the staid and stifling Soviet intellectual climate, so did Czechoslovakia and its culture stand for a merry freedom against the Reich's 'racially pure' art and its brutally enforced norms. In March 1938, the opera *Julietta* by Martinů would premiere at the Prague national theatre: it was a roaring success, and it played for many nights to an enthusiastic audience.[42] What the Prague public cheered for nights on end, though, was not just Martinů's score; it was the opera's cosmopolitan and progressive associations; it was a liberal spirit that, under pressure from the Reich, proclaimed as best it could its defiance.

Likewise, finally, the refugees who possibly mattered most were the small group of German writers and artists in flight: they were the ones who could thumb their nose at the Nazis and get public attention for it. In Czechoslovakia, they found a country where books were not burnt and their works not banned. Perhaps the best known of the German exiles, strangely enough, was someone who had assumed Czechoslovak nationality but did not live there: Thomas Mann, the Nobel prize-winning author of *The Magic Mountain* and *Buddenbrooks*. Stripped of his German citizenship, Mann had been offered a Czechoslovak passport in a move endorsed by Masaryk and Beneš themselves. Mann had visited his new country in 1937, and he would defend Czechoslovakia from afar after moving to the US in May 1938.[43]

Prominent exiled German artists on the Prague scene included Helmut Herzfeld, also known as John Heartfield, and Oskar Kokoschka. Kokoschka, who would eventually move to England, was an expressionist known for haunted canvases that were nevertheless packed with colour. Other than a number of memorable Prague landscapes, he would paint a famed self-portrait as a 'degenerate artist'.[44] Heartfield, originally a member of the Dada movement, was celebrated for his photomontages, which often carried a political message. He was a feature of a major caricature exhibition at the Mánes Gallery in 1934, alongside such international celebrities as Jean Cocteau and Otto Dix. Typical Heartfield photomontages showed a woman crucified on a swastika, or a tiny Hitler with an outsize head watering an oak whose acorns were giant artillery shells. The show was violently condemned in Germany, and it was the object of official protests from Italy and Poland. This did not prevent the Mánes from having a re-run in 1937, with both Kokoschka and Heartfield as its stars.[45] Alongside these worthies, finally, were a host of minor artists and illustrators, such as the contributors to the satirical journal *Simplicissimus*. A cross between a literary journal and *Punch*, this was revived in Czechoslovakia under various names such as *Simplicus* and *Simpl* in initiatives that were calculated to keep the Nazis, across the border, in a state of constant exasperation.[46]

ON 20 FEBRUARY 1938, Prokop Drtina tuned in to a speech given by Hitler in Berlin's Kroll Opera House, the first such speech to be transmitted on Czechoslovak radio. His immediate impression was of the vulgarity of the German leader, his strong accent, uneducated choice of words, and street-level manner.[47] 'In his whole demeanour, he recalled the Austrian petty official or warrant officer,' observed a fellow listener, 'including his crooked nose, toothbrush moustache, and bowed legs. Hitler barked in an Austrian accent and only his international recruits (of all years) were afraid of him. Among us, people laughed at him.'[48] Yet as both recognised, Hitler's words were serious. 'Over ten million Germans live in two of the States adjoining our frontiers,' had said the German chancellor. 'It is intolerable for a self-respecting World Power to know that across the frontier are kinsmen who have to suffer severe persecution, simply because of their sympathy, their feeling for union with Germany. [...] To these interests of the German Reich belongs also the protection of those fellow Germans who live beyond our frontiers and are unable to ensure for themselves the right to a general freedom, personal, political, and ideological.'[49] The two unnamed states were unmistakably Austria and Czechoslovakia. The Nazis had attempted to take over Austria once already, in 1934, and it was an open secret that Hitler wanted to annex it to the Reich. Now Czechoslovakia was lumped together with it.

The third reason Czechoslovakia was in Hitler's sights was that it contained a community that the Reich could plausibly call its own. Bohemia and Moravia, the historical Czech lands, contained a number of heavily Germanised regions and enclaves, especially along their borders. Many or most people in these areas spoke German as their mother tongue. Though they were Czechoslovak citizens and had never belonged to Germany as a state, they called themselves German and were called German by others. Together, these regions formed a geographically never quite defined province named the Sudetenland. (The Sudetenland lacked both territorial cohesion and a natural capital, and, indeed, as that capital could only be Prague, the Prague Germans were typically also counted as Sudeten Germans.[50]) The Sudetenland was to be Hitler's lever, the excuse for his campaign against Czechoslovakia.

Drtina, a lawyer by education, had pursued a career as a civil servant and joined the president's staff, serving as Edvard Beneš's private secretary. He was an important witness to the events of 1938, and his observations will appear several times in these pages. Scarcely was the broadcast over than he received a call from a friend. 'Did you hear Hitler's speech?' Later that afternoon, Czechoslovakia would beat Germany 3–0 in the world ice hockey championship. Beyond such minor mercies, the atmosphere had darkened. 'Anyone who had heard Hitler's threats had understood them, without exception. It was the end of our illusions,' Drtina wrote.[51]

The Sudeten Germans organised themselves politically into their own parties, as had been common practice in Austria-Hungary. These included a German Social-Democratic Party, a Christian-Social Party, a German Agrarian Party, and so on. The only exception was the Communist Party, whose membership spanned all national identities. In the mid-1920s, the main German parties of Czechoslovakia had participated in ruling parliamentary coalitions, and their representatives had entered government. These were called 'activists', and for a time they had received the vast majority of Sudeten German votes at elections. As 1938 dawned, there were three Sudeten German ministers in the Czechoslovak government: Franz Spina, an Agrarian, Erwin Zajicek, a Christian-Social Party member, and Ludwig Czech, a Social-Democrat.

At one point Czechoslovakia had also had a German National Socialist Party, known as the DNSAP. It had existed since 1918, before Hitler's political career had even begun, and in the parliamentary elections of 1929 it had managed to pick up about 10 per cent of the Sudeten German vote.[52] From the late 1920s, though, it had increasingly modelled itself on its bigger cousin across the border, creating a paramilitary organisation named the *Volkssportverband* ('People's Sports Organisation'), complete with brown shirts, swastika-bearing accessories, and training sessions in Germany. In 1933, as Hitler came to power, the Czechoslovak authorities began to worry about this party calling so hoarsely for a Sudetenland *Anschluss*, and they initiated a ban. The state lifted the parliamentary immunity of five of the DNSAP leaders and arrested various members of the *Volkssport*, some of whom fled to Germany. The DNSAP itself pre-empted its inevitable demise by dissolving voluntarily.[53]

Before that final break-up, however, and before making his escape to Berlin by canoe down the Elbe, Hans Krebs, one of the DNSAP chieftains, met with the promising leader of another gymnastics organisation, Konrad Henlein. Together they hatched a plan for a *Sudetendeutsche Heimatfront* ('Sudeten German Home Front') which, though it absorbed the DNSAP's remnants, was originally not constituted as a political party – the DNSAP leaders having learned discretion the hard way. The *Heimatfront* promptly merged with another right-wing association known as the *Kameradschaftsbund*. This claimed inspiration from a Viennese university professor and ideologue named Othmar Spann, whose philosophy is best described as an extreme form of Austrian clerical fascism. (Clerical fascism, while rooted in fascist ideology, eschewed fascism's modernist godlessness to borrow ideas and endorsements from the Catholic hierarchy.) To the modern observer, the doctrinal differences between Spannism and Nazism can be hard to discern, and Spann himself was a member of the Nazi Party, but the merger enabled Henlein and the *Heimatfront* to claim distinction from Hitlerite ideology and avoid designation as a direct successor to the DNSAP. It also helped to establish the notion that Henlein's movement was composed of an extreme and a more moderate wing – a notion more rooted in factional rivalry than in differing aims – which was to play an important role in British perceptions of it in 1938. The next step, taken in 1935, was to transform the *Heimatfront* into an actual party, the *Sudetendeutsche Partei*, or SdP.[54]

The *Daily Express* correspondent George Eric Gedye, who met Henlein in his home town of Aš, thought he looked like 'an athletic bank clerk'.[55] Born to a Liberec book-keeper in 1898, Henlein had fought in the First World War (he was captured by the Italians) before spending the early 1920s in a bank.[56] He soon got involved in the gymnastics association known as the *Turnverband*, first locally and later as coordinator for the Sudetenland as a whole. Henlein was not, Gedye felt, a charismatic leader. At rallies, he read from notes, lacking Hitler's oratorical power.[57] He declined to take a parliamentary seat and often let others act as his spokesmen. Yet he must have possessed notable organisational talents. By the end of 1935, he found himself standing at the head of by far the largest Sudeten German party. From the depths of the Depression, bathed in the reflected glory of the Nazi Reich's vaunted reconstruction programme, the SdP had won a majority of Sudeten German votes. As 1938 opened, forty-four of its members would be sitting in parliament, in Prague: more than all the 'activist' Sudeten German parties combined.[58]

Whether Henlein was a committed Nazi from the very beginning or whether he was initially better aligned with clerical fascism is a matter of historical debate.[59] Perhaps a hint is given in his choice of names for his children: Gudrun, Ingrid, and Horst, Horst being a quintessential Nazi name, as in the pet Nazi song the 'Horst Wessel Lied'.[60] He was also capable of ruthlessness. Two men helped him more than anyone else up the ladder of the *Turnverband* and to the leadership of the *Heimatfront*: Walter Brand and Heinrich Rutha. Both faced the problem, in Nazi eyes, that they were members of the *Kameradschaftsbund* faction. In October 1937, Rutha, a long-time personal friend of Henlein, was arrested for homosexuality and having sex with young men after an enquiry helped along by leaks from his Nazi rivals. On 5 November, he was found hanged in his cell, just as Henlein was about to leave for Berlin to be sworn in by the Führer. The SdP chief likewise refrained from interfering when Walter Brand got sidelined, on the initiative of the Gestapo chief Reinhard Heydrich, and two years later arrested.[61]

Sometime towards the end of 1934 or the beginning of 1935, Václav Maria Havel – a successful architect and the father of the future dissident and president of the republic Václav Havel – hosted a special encounter behind the closed doors of his home, a flat in a florid, pastel art nouveau building with a Castle view, on what is now Rašínovo nábřeží. Konrad Henlein and a few of his acolytes came to meet a group of Czech political and intellectual luminaries, including Prokop Drtina, Hubert Ripka, editor at *Lidové noviny* and a friend and adviser to Beneš, and Hubert Masařík, an essayist and diplomat. Members of that group had recently gone to the town of Česká Lípa to witness Henlein's first major public appearance. Their impression had been that the *Sudetendeutsche Heimatfront* was just another incarnation of the DNSAP, the Nazi Party, but they wanted to judge things more closely. Henlein spoke at length. He made the same protestations of distance from Nazism and belief in democracy he had made in Česká Lípa. His interlocutors wavered, until at last Ripka asked point-blank: 'And what would you do if Hitler and Germany attacked Czechoslovakia, if a war arose between us and Germany? Would you invite your supporters to fight against Germany and participate loyally in the war against it?' Henlein stammered and in that moment lost the trust of his hosts.[62]

What is not in doubt is that Henlein's party was from the beginning supported by and as time went by increasingly run from Berlin. From the date of their electoral success, Henlein and his SdP received funds from the *Volksbund* for the promotion of German culture abroad, then from a parallel organisation named the *Volksdeutsche Mittelstelle*. This was not necessarily incriminating as such: though also engaged in foreign spying and subversion, the *Volksbund* and *Mittelstelle* were ostensibly set up to aid Germans abroad. But Henlein was receiving subsidies from more questionable sources too, including the German foreign ministry, the *Deutscher Arbeitsfront* or Reich Labour Front, and Goering's economic planning bureau. The Reich financed the party newspaper and main propaganda organ, *Die Zeit*, to the point that it even fixed the salaries of its editorial staff. Krebs, finally, having landed a job as press chief at the German interior ministry, helped coordinate Henlein's activities and contacts in Berlin.[63]

It is established that Henlein met Hitler personally for the first time at the latest at the 1936 Berlin Olympics.[64] By the end of 1937, he and his party were unambiguously on orders. A couple of weeks after Rutha hanged himself in his cell and the day after Halifax's visit to Berchtesgaden, on 19 November, Henlein met again with the Führer to make plans. Henlein assured his chief:

> The Sudeten Germans are today imbued with National Socialist principles and organized in a comprehensive, unitary National Socialist Party, based on the Führer concept. [...] The Sudeten German Party must camouflage its profession of National Socialism as an ideology of life and as a political principle. As a party in the democratic parliamentary system of Czechoslovakia, it must, outwardly, alike in writing and by word of mouth, in its manifestoes and in the press, in Parliament, in its own structure, and in the organization of the Sudeten German element, employ democratic terminology and democratic parliamentary methods. [...] At heart it desires nothing more ardently than the incorporation of Sudeten German territory, nay of the whole Bohemian, Moravian, and Silesian area [the totality of the Czech lands], within the Reich.[65]

2

The struggle begins

IN THE EARLY HOURS of 12 March 1938, German troops crossed the south-eastern border into Austria. Hitler had already threatened and browbeaten the chancellor, Kurt Schuschnigg, into accepting a Nazi government at the last minute, and the invasion went unresisted. Famously, the crowds greeted the German soldiers with flowers and Nazi salutes, and Hitler appeared to ovations in Linz, the town of his childhood, and Vienna. The Reich swallowed up Austria after the performance of a plebiscite, though since the whole exercise had been timed to pre-empt a vote originally proposed by Schuschnigg, perhaps this did not carry complete conviction democratically. Tens of thousands of people, actual or potential political opponents, were promptly imprisoned or sent to concentration camps. A few desperately attempted to clear out, some joining an existing community of exiles based in Brno. They were soon followed by the bulk of the foreign press corps, which, faced with Nazi censorship and Gestapo harassment, headed for Prague.[1]

On the Czechoslovak side, the immediate product of the *Anschluss* was a gush of peaceful gestures from the Reich. Leading Nazis competed to assure their chancellery counterparts of their entirely benevolent intentions. The night before the invasion, at a reception at the 'airmen's house', Goering had taken the Czechoslovak ambassador, Vojtěch Mastný, aside and assured him that 'Germany has no unfriendly intentions towards Czechoslovakia and that on the contrary, after the completion of the *Anschluss*, it expects an improvement in relations with it – as long as you don't mobilise.' Goering threw in his 'word of honour' and, for good measure, Hitler's as well. Such assurances were repeated by the German ambassador in Prague and the newly appointed foreign minister, Joachim von Ribbentrop.[2] Ribbentrop's predecessor, Konstantin von Neurath, even took the trouble to confirm that Germany still considered the 1925 Locarno arbitrage treaty as valid – interestingly in the light of future developments, as the Czechoslovaks would only be ridiculed when they tried to invoke it a few months later.[3]

In Prague, though, no one rejoiced. Mastný himself was unimpressed, and neither was anyone fooled at the foreign ministry. The shock of Hitler's 20 February speech, in which he had lumped Austria and Czechoslovakia together, was all too fresh and Nazi hostility too longstanding for Goering's sudden bonhomie to convince.[4] As was well understood, the Nazis were anxious lest a Czechoslovak mobilisation derail their assault on Austria, either by encouraging international resistance to it or simply by throwing a spanner in a military exercise that was not going as smoothly as they liked to pretend.[5] Italy, once the protector of Viennese independence, had furthermore become acquiescent in and even supportive of German expansionism. The Czechoslovak border system of defensive bunkers, finally, now lacked a strong enough section on the south side against the old Austrian frontier.

It was clear to all that Czechoslovakia was only more exposed, and that it was next on the list. In *Přítomnost*, a bi-weekly that perhaps best reflected thinking among the Prague intelligentsia and ruling political class, the editor Ferdinand Peroutka spelt out the threat in an issue that made short shrift of sudden assurances of peace.[6] The foreign press corps itself, indeed, with its unfailing nose for upcoming trouble, made the same point by moving en masse to Prague.

Political decision-making in the Czechoslovak Republic was ultimately vested in the government, but in practice power was shared among a variety of overlapping groups of people. The constitution, loosely modelled on America's, involved two elected assemblies plus a president, but the president, elected by these assemblies rather than by popular vote, had a more regal than executive role. Because governments were reliant on parliamentary coalitions, power could be diffuse. A core of 'political ministers' acted as a compact executive committee, sometimes with the addition of non-governmental experts or figures such as the chief of staff on military matters. Conversely, because parliamentary representation was fragmented among a large number of political organisations, plus the German parties and a Slovak nationalist party, the secretariats of the parties in power and their parliamentary whips were able to exercise significant influence. They sometimes operated behind the scenes and appealed straight to individual ministers, especially on matters dear to their particular bases. Behind and among them moved figures from the business and media world – such as Jaroslav Preiss of Živnostenská banka, the largest financial–industrial conglomerate in the country, or Hubert Ripka of *Lidové noviny*, a powerful, centre-left but independent daily.[7]

In the crisis year of 1938, foreign policy would be led by a trio consisting of President Beneš, the premier Milan Hodža, and the foreign minister Kamil Krofta. The premiership had for its centre the Kolowrat Palace, on the Malá Strana or 'small side' of the river in Prague, while the foreign ministry was situated higher up the Castle hill, in the Czernin Palace. The president resided in the Castle itself, the seat of Bohemia's erstwhile kings, and collectively the president's formal and informal entourage came to be known as 'the Castle'. The Castle, indeed, with its contrasting stone turrets and plaster façades, its baroque reception halls and maze of interlocking courtyards, and standing amidst its own quarter of old houses, pubs, and palaces, was apt to dominate the Prague landscape figuratively as much as it did physically.

Beneš had replaced Tomáš Garrigue Masaryk – who died in 1937 – as president in 1935. Before that he had long been the republic's international face, both as foreign minister and as a League of Nations delegate. As the *Daily Mirror* correspondent Sydney Morrell describes him, he was small, had a Maurice Chevalier smile, and looked deep into the eyes of his interlocutors. He drank 'innumerable cups of tea', and at the weekends he gardened at his country house, both qualities that ought to have endeared him to the British public, though perhaps not with the upper-class ambassadorial and political corps with which he interacted.[8] Beneš, born into a middle-class farming family, had studied philosophy and political science in Prague, Berlin, and notably Paris and Dijon, before working as a teacher and academic writer.[9] His strengths were his clarity of vision and his thorough knowledge of the diplomatic trade. Yet he never entirely lost his professorial calling, and he was prone to lecture. While laudably high-minded, this was not always tactically apt. At the height of the crisis, later in the year, Beneš could not resist interrupting the delivery of a crucial and final offer of terms to sermonise Ernst Kundt, his antagonist: 'Nazism is but poison and ruin. In Germany this will only end with another revolution or a catastrophic war. [...] This is not just about us. What is at stake is a great European ideological and power contest, and Nazism will not win it in the end. It will finish with its dreadful demise, and the fall of all of those who stand with it today.'[10]

Hodža mattered, of course, because he was head of the government and the situation presented by the collusion of Hitler and Henlein had extensive domestic ramifications. But Hodža was also a Slovak, helping prove that at the heart of the matter was not simply a dispute between Czechs and Germans. 'The son of a wealthy peasant, stocky, well dressed, precise, with pince-nez and a stubborn chin', he had the look of a successful businessman.[11] He was the glue that kept together the political parties in government. Krofta, finally, 'a white-haired, low-voiced man of sixty five', was a historian and university professor who had also served as ambassador to the Vatican and to Berlin before rising to the head of the diplomatic service. A 'kindly, unostentatious man who could be seen in the mornings taking his dog for a walk in the park at the back of the Czernin Palace, prepared to wait his turn at the corner stall to buy a bag of fresh apricots or strawberries from the peasant woman who ran it', his energies would nevertheless be tested severely in facing both the public needs and the private pressures of Czechoslovak diplomacy under assault.[12]

This trio had responded energetically to Hitler's 20 February challenge. Hodža declared, in a parliamentary speech, that Czechoslovakia's frontiers were unalterable and that Germans already enjoyed full rights in the country. 'Czechoslovakia and its people cannot nor will under any circumstances entertain any foreign interference in its internal affairs.'[13] Beneš repeated the same message for British audiences, in a more subtly scripted version, in an interview with *The Times* that came out in early March. This combined warnings that the Sudeten issue was 'an internal issue which can never be the subject of direct official negotiation or discussion with a foreign Power' with a recognition of 'the moral right of Europe to take an interest in our minorities' because it was important to peace.[14] Krofta meanwhile warned his own ambassadorial teams that Henlein was 'directed from Berlin', and that 'interventions in Austrian politics and similar attempts in our country are merely part of a plan whose execution would lead to the creation in central Europe of a new Holy Roman Empire of the German Nation.'[15] Finally, driving the point home, the chief of the general staff, Ludvík Krejčí, called a press conference on military strategy and stressed the mobility, speed, and offensive striking power achieved by Czechoslovakia's mechanised units, as well as the strength of the country's fortification barrier.[16]

Initially, this defiance seemed to work. If anything, the *Anschluss* made the Czechoslovaks more resolute and the argument for their allies to stand by them more urgent. Trouble, however, was not confined to the field of foreign relations. As would prove the case throughout the crisis, domestic events were about to interact with international affairs in a feedback loop. In late March, the government's German-speaking activist ministers suddenly resigned.

Hitler's tactics, and with him Henlein's, were brilliant at surprising and wrong-footing their opponents, if nothing else. Building on momentum acquired by the first blow, they left their antagonist no time to recover before dealing the next in quick succession. Rather than taking time to 'digest' Austria, as so many analysts expected, the Führer and his henchman used its shock value to crush their opponents on the Czechoslovak German political chessboard.

Franz Spina resigned his cabinet post on 22 March. Two days later, Erwin Zajicek followed suit. Spina represented the *Bund der Landwirte*, the German Agrarian Party and the most important of the activist parties on the right. Zajicek was from the Christian-Social Party, the vehicle for Catholic German opinion and potentially an important strand of opposition to Nazism. On 24 March, the *Bund der Landwirte* announced its merger into the SdP. The Christian-Social Party immediately followed. So did the DGP, a smaller party standing for trades and business people.[17] All this had taken place within less than a fortnight of the Austrian *Anschluss*.

Nor did the Henleinists just swallow up the quasi-totality of their party opponents (all that still stood against them were now the Social-Democrats and a small, mostly Prague-based German Democratic Freedom Party). They took over their newspapers, their youth organisations, their cultural associations, their student unions, with their assets, staff, and capacity for moulding the Sudeten German community to their own ends. They also automatically assumed their parliamentary mandates, bringing the SdP's number of MPs to fifty-five, or 83 per cent of the German total.[18] Most importantly, they could now plausibly claim to be the true representatives of the Sudeten German people.

Behind this remarkable coup stood a systematic *razzia* by the SdP. No doubt the Sudeten German community was impressed by the annexation of Austria. Whether they now expected Hitler to swallow up their own region or whether they only thought the *Anschluss* would help win them a more elevated status within Czechoslovakia is unclear. Perhaps they merely gazed in wonderment at the scenes of celebration across the border. If so, they were not given the chance to wake up and think things over. On the contrary, Henlein immediately upped the pressure. On the very day of the *Anschluss*, he issued a speech calling for all Germans to leave the 'splinter' parties, meaning the activists, and join the SdP. 'Fight under the banner of the SdP for the living rights and honour of our people!'[19] Party members spread the rumour, broadcast on the Reich radio, that Hitler would soon annex the Sudetenland. The party built on the momentum to organise more than one hundred rallies in places as widespread as Cheb, Liberec, Jihlava, Teplice, Marienbad, Litoměřice, Trutnov, Znojmo. In many towns, Henlein sent representatives from house to house to warn of the coming annexation and to ask people whether they were with the party or against it. He then gave a deadline for joining his organisation: the end of May. Everything was designed to encourage those who were susceptible to his party and terrify those who opposed it.[20]

At the grassroots level, there was support within the German Agrarian Party for a merger with the SdP. The Christian-Socials were encouraged by pro-Nazi declarations by senior Austrian clergy. In places, local party cells acted before their leadership had time to react. It was a particular individual, though, who orchestrated the defection of the *Bund der Landwirte*, the keystone in the whole matter. Gustav Hacker, the chairman of the German Agrarian Party, called a conference just four days after the *Anschluss*. Given powers to explore the situation and open a dialogue with all sides, including the government, he decided instead for the SdP option. Spina was against the idea, as he went to tell Beneš before retiring from political life. So was Robert Mayr-Harting, who alongside Spina had been one of the very first activist ministers. Within *Bund der Landwirte* ranks, meanwhile, there were protests and accusations of treason against Hacker. A group of party members including two MPs refused to join the SdP and instead set up their own organisation. For this they would be hounded, and their secretary was gruesomely murdered in his office on 25 September.[21]

Hacker's motivations are not entirely clear, but the party newspaper and his pronouncements within it offer a glimpse of his logic. Though he greeted the *Anschluss* as the achievement of 'freedom in the German sense', this only acted as the trigger for requests for more Sudeten rights, such as recognition of the Germans as a state nationality, not just a minority, and autonomy in the fields of culture and social policy.[22] By taking the early initiative to bring his troops into the SdP, he appears to have calculated he would gain influence for himself and for his base.[23] In any case, in April the German Social-Democrat Ludwig Czech, the last remaining activist cabinet member, also resigned. The Social-Democrats were not reconcilable with Henlein's party, but they felt they would fare better in the expected bargaining and in upcoming municipal elections if they were independent.

At the end of March, Henlein met Hitler again and received new instructions. The *Anschluss* now completed, the Reich's attention would turn to Czechoslovakia. The SdP was to make political demands of the state which it could not accept. In tight cooperation with Berlin, it would ask for measures amounting to a carve-out of the Sudetenland from the republic. Henlein would place Czechoslovakia in the wrong, providing an excuse for intervention.[24] If the government was willing to go so far as to cede control of the Sudetenland to the SdP, Henlein offered in a subsequent Berlin meeting, 'I shall answer "Yes" with the demand that the foreign policy of Czechoslovakia be modified. The Czechs would never accede to that.'[25] Meanwhile domestic tensions were to be stoked to fever pitch. If necessary, a violent incident could be manufactured or exploited to provide an excuse, when and if the time came, for invasion.

THE *ANSCHLUSS* HAD AWAKENED the international community to their danger, or so the Czechoslovaks had reason to believe. Admittedly, the annexation of Austria had gone unopposed by Britain or France, helping Hitler's success look effortless. Britain had confined its actions to official protests, and France was without a government, having found itself in the middle of a recombination of its ruling parliamentary coalition. Soon thereafter, though, the statesmen of both countries publicly let it be known that Czechoslovakia must not fall to the same fate.

The new French government brought the socialist Léon Blum to the helm and made the hawkish Joseph Paul-Boncour foreign minister. As soon as they were in office, they reiterated France's commitment to Czechoslovakia, prompting the Soviet foreign affairs commissar, Maxim Litvinov, to follow suit.[26] The joint diplomatic services initiated steps towards mustering a common defence of the country. Paul-Boncour even sent a shot across the bows to London, warning that the Sudetenland dispute was not at heart about the German minority but about Czechoslovakia and indeed Europe itself. He requested that Britain undertake a direct commitment on its behalf.[27] This all came to naught when Blum fell in the following month and was replaced by Edouard Daladier. His new foreign minister, Georges Bonnet, came from the right wing of their party and was known to be less hostile to Germany. Daladier nevertheless inaugurated his tenure with a forceful address in parliament. Though he did not name Czechoslovakia specifically, he warned: 'France's national energies will be mobilised in cementing existing friendships, in attesting its fidelity to existing pacts and treaties, as well as in participating in just negotiations. We want peace with all peoples whatever their political regime, [but] peace with respect for legality and not some sort of abdication of France, a preface to servitude.'[28]

On 24 March, meanwhile, Chamberlain made a much-awaited appearance in the Commons. The speech refused to commit Britain on behalf of Czechoslovakia. This reluctance was, however, placed in the context of Britain's traditional reluctance to enter into hard alliances, especially on the European continent. In practice, France was bound to defend Czechoslovakia, and Britain was likely to find itself fighting at France's side. Chamberlain declared:

Where peace and war are concerned, legal obligations are not alone involved, and, if war broke out, it would be unlikely to be confined to those who have assumed such obligations. [...] The inexorable pressure of facts might well prove more powerful than formal pronouncements, and in that event it would be well within the bounds of probability that other countries, besides those which were parties to the original dispute, would almost immediately become involved. This is specially true in the case of two countries like Great Britain and France, with long associations of friendship, with interests closely interwoven, devoted to the same ideals of democratic liberty, and determined to uphold them.[29]

Perhaps this was not the boldest foreign policy speech ever pronounced in the Commons. Yet it left hope that the cabinet might heed Beneš's warning to his partners to stand firm against Hitler in their own interest.[30]

In April, though, the premiers and foreign ministers of Britain and France were scheduled to meet in London for a review of joint policy. The talks did not just concern Czechoslovakia, but central Europe was the principal item on the agenda and it is worth quoting in some detail what was said there.

Halifax opened the talks with the opinion that the situation was becoming dangerous and that 'The German minority were forming themselves more and more closely into a compact body under the leadership of Herr Henlein.' Furthermore: 'On the other side of the frontier German opinion was also in a high state of exaltation, and the momentum generated by events in Austria might well, in certain circumstances, carry the German Government forward to further operations.' Because of France's engagements, this could lead to war, a prospect causing the foreign secretary 'considerable disquiet' due to the unreadiness of the Entente partners. Halifax went on to dismiss the military contributions of Soviet Russia, Poland, and Czechoslovakia itself. The upshot was that 'every effort should be made by Dr. Benes to reach a settlement of the German minority problem', that it was the role of Britain and France to make that as clear as possible to the Czechoslovaks, and that 'he regarded it as essential that such a settlement should be reached in direct negotiation with Herr Henlein's party.'[31]

Daladier, to whom this came as a surprise, spoke next. 'He was of the opinion that Czechoslovakia had done more for the minorities than any other European State. He had himself visited Czechoslovakia several times. He had been to the Sudeten districts and everywhere he had seen German schools and officials. If, therefore, Czechoslovakia was compared with other countries, it must be recognised that nowhere else had greater concessions been made to minorities.' As the French premier opined: 'He was himself convinced that Herr Henlein was not, in fact, seeking any concessions, and that his real object was the destruction of the present Czechoslovak State.' As proof, the SdP had attempted to hide from the press the proceedings of its recent congress, so 'violent and negative' were they. 'M. Daladier considered, however, that it was not really at Prague that it was necessary to bring pressure to bear. [...] We were confronted by German policy readily translated into action, designed to tear up treaties and destroy the equilibrium of Europe. In his view, the ambitions of Napoleon were far inferior to the present aims of the German Reich.' Daladier contradicted Halifax on the military situation and maintained that it was Germany that was not prepared for war. 'M. Daladier agreed that every effort should be made to avoid war, but he could only profess his profound conviction that, confronted as we were with such a situation, war could only be avoided if Britain and France made their determination quite clear to maintain the peace of Europe by respecting the liberties and the rights of independent peoples. [...] If, however, we were once again to capitulate when faced by another threat, we should then have prepared the way for the very war we wished to avoid.'[32]

Chamberlain, however, thought this at once too gloomy and not sufficiently well informed of conditions in the country in question. Henlein, he affirmed, was 'a moderate' who had not asked for

31

an *Anschluss* with Germany. Besides, Czechoslovakia was so dependent on Germany economically that the Reich could dictate policy to
it 'without moving a single soldier'. (Why it had not done so already
and prevented Czechoslovakia, say, from becoming a Soviet ally was
not explained.) As it did to Halifax, he added, the military situation
caused him 'serious doubts'. Neither France nor Britain were ready to
fight a war. But the point to stress was the moderation of Hitler himself.
'Mr. Chamberlain had asked himself whether the picture was really so
black as M. Daladier had painted it. For his part he doubted very much
whether Herr Hitler really desired to destroy the Czechoslovak State.'
Indeed, he thought that the reason why Henlein had not demanded an
Anschluss of the Sudetenland, as desired by his own followers, was that
Hitler had advised him not to do so. He urged his French partners to
look at things from Germany's perspective, and to be more sensitive to
its fears of encirclement.[33]

Bonnet, the French foreign minister, lectured his British partners:
'France must respect her signature and Great Britain, whose school-
children were taught the importance of honouring their promises,
would readily understand that attitude of France.'[34] The Frenchmen
lobbied for a firm message to be conveyed to Hitler lest he be tempted
by a repeat of the *Anschluss* on Czechoslovakia. Chamberlain and
Halifax, though, were adamant. What they now disclosed was that
they had been urging the Czechoslovaks to accommodate Henlein for
a while already. Further pressure must be applied in Prague. At most,
the British diplomatic service in Berlin would be instructed to sound
out the Germans as to what terms they thought it advisable to push for
in the Sudetenland.

France was an ally of Czechoslovakia but Britain was not, and the
French were not prepared to fight or confront Germany without British
backing. Daladier and Bonnet had effectively come, in this matter at
least, as supplicants. In the end it was agreed that the British ambassador would sound out the chancellery in Berlin, with the possibility of a
subsequent warning if the Germans proved unreasonable.

AT SOME POINT in the London talks, Daladier interjected that: 'He regretted that he must say that the French Government could not agree that German policy should be allowed to continue to develop freely. [...] He felt that time was not on our side, but rather against us, if we allowed Germany to achieve a new success every month or every quarter, increasing her material strength and her political influence with every successful advance. If this continued, countries which were now hesitating would feel compelled to submit to the hegemony of Germany and then, as we had been warned in "Mein Kampf", Germany would turn to the west.'[35]

It is sometimes assumed that contemporaries were ignorant of Hitler's magnum opus or that, not without intellectual justification, they dismissed it as a youthful work that could not be taken as a serious key to his intentions. That *Mein Kampf* was not programmatic in the detail is correct, and it said little specifically about the Czechoslovaks. Yet that it offered essential insights into both Hitler's ultimate aims and his manner of proceeding was obvious, and it was actually cited by an alarming number of participants in or observers of the Munich drama. Daladier would return to it in conversations with his London counterparts later in the year. It was commonly mentioned in the Czechoslovak press and by Czechoslovak diplomats. Even on the British side it was repeatedly cited, for example by Basil Newton, the ambassador in Prague, in a May warning about the risks of placing too much pressure on the Prague government, or in a discussion with Masaryk by the senior civil servant Alexander Cadogan.[36] A reader of the *Manchester Guardian* listed, in a letter, Hitler's objectives as outlined in *Mein Kampf*, suggesting at least some awareness of it among the general public.[37] The book had been translated and was available in print in English, albeit in an imperfect, abridged version. Within months of Hitler's rise to power, the Foreign Office had become interested in it and submitted it to a detailed analysis. One of the points this highlighted was Hitler's explicit endorsement of lies as a policy tool. Anthony Eden had circulated a note when still foreign secretary, including extracts of the book itself, which Chamberlain is known to have read.[38]

What the protagonists understood to be Hitler's intentions was central to the drama that was to lead to Munich. 'We were in these years – perhaps the only people in Europe – in the "lucky" situation of knowing of Hitler's full plans as much as he did *himself*,' wrote one memoirist, the writer Václav Černý.[39] '*Dr Otto Strasser* was to thank for this,' he added. This was an exaggeration. Admittedly Strasser was valuable for his knowledge of the Nazi system from the inside. Evidence is that he was recruited by the secret service and that he was protected by Beneš personally, and, in August, he would inform the Czechoslovaks of a budding army plot against Hitler.[40] More broadly, the presence of the German exiles made it difficult to ignore the brutal nature of Hitler's regime. But Czechoslovak familiarity with the character and ambitions of Nazism was more basic than this. Indeed, it was well-nigh universal, tied at an instinctive level to the Czech nation's history of episodic conflict with German rulers and to a long-time, first-hand acquaintance with pan-Germanist movements such as the DNSAP and now the SdP. The Czech press routinely mentioned *Mein Kampf* in connection with SdP demands and policies.[41] The Czechoslovak foreign ministry never ceased to warn that France and Britain must 'be firm, or they will end up being threatened themselves'.[42]

As to the SdP's subservience to Berlin, in his early public appearances, such as in Česká Lípa in 1934, Henlein had protested that 'both Fascism and National Socialism lose the natural conditions for their existence at the frontiers of their respective states. [...] We shall never abandon [...] the unconditional respect for individual rights.'[43] He continued to make professions of loyalty to Czechoslovakia to the press and public in the following years. Domestically, though, few were under any illusions. A public debating society run by *Přítomnost* had long been hosting distinguished members of the Bohemian German community: people such as the liberal academic and journalist Bruno Kafka, the writer's cousin, and activist politicians. As early as 1934, when that club had wanted to invite Henlein, Beneš himself intervened, warning in quite vivid terms that Henlein was a Nazi, that he would only lie, and that there could be negative foreign policy implications. It was all a ploy, anyway, so that he would not be barred from participating in the upcoming elections.[44]

The government had debated banning the SdP's *Heimatfront* predecessor in 1934 and early 1935. The police had a thick enough file to justify doing so and had briefly arrested four of the front's leaders a year before. The interior ministry kept tabs on and knew what Henlein's organisation was up to, including that it received money from Berlin.[45] A ban had only been rejected out of concern that internal German opposition might take even more drastic and subversive forms and because it was judged that party bans were undemocratic.[46] The Agrarian Party leader Rudolf Beran briefly considered bringing the SdP into the coalition and government at the end of 1937; this would have had the advantage, from his perspective, of ceasing to rely on a left-to-right grand coalition and ushering in a true right-wing majority instead. Even Beran, though, was compelled to float the idea in veiled terms in a new-year speech.[47] His own party shot down this trial balloon, and he beat a hasty retreat.[48] By 1938, before the confrontation even began, it was generally understood that the SdP's totalitarian inspiration, its reliance on the Führer or 'leadership' principle, was not congruent with republican practice, and that 'Mr Henlein's movement, whatever his opportunistic statements about the state and his loyalty to it, does not agree with the spiritual values based upon which our public life has flourished.'[49]

As Halifax had revealed to his French partners, his messages to Prague had since the *Anschluss* been less than benign. Newton, the ambassador, was from the start no friend of the Czechoslovaks. He had been posted in Berlin prior to Prague, and he routinely addressed his counterparts in German. From March already, Newton had been complaining to Beneš about supposed police abuse in the border regions. In his view, the president was 'cherishing illusions' about opposition to Henlein from Social-Democrats and Catholics.[50] In advance of the Anglo-French talks, his advice to Halifax was to drop Czechoslovakia entirely and, in tandem with far-reaching concessions to Henlein, to let it fall in the German orbit.[51] Halifax needed no encouragement. Ahead of Chamberlain's Commons speech, he had hurried to gloss that British obligations to Czechoslovakia were no more than 'those of one member of the League to another'. Even to France, Britain was tied only by the Treaty of Locarno, and therefore only bound to intervene 'in the event of an unprovoked act of aggression upon her by Germany'. His government regretted that it was 'unable to take any further direct and definite commitment in respect of Czechoslovakia'.[52] Faced with Newton's neutralisation proposal, Halifax urged that the Czechs make 'a supreme effort' and 'do their utmost to reach a settlement by direct negotiation with Herr Henlein'. Newton was encouraged to link up with his French counterpart, Victor de Lacroix, the better to drive the point home.[53]

The Czechoslovaks needed to persuade the Entente partners of the underhand character of Henlein's tactics and the irreconcilable nature of Hitler's aims. This moreover involved appealing not just to the decision-makers, but to their respective publics. The British and French felt they could only resort to arms if the case could be made clearly and convincingly enough to their home bases – and in the British case, to the Commonwealth allies. Only if they could broadcast their story in Britain and France might the Czechoslovaks undercut arguments that their domestic constituencies were not ready for war.

Hitler was trying to whip his own population into a warlike mood. Domestically, the Czechoslovaks faced the difficult task of uniting the nation while trying to conciliate what portions of the Sudeten German community remained hostile or lukewarm towards Henlein – and they had to do this while remaining responsive to Allied demands. A triangular contest began involving the Entente partners, the Sudeten Germans, and the Czechoslovaks. The Czechoslovaks strained to ensure their western partners remained on board, while the Henleinists sought to instil enough doubt and room for manoeuvre to ensure they were not. Behind them stood Hitler, ready to resort to threats whenever Henlein's tactics came unstuck.

This is not to say that the Czechoslovaks were friendless. Many of the foreign correspondents in Prague were well disposed towards them, including George Gedye, Sydney Morrell, Geoffrey Cox, and Alexander Henderson. Morrell wrote for the left-wing *Daily Mirror* and Henderson for the high-circulation *Daily Herald*. Gedye wrote for the *Daily Express* and *Times*, and Cox for the *Daily Express*. Domestically, the Labour-leaning *Daily Herald* and the Tory *Yorkshire Post* were critical of Chamberlain, and the Liberal *Manchester Guardian*, while prepared to give voice to conflicting views, clove to a policy of firmness against the dictators.[54] The *Guardian*'s diplomatic correspondent regularly issued lucid analyses of the crisis, writing, for example, under the title 'Reducing Czechoslovakia to a vassal state', that Henlein was 'an instrument of German foreign policy' and that there could be no question of a war because Germany was not prepared for it.[55]

Several powerful press organs were nevertheless famously friendly towards Hitler and his regime: those of the media barons Lords Beaverbrook and Rothermere, for example.[56] Beaverbrook's titles included the *Evening Standard* and *Daily Express*. Rothermere's main newspaper was the *Daily Mail*. Beaverbrook had attended the Berlin Olympics as Ribbentrop's guest and gushingly congratulated him when he became foreign minister. Rothermere liked to entertain top Nazi leaders at his hotel when in Berlin, and he had visited the German dictator several times at his Berchtesgaden mountain retreat. *The Times*, edited by Geoffrey Dawson, a childhood friend of Halifax, was likewise pro-appeasement. On 3 June it suggested that 'the Germans of Czechoslovakia ought to be allowed, by plebiscite or otherwise, to decide their own future – even if it should mean their secession from Czechoslovakia to the Reich', causing an outcry and forcing the Foreign Office to issue a rebuke.[57]

Of particular note was the *Daily Mail*'s central European correspondent, George Ward Price. Price had been granted the honour of standing in proximity to the Führer when he addressed the Viennese crowds from the Hofburg.[58] František Kubka, a press attaché at the foreign ministry in Prague, writes that sometime after the *Anschluss*, he called at the Czernin Palace and claimed to be carrying a message from Hitler for the president. In the evening, they met in the company of other journalists; Price boasted over drinks that he was Hitler's best friend in Britain, and that his message was that Czechoslovakia would be annihilated if Beneš did not go to Berlin and agree to hand over the Sudetenland within ten weeks.[59]

If Britain's media were divided, so were France's. There was some consistency at the extremes. The far right was uniformly anti-Czechoslovak, the communist press virulently anti-German. Sympathetic centrist organs included the high-circulation *Le Petit Parisien* and the high-impact *Le Temps*, a business newspaper. Broadsheets loyal to the *Parti Radical*, the main party in power, wove between pacifism and a nationalistic readiness to denounce German expansionism.[60] The newspaper *L'Epoque* interviewed Konrad Henlein, but also the leader of the Sudeten German Social-Democrats, Wenzel Jaksch, in April. The interviewer described Henlein as the '*"petit Führer" des Allemands Sudètes*', while at the same time giving him a flattering biography. The article reminded the reader that Henlein was 'but an instrument of Hitler, like Seiss-Inquart [*sic*] in Austria [the Nazi Party chief who had subverted the country in preparation for the *Anschluss*]'. Jaksch separately opined that 'Czechoslovakia cannot grant what Henlein is demanding'.[61]

Goebbels meanwhile did all he could to inflame domestic anger against Czechoslovakia and prepare the German population for a war. The Reich media denounced Czechoslovakia as 'Bolshevik', a violent police state that provided haven to Germany's enemies. Books described the Czechs as tainted with 'wild Asian blood' inherited from the Avars (a steppe invader of the sixth century). Bestial and rotten, they were the 'burning and killing Hussite horde', a semi-civilised people whose role was at best one of passive profiteer from German culture and at worst that of traitorous foe. Czechoslovakia was a monster born of Versailles, an impossible mix of nationalities that had fallen – its gravest sin – to cultural, economic, and political 'Jewification'.[62] In 1938, a favourite tactic became *Gräuelpropaganda*, or 'atrocity propaganda'. Goebbels's accounts built up the slightest incidents into rape-and-pillage stories, and if there was no incident, one could always be made up and placed under headlines such as 'The Hussites plunder the town' or 'Women burnt alive', in a gory *Blut, Tot, Leid*, or 'blood, death, pain', style.

The primary audience for this material was domestic. It did not necessarily go down well with international audiences or give a peace-loving image of Germany, even if it did make it look all the more irreconcilable and dangerous to provoke.[63] A secondary target for Reich propaganda, however, were the Sudeten Germans. For this, since most Reich newspapers were banned in Czechoslovakia, the main organ was the radio. There was a Czechoslovak German-language radio station, but reception was often better from Reich transmitters, and this was what many or most people listened to. German radio actively diffused anti-Czech programmes – 922 in total just between 21 May and 21 July 1938, by one count – including attacks on the president, the administration, the army, or programmes in praise of Henlein, as well as the *Gräuelpropaganda*. The principle was that expounded in *Mein Kampf*: the bigger the lie, the more it was likely to be believed. This was supplemented by the local distribution, undercover or not, of German film, press, pamphlets, flyers, and newsreels, and by the SdP's own press titles and a host of cultural organs, including its main daily, *Die Zeit*, and a magazine, *Rundschau*, plus the use of such tools as the theatre or the organisation of exhibitions of 'degenerate' and 'racially pure' art.[64]

The Czechoslovaks ran their own public relations services, with a press bureau at the foreign ministry issuing regular releases and inter-acting with foreign press correspondents. They placed interviews with Krofta and Beneš abroad. In London, this was run by Jan Masaryk himself, even if he complained in his jocular style that his budget was insufficient and that 'for too little money, too little music'.[65] Masaryk, though, and the foreign service with him, were outplayed by Henlein, who issued news from his own parallel press office in the capital. In Sydney Morrell's view, the Czechs were 'hopelessly outclassed' with their complicated, historical arguments. 'They put too much faith in the truth. Pravda Vitezi – the truth prevails – was their country's motto.'[66]

At the beginning of April and as part of a policy of keeping the Entente powers on side, the Czechoslovaks bowed to the inevitable and invited the SdP in for talks. On 28 March, Hodža had announced on the radio that the government would be preparing a new nationalities statute.[67] The collapse of German activism domestically made Henlein's party unavoidable as a partner for political dialogue. Hitler's propaganda and pressure politics among the Sudeten German community also called for a response. Above all, Czechoslovakia had to be seen to be extending a hand to its internal antagonists because this was the price its friends demanded for their support.[68]

The premier announced that the government was working on proposals to include a new language law, special budgetary allocations for minorities, the appointment of civil servants from their ranks, and autonomy in school policy. His government invited the SdP to make its own suggestions along these lines. On 1 April, a delegation of SdP representatives arrived to meet with Hodža. Once the meeting was over, however, faithful to the strategy laid down by Hitler, the SdP issued a communiqué refusing to negotiate on such terms.[69] The Czechoslovak government separately continued to work on the measures in planning through April and early May, informing the French and British of its progress step by step. The SdP meanwhile released its own entirely different demands through the pulpit, while spurning new invitations to dialogue.

Domestically, the SdP bothered less and less to hide its Nazi allegiances. Henleinist deputies boldly strode into parliamentary chambers in jackboots and were prepared to greet their parliamentary whip with the Hitlerite raised arm.[70] They attended public events 'in grey uniforms which were exact copies of the black German SS uniform'.[71] Gedye describes an SdP rally he attended in Liberec. 'Today Germany belongs to us, tomorrow we shall rule the world,' sang the crowd. The party faithful wore white shirts and jackboots instead of brown shirts and jackboots and stood under a banner bearing a gothic-script SdP monogram instead of the swastika, but this otherwise looked very much like a Nazi Party event. 'As the loudspeakers announced "Der Führer kommt" the roaring of the open exhausts of twenty motor-cycles of Konrad Henlein's motorised bodyguard heralded the arrival of the Führer, Czechoslovak edition.' As Henlein arrived 'every hand shot out in the Hitler salute and every throat roared "Heil".'[72]

In its language, too, the SdP was increasingly brazen. Its pronounce-ments about the Czechs and Czechoslovakia now made Henlein's old expressions of loyalty look positively outmoded. This, however, was as much as possible shielded from foreign audiences. Daladier had been close to the mark when he had offered the information, at the April Anglo–French meetings, that Henlein's party had attempted to hide its congress proceedings from the press. Some journalists had been present, but only local or German. This was not for lack of interest from foreign correspondents: to prevent the exact text of the speeches from being reported, the party barred non-German foreign journalists from attending.[73]

Abroad, Henlein was likewise playing a very different role. In the interview by *L'Epoque*, for example, the SdP leader was cautious to limit his claims to autonomy, and he studiously avoided any mention of ideology.[74] Yet his greatest success occurred on the London scene. Henlein visited London four times on official or semi-official visits: December 1935, July 1936, October 1937, and May 1938.[75] In both 1935 and 1936, he had spoken at the Royal Institute of International Affairs (Chatham House), and on these visits he met with various political per-sonages, in or outside office, and gave newspaper interviews, notably to the *Daily Telegraph* and *Evening Standard*.

Henlein reiterated his loyalty to the Czechoslovak state and denied, in response to questions, having any links with Nazism or receiving any funds from Germany. He accepted 'the existing Constitution, treaties and Minority Treaty', declared himself in favour of an 'honest democ-racy', and repudiated anti-Semitism.[76] The Chatham House audience did not always give him an easy ride. Likewise, when Henlein came in May 1938 and met with such people as Winston Churchill and Harold Nicolson, a retired diplomat and politician and an anti-appeaser, he was grilled over his sympathy for Nazism and its compatibility with his professed Czechoslovak loyalties. The SdP leader was forced into the odd statement that 'he claimed the right to profess the Nazi ideology, but he did not claim to impose it on others'.[77]

Overall, though, Henlein impressed his hosts with his supposed moderation. The SdP leader met in particular with Robert Vansittart, who was under-secretary of state at the Foreign Office, in 1936, 1937, and 1938. On his last visit, over a four-hour dinner, Henlein made himself more threatening, mentioning the possibility of a plebiscite if his demands were not met, and even the prospect of war. Vansittart nevertheless found that he 'retained the general impression that I derived from the whole conversation, that I was, as in previous years, speaking to a wise and reasonable man'.[78] This was all the more ominous in that Vansittart was actually a rare hawk at the Foreign Office, and not a champion of appeasement. The Sudeten German Social-Democratic leader Wenzel Jaksch was also received in London in 1937, but not by the under-secretary, who dismissed him as insignificant.[79]

3

Faithful we remain

'HENLEIN THROWS AWAY THE MASK,' posted *Český deník* in bold letters.[1] 'Henlein identifies with Nazism,' splashed *Lidové noviny* on its front page.[2] The SdP congress had taken place, in Carlsbad, and however much foreign journalists might have been kept out of the room, domestically it was a bombshell.

The SdP's annual congress opened, that year, on 23 April and lasted two days. The town was bedecked with the party's Gothic-script emblems. Henlein was met at his hotel with cries of '*Heil Henlein*' and '*Sieg Heil*'. Crowds greeted him again as he came out and proceeded to the spa and conference centre, chanting songs such as: 'In April Hitler does what he wills, in May he picks up the Czechs, in June Prague is as German as Vienna in bloom.' Inside the conference room 450 party members, MPs, and senators were waiting.[3] Henlein's allocution was booked for the second day, designed to close the proceedings.

The participants' speeches, even before the leader rose to the pulpit, were explosive. Wilhelm Sebekowsky, a party secretary, spoke on the topic of 'Czech expansion and its spiritual-historical basis'. This virulently denounced Czech nationalism as the enemy of all things German. Czech nationalism did not aim at the development of its own people, but existed purely in enmity with the Germans, even though, or rather because, the Czechs owed everything to German civilisation in the first place. Czechoslovakia as a state strived, in its very foundations, towards the forceful assimilation of Germans, and the Sudeten Germans were the victims of Czech 'imperialism', through which their lands had been 'conquered'. Sebekowsky concluded: 'With this Czech imperialism, there can be no understanding because it leads not to peace but to war.'[4] Ernst Kundt, another senior party official and an MP, suggested that the creation of the republic had violated the Sudeten German right to self-determination. Like the preceding intervention, his speech belittled the republic's democratic freedoms, closing with threats of separation.[5] Kundt and Sebekowsky would be put forward as the two main interlocutors in subsequent negotiations with the government.

In passing, Henlein criticised the 1933 dissolution of the Nazi Party in Czechoslovakia as undemocratic. How long will the Czechs continue to consider it the Slavic historical mission to bar a German advance into the south-east? he asked. The Czechs owed everything to the Germans, and they must revise their national 'historical myths'. Correspondingly, so should they alter their foreign policy. Then came a list of eight demands, which would come to embody the SdP programme and form a fixed point of reference in future talks: the Carlsbad demands. These were succinctly: (1) the recognition of the Germans as an equal national group; (2) the constitution of the Sudeten German community as a legal entity with its own communal, not just individual, rights; (3) the delimitation of the Sudetenland as a self-contained region; (4) the encouragement of autonomy and self-rule in all fields of public life within that region; (5) specific legal protection for Germans living outside the area; (6) the rectification of or compensation for all 'injustices' dealt to Sudeten Germans since 1918; (7) the application of the principle that the Sudetenland should have German civil servants; and (8) the complete freedom to adhere to the 'German world outlook'.

Though some of these points – for example, the first – contained nothing a democratic state was likely to find offensive, together they formed a programme for an SdP-run, totalitarian enclave within Czechoslovakia. Henlein clarified that the 'world outlook' meant Nazism. 'Every people is unique and indivisible. It carries within itself its own, inner laws, and its world outlook is nothing else than the expression of its very being,' he insisted. Nazism being an avowed pan-Germanist creed, the eighth point clearly implied the right to secede and unite with the Reich. As to what would happen if this were not granted: 'We want neither a foreign nor a civil war, but we can no longer tolerate a situation which for us only means war within peace.'[6]

Domestically the reaction was a mix of scorn, fury, and satisfaction that Henlein's nature had at last been laid bare. 'Are Henlein's demands meant seriously?' asked *Lidové noviny*. 'It was Berlin speaking through Henlein's mouth. These demands are neither a maximum nor a minimum programme for the German minority, but simply the foreign policy programme of the Third Reich.'[7] The newspaper argued that there was no hope of agreement with Henlein, but that the government should go on with its new statute nevertheless, both in the interests of peace internationally and because this was what a democratic state should do.[8] The SdP's own daily, *Die Zeit*, had loyally run the headline: 'Recognition by Konrad Henlein of the National Socialist world outlook'. *Přítomnost* replied: 'There is no debate that a basic demand of Nazism is the integration of all Germans into the Reich. We can read the details in Hitler's *Mein Kampf*, or in the records of the high court of our own republic. He recognises Nazism, therefore open antagonism towards everything that is called democracy in Czechoslovakia and elsewhere. The congress even resolved that from now on the Reich's racial laws will apply to its membership.' Observing that Henlein's policy was reliant on 'the strength of a foreign state', the piece closed on a truculent note.[9]

The Carlsbad congress and SdP agitation elicited their own counter-reaction. From April onwards, a tide of popular indignation began to gather on the Czechoslovak and loyalist German side. The 1 May demonstrations, traditionally left-wing marches, now took on a national dimension. A picture of Wenceslas Square that day shows it black with people. Yet what turned into demonstrations for the defence of the republic far exceeded the confines of Prague: 20,000 people came out on the streets in Bratislava, 50,000 in Brno, and 35,000 in Ostrava, among numerous other towns as far as Ruthenia.[10] Whether the left-wing *A-Zet* or the right-leaning *Národní politika*, the newspapers welcomed these events as national, with titles such as '1 May – the victory of unity' or 'The new spirit of 1 May'.[11] Czechs and German Social-Democrats demonstrated jointly in a number of Sudetenland locations in an 'antifascist front'.[12] Not by coincidence, Wenzel Jaksch, the Sudeten Social-Democratic leader, chose Carlsbad for his own rally that day. The spa town was deserted of foreign visitors, but many Czechs came, so that together with the local Germans they made a strong crowd at the afternoon speeches and marches. The former legionary and editor of the periodical *Národní listy* Vojtěch Holeček spoke alongside Jaksch and a visiting British Labour MP, to cries of '*Freiheit*' and '*At' žije republika*' ('Freedom' and 'Long live the republic').[13]

The notion of concessions to the SdP and its secessionist programme was not popular. On the contrary, petitioners had been writing to the government to urge it to hold firm since the beginning of the year. An appeal from trade and sports organisations in Rousínov, Czech and German, dated 15 April, warned about the SdP's attempts to cow its opponents and proclaimed its attachment to democracy. Another, from multi-party Czech representatives in Český Krumlov, urged the government not to give in to German pressure. On 13 February, the people of Lidice had proclaimed: 'We will defend our independence together and guard it with our lives.'[14] (In 1942, the SS would gun down the village's entire male population and deport its women and children in reprisal for the assassination of Heydrich.) A joint Czech–German petition from Jablonec dated 17 May: 'We proclaim emphatically that the democratic population will never and under no circumstances give in to terror from whatever side, for it is firmly resolved to defend the integrity and democratic nature of our republic whatever the consequences.'[15] The textile workers' unions of Brno, Rybárpole, and Ružomberok issued a Slovak petition rejecting all interference from Germany, and there were many more such appeals from Kutná Hora, Žilina, and smaller places such as Netřebice, Libkovice, and Röhrsdorf.

By far the largest and most significant such initiative, though, was the mass gathering of signatures initiated under the banner 'Faithful we remain!' by the PVVZ (*Petiční výbor věrni zůstaneme* – 'Petition committee faithful we remain'). Started by a few hundred scientists, academics, writers, actors, filmmakers, and journalists, by September this would exceed a million signatures. It was paralleled by a mass collection for the defence of the republic which, by the same date, managed to raise half a billion crowns from more than 200,000 donors.[16] The PVVZ would survive Munich to act as the conscience of the rump republic and, during the war, become a kernel of the Czechoslovak underground movement. The petition stated: 'In the name of the national freedom and independence which we fought for twenty years ago, we call on all the loyal citizens of the Czechoslovak Republic: with firm resolve, unbreakable faith, and a preparedness for self-sacrifice, we will maintain the integrity and sovereignty of our state. Only in unity can we remain strong and ensure we cannot be overcome. Let us remain faithful to ourselves and faithful to the principles upon which our independence was founded.'[17]

In conformity with SdP tactics, the verbal violence of the Carlsbad congress was pressed home through an active grassroots campaign. The day of national demonstrations, 1 May, was also the occasion for fresh SdP festivities in Carlsbad and other towns. Party representatives openly displayed their Nazi allegiances, such as in Cheb, where the SdP delegate proclaimed to the assembled public that 'Henlein and we all recognise Nazism, because the Reich stands behind us.' Some Czechs came out to sing '*Hej Slované*' ('Hey Slavs', a nineteenth-century pan-Slavic anthem) against cries of '*Ein Reich, ein Volk, ein Führer*', the two groups demonstrating in front of each other's buildings and throwing firecrackers at one another. Henlein's birthday, 6 May, was celebrated with a 20,000-strong demonstration in Aš, where all important buildings were festively decorated except for the district court, the cooperative, and the working-class cultural hall. Uniformed men marched around all day chanting Nazi slogans. The Social-Democrat Andreas Amstätter commented: 'What is going on over there is not for the politician to solve anymore, but for the psychiatrist.'[18]

NONE OF THIS DID anything to ease the pressure from the British or French to accommodate Henlein. Krofta met Newton and Lacroix on 7 May. He tried to explain to the British ambassador that compromising with Henlein would only produce fresh demands. The Sudeten German leader was a Nazi, and his allegiances were to Germany. Newton, in return, lectured the foreign minister on Czechoslovakia's military weakness. France could not help it because it faced impregnable fortifications in the Rhineland, the German 'West Wall', and it was a mistake to rely on Soviet support. Besides, even in the assumption of a long yet victorious war, Czechoslovakia should not necessarily count on retaining its present borders. When Krofta replied that this was too pessimistic, Newton admonished him and his government for being overly timid in their accommodation of Henlein, urging them to be more conciliatory.[19] Lacroix drove the nail in, confirming that the French and British governments had agreed the Czechoslovaks should go to the 'extreme limit' of what was compatible with national integrity in their discussions with the Sudeten Germans. British support was essential to France, and only when the Czechoslovaks could show that they had done their utmost could any useful admonitions be made in Berlin.[20]

It was proving difficult to get the message across that Henlein was playing a double game. On 20 May, two weeks after Krofta's visit to Newton, an incident took place that threatened to make the whole question moot. That evening, two Sudeten German motorcyclists who were driving across the border in Cheb ignored a warning by Czech guards and were shot dead. That they had been smuggling a large quantity of propaganda leaflets attacking the government was unlikely to be painted as an extenuating circumstance by Goebbels's propaganda services. This was just the sort of incident that Hitler could use as pretext for an *Anschluss*-style invasion.[21]

The Czechoslovak secret service had freshly warned that the *Abwehr* was looking to foment trouble. That same day, a Czechoslovak intelligence asset in the Reich alerted Prague over the movement towards the frontier of various German army units.[22] This tallied with reports from the British consul in Dresden of a military build-up at the frontier in Saxony, Silesia, and northern Austria, and with similar information collected by the French in Berlin. The Germans denied that any troop concentration was in progress, but this was only to be expected.[23]

The Czechoslovaks feared a surprise attack more than anything else. This would render their fortification line useless, since it risked being overrun before they could mobilise sufficient troops to man it in strength. On 20 May, the Czechoslovak chief of the general staff, Ludvík Krejčí, having been appraised of the reported German troop movements, asked for an audience with Beneš. Krejčí requested the immediate mobilisation of five army classes. There followed the typical consultations with the 'political ministers' and other government members, as Beneš was worried of being accused, internationally, of stirring up trouble. In the end, the president agreed to mobilise one army class, starting the same evening. The standing army and general staff were put in a state of readiness, and special defence and army units moved into light fortifications and border positions. By the evening of 23 May, 371,000 men would stand under arms and be ready to fight.[24] Meanwhile, 'barricades were flung across roads from Germany, bridges mined, anti-aircraft guns set up round big cities. For four days and nights fighter planes roared above Prague, searching the cloudy skies.'[25]

At the Castle and at the Czernin Palace, the staff were on edge throughout the night.[26] The operation, though, was a success. It proved that the republic intended to defend itself. It had the benefit of acting as a dry run for a more complete, general mobilisation and a trigger for the dusting up of military plans.[27]

No one doubted the risks of confronting Henlein and his Nazi backers. On 23 March, a twenty-four-hour air-defence exercise had been carried out in Prague. The mock attack began at 6:30 a.m. with a raid by forty-nine aircraft which 'attacked' the central post office, followed by a gas alert on the shopping artery of Na příkopě involving the distribution of masks. The aircraft carried on to the Žižkov area, and a second and third attack took place before midday and at 6 p.m. in the industrial suburb of Nusle. Sirens sounded and the streets were evacuated and a black-out tested in the evening. The exercises were repeated in large parts of Bohemia and all of the border regions, serving to identify gaps in air defences as well as to prepare the population. Instructions were circulated: 'Do not stay on the street during an attack, or on the higher floors of buildings. Do not smoke in shelters. Do not pour water on an unexploded bomb: this may cause it to explode. Do not touch any object that has come into contact with poison gas.'[28]

The 20 May mobilisation galvanised a population that was already busy organising against Henleinist bullying. Domestically it reassured the public that the government was able and prepared to resist aggression. However transitory the effect was to prove, moreover, Czechoslovakia's partners responded firmly to the perceived German threat. Though Bonnet privately met the news with panic, he felt bound to declare to the press that an invasion of Czechoslovakia would 'automatically' trigger war. On 22 May, Halifax followed up with a message to Berlin that Britain was unlikely to stand by in a European conflagration.[29]

The effect was likewise electric in the Sudetenland, where Nazi-style white stockings, Hitler salutes, and SdP uniforms were quickly pulled away.[30] The troops which Henlein supporters were given to peek at from behind curtains were Czechoslovak, not Nazi, after all, and war suddenly became something to be feared. A Czech observer recalls: 'A big surprise arrived on 21 May. Around us marched one column after another with their full contingent of weapons towards the border. [...] Practically this meant that military units settled in all the border towns and villages, requisitioning pubs, associative buildings, and even barns. Alongside the fortifications, the soldiers built road blocks and gun emplacements. The Henleinists had been expecting the arrival of the Hitlerite armies.'[31]

Hitler was furious. On 21 April he had ordered General Wilhelm Keitel to flesh out Plan Green, the plan for the invasion of Czechoslovakia, and Keitel had handed in his report on 20 May. There hangs the intriguing possibility that Hitler's instructions somehow filtered through to the Czechoslovak secret services, prompting the alert. The army troop movements had genuinely been mere manoeuvres. Czechoslovak fears were nevertheless on the mark: Plan Green counted on a surprise attack and emphasised the importance of a swift victory. Surprise was to be achieved by the manufacture of some 'convenient apparent excuse' and use made of cooperation from the Sudeten Germans behind the lines. Czechoslovak industrial establishments were to be spared. 'It is my unalterable decision to smash Czechoslovakia by military action in the near future,' Hitler now told his generals. The Führer set an October deadline for invasion, having determined to solve 'once and for all, and this radically' the Sudeten question.[32] The Czechoslovaks' unexpected show of force was meanwhile good evidence of their anti-German tendencies and wanton war-mongering, a theme the Nazi dictator would return to in his September speeches.

After having refused to negotiate with the Czechoslovak government for so long, the SdP finally came to the table on 23 May. Henlein arrived in a 'long grey Mercedes car' to visit Hodža at the Kolowrat Palace in the company of Ernst Kundt.[33] Subsequent discussions would mostly be led, on the SdP side, by Kundt and Wilhelm Sebekowsky. Kundt, weathered-looking and sporting a Hitler moustache, was the self-educated son of a washerwoman, while Sebekowsky was an internationally educated jurist who had practised as a lawyer before becoming an MP and secretary of the SdP.[34]

More meetings followed on 27 and 28 May. Since the SdP still refused to negotiate on the basis of the plan under preparation, Hodža asked its representatives to submit their own proposals. They did so on 8 June, in the form of a memorandum that repackaged the Carlsbad demands. According to the document, the Germans were to have their 'own sovereignty', separate from the organs of state, whose powers were to be severely circumscribed. The Sudetenland was to be granted a very broad self-administration covering the areas of finance, police, education (including 'pre-military training'), social affairs, and health, among others. Even legislative powers were to be divided between the national assembly and the diets of each nationality, and likewise the courts. Sudetenland civil servants were to be exclusively German. What the Henleinists were asking for was the establishment of a separate, exclusively SdP-run territory within the republic, with responsibilities covering basically all public administration and governmental tasks. Formulas proposed for sharing residual powers with the centre were so complex as to be effectively impossible to carry out. The Sudetenland, already endowed with its own German sovereignty, would be available for detachment at any moment.[35]

Intransigent though it remained, the SdP had at least joined talks with the government. Hitler's surprise attack and annexation had not happened. The Czechoslovaks were showing that they were perfectly prepared to resort to arms. Their troops were positioned in Sudetenland territory, since this was mostly situated on the borders, curtailing Henleinist room for creating havoc. If any proof was needed that the Henleinists only responded to force and points scored against them and Hitler, surely this was it.

The talks over the Sudetenland proceeded, regardless, to an accompaniment of continued sniping and exhortation from the Entente partners. By June, the jolting effect of the mobilisation had faded, the war alert retrospectively causing the British and French an even greater degree of anxiety and raising their eagerness to see Prague find a compromise with the SdP. Neville Henderson, the ambassador in Berlin, had informed the Germans that 'His Majesty's Government are now using their influence urgently with the Czechoslovak Government to bring them to seek without delay a solution of the problem on comprehensive lines by direct negotiation with the Sudeten Germans.'[36] At the end of the month, Newton came to visit Krofta and, warning that Czechoslovakia should not 'misuse' the advantage it had gained in the May crisis, he asked for 'a significant gesture' towards the Sudeten Germans.[37] Lacroix also weighed in; as soon as the alert had passed, the two ambassadors asked that the Czechoslovaks withdraw their troops to pre-empt agitation in Germany about 'Czech imperialism'.[38] In the background, Halifax was reproaching Bonnet for ascribing French pressure too much to British desiderata and British opinion. France must put 'the greatest possible pressure, without delay, upon Dr. Benes' and convey the 'specific warning that France would have to reconsider her treaty position if the Czechoslovak Government were unreasonable on the Sudeten question'.[39]

Beneš and Hodža decided that they had no choice but to accept the SdP proposals as a basis for further consultations. While in bulk the provisions contained in the SdP's June memorandum were unacceptable, some of them could be adapted in the form of local autonomy measures, such as in the fields of education or social policy. Hodža told the cabinet: 'My position: broad concessions to the Germans in order to show a clean conscience in London. Not to fragment the legislature. Decentralise the administration – by allocating day-to-day responsibilities to localities.'[40] The nationalities statute that had been in preparation in April, a so-called 'First Plan' that had been intended for legislative approval by the end of June, was now dropped in favour of a 'Second Plan', yet to be specified but to incorporate such measures as inspired by the SdP document.[41]

Jan Masaryk made a blunt suggestion that month: the government should adopt a programme of thorough but quickly implemented concessions, designed to prove Czechoslovakia's goodwill, but then dig in its heels with the British and French. 'I consider it necessary to show the French and the British immediately how far we are prepared to go in concessions, but then to adopt a manly stance and point at our duty to defend our sovereignty.'[42] Since Henlein was sure to turn down whatever was offered to him, this was never going to work on the Entente decision-makers, who were set on Czechoslovakia coming to an agreement with him. It might, however, have had the desired effect on the British and French publics, whose understanding of the issues could only ever be foggy but who might have grasped the concept of substantial but final concessions.

Another tantalising hypothetical concerned a planned trip of Beneš. As Štefan Osuský, the ambassador in Paris would warn in September, there were deep divisions within the French cabinet, which was far from being uniformly pro-appeasement. Osuský, a Slovak, was a seasoned diplomat with a long career in Paris who knew his interlocutors well. 'Do not allow yourself to be overly scared by Anglo–French interventions. [...] If we are strong, we will have value to ourselves and to others. Therefore judge the situation coolly and without regard to what they are saying,' he would urge Beneš, much as Masaryk had done.[43] There existed key differences between the French and the British in their perception of the problem, but also subtly distinct positions between the decision-makers themselves. Bonnet may have thought a rapprochement with Germany possible, but he faced the dilemma that France's honour and credibility were on the line. Daladier, who wavered throughout, almost certainly knew that compromise was impossible and even self-defeating, and that only the threat of war or indeed war itself could stop Hitler; in his conceptions, though, war meant a long war, something like 1914–18, and this could only be won with British participation. It is also worth noting that ultimately the Czechoslovaks had a French, not a British, problem: it was France, with its large army, that was committed to coming to its aid if Germany attacked, not Britain, which had virtually no land forces and owed it no diplomatic commitment. If the French could be kept on side, their eyes firmly on their treaty duties, what Chamberlain or Halifax thought need not, in the last resort, matter.

Beneš, however, was paradoxically capable of being quite narrowly focused on diplomacy, and strangely indifferent, for a politician, to the fissile character of opinion. The Czechoslovak president went on trips to Romania and Yugoslavia to bolster his alliances there in June. He had been booked to visit France officially in the same month. The occasion was the unveiling of a monument to commemorate the handing of flags, during the Great War, to a Czechoslovak regiment that had fought on the Western Front under French command. But just as he was about to take the trip, the Quai d'Orsay asked the embassy to delay it on the grounds that the ceremony might be perceived as a provocation in Berlin at a sensitive time.[44] Perhaps it might have made an impression on the French public or provided an occasion to stiffen Daladier's spine had Beneš insisted and gone regardless.

THE STATE OF DOMESTIC OPINION likewise supported a firm, even belligerent stance. Few people outside policy-making circles realised the kind of pressure the Entente partners were applying on their government to come to a deal with Henlein. The press typically failed to highlight the conditional nature of their support, and it tended to gloss all pronouncements from them as proof of interest in the Czechoslovak cause. As Beneš and the government were being forced into negotiations with the SdP, the mass movement in favour of resistance was actually gathering strength.

On 21 May, the very day of the mobilisation, Beneš made a speech in the south Bohemian town of Tábor. The timing was fortuitous, but the venue had an almost mythical status: it had been the focal point of the fifteenth-century Hussite movement, which itself occupied an important place within Czechoslovak, and specifically Czech nationalist, discourse. The Hussites took their name from Jan Hus, a religious reformer, follower of the English medieval theologian John Wycliffe, and a Protestant before Luther. The Hussites were strong nationalist material because under their leadership, the nobility and people of Bohemia had fought long and victorious wars against the Catholic German emperor, culminating in the election of their own Czech king. In Nazi propaganda the Hussites stood for destruction and anarchy and were a pillaging horde. In Czech iconography, they were an idealistic movement motivated by purity and probity that had, moreover, united the people in an early incarnation of the nation.

'We [...] are determined to defend our State to the last extremity,' said Beneš, but the president also called for forbearance and mutual understanding between the communities and warned that 'nothing, nothing whatever, can shake or jeopardize our democratic regime'.[45] Czechoslovak nationalism had always had a dual character. It was at once a vehicle for the defence and development of a particular group, or two groups – the Czechs and Slovaks – and the embodiment of humanist ideals, Czechoslovakia defining itself as the heir to Jan Hus, Comenius, and Renaissance humanism, and to their Czech and Slovak continuators in the nineteenth-century National Revival. There was a small Czech fascist league, led by the war veteran Radola Gajda, but it was the object more of ridicule than fear. Slovakia had a nationalist party, the HSĽS, whose ideology flirted with Austrian clerical fascism, but support for it owed more to disappointed aspirations for an autonomy that had been promised the Slovaks in 1918, and even the HSĽS only polled a quarter or so of the Slovak vote.

The same blending of Slavic celebration and democratic idealism came to the fore in the Sokol festivities that took place in June and early July: the third contributor, after the 1 May events and the mobilisation alert, to the popular groundswell. In the nineteenth-century Czech lands as in Germany, gymnastics societies had been crucibles for national movements which, in the absence of a nation-state and in the face of active censorship, often struggled to find other outlets. Originally founded in Bohemia in 1862, the Sokol gymnastics organisation had branched out throughout the Slav world and beyond at the turn of the century. Clad in uniforms (grey tunics, red shirts, dark trousers, and a brimless semi-top hat with a falcon's feather, *sokol* meaning 'falcon' in Czech), the Sokol had helped to form a national guard to maintain order during the revolution. They naturally stood for republican nationalism.[46]

All-Sokol games or festivals were held every six years, and this was the tenth such occasion. The all-Sokol festival (or *slet*) of 1938 was the scene of a massive coming together in a cry of defiance to Hitler. For days, the press wrote of almost nothing else. The event was propagated through film, newsreel, and radio. It popularised the slogan 'We won't surrender!', launched by the army during the May mobilisation and repeated everywhere during the festivities. The games even brought the nation together physically: Prague was completely packed by the time of the final celebrations on 6 July (the anniversary of Jan Hus's martyrdom), when more than a million tourists flocked to the capital.[47]

It had all begun the year before, on 26 October 1937, when the Prague Sokol had launched a group of torch-bearers to the four corners of the republic, involving 100,000 people in an even grander replica of the Olympic torch ceremony (itself an invention of Goebbels for the 1936 Olympics). Yet the *slet* proper began with a set of marches through Prague in the last weeks of June.[48] The first international units, from the United States, had arrived appositely at Wilson Station on 18 May. Sydney Morrell watched the participants walk past his hotel window in their picturesque costumes for four hours, 'Bosnians from the Albanian border, tasselled fezzes on their heads, their loose red silken trousers gathered in at the ankles, great old pistols stuck diagonally into scarlet sashes [...] Ruthenians in coarse homespun linen, leaping and twirling in the air, brandishing their long small-headed forest axes', and finally American Czechs, 'very modern and western in white vests and shorts'. Beneš sat on a stand outside the Old Town Hall by the astronomical clock, surrounded by Czechoslovak, Yugoslav, and Romanian army officers in uniform.[49] Throughout, 'the houses were decorated with bunting, flags were floating in the mild breeze, and at night the baroque and Gothic steeples of the churches of golden Prague with her hundred spires were floodlit. The open-air cafés were crammed full and so were the pubs. Brass bands played Smetana and Dvořák and the latest hit: "We won't give Prague away / Rather not let her stay / Rather not let her stay / Let's pull her down."[50]

The centrepiece of the festivities was a set of athletics displays performed in Strahov Stadium, the largest in Europe. On 3 July, at three minutes before three, the games were launched as a cannon fired and 3,000 doves were set free. As the president, his wife, and various government members and foreign ambassadors sat in the tribune, the participants took up the Hussite hymn, 'We are God's warriors,' and swore fidelity to the republic. Thousands of gymnasts poured into the stadium. Participants entered through two wide gates into the arena, marching in line and splaying out to fill it and perform their calisthenics in perfect coordination. The pictures show them clothed in the same way with white sleeveless shirts, dark trousers, and a striped belt, forming gigantic squares and various geometric figures and signs of stadium length.[51]

The games' pageantry mixed symbols of peace, defiance, Slavic solidarity, and reminders that Czechoslovakia's allies, especially from the Little Entente but also France, stood by its side. The 4 July displays thus involved athletes from an International Gymnastics Federation championship that had just taken place, including French and British athletes.[52] There was also a 'day of our army', 6 July, involving Czechoslovak as well as Yugoslav and Romanian soldiers. This had military performances in the stadium by infantry and cavalry and a march by motorised and air defence units before the president, with, as the closing spectacle, an over-flight by military aircraft, one squadron forming the words 'X. slet'.[53]

The slet bolstered a popular rally to the flag that would play an important role during the events of September. Its enthusiastic attendance conversely helped convince the decision-making elites that a military solution was within their grasp. Kurt Weisskopf, a Czecho-slovak citizen but also a German Jew, cast an at once detached and concerned eye on these displays. He describes one of the set pieces as follows:

> For a minute or two the searchlights were turned off at the start of the spectacle and onlookers and actors in the large stadium waited in complete silence under the dark silver-sprinkled velvet canopy of the night sky. A fanfare from Smetana's *Libuše* signalled the beginning. As if born by a mobile cone of white spotlights a large group of Sokols marched or, as it seemed, floated into the centre of the arena. It was an orderly, well-drilled entry, yet rather more graceful and easy than the march of a military unit. The scene was to symbolize the birth of Czechoslovakia. It was, of course, almost unbearably naïve but at the same time, despite its triviality, it was movingly dignified and simple.

> [... There entered] a column of cardboard tanks and armoured cars followed by hordes armed with staves symbolizing rifles. [...] Sombre music emphasized the sinister intentions of the invaders. [...] All seemed lost. [But] the spotlights focused on a distant and dark corner of the wide field. There they were, our Sokols, busily engaged in eurhythmics, body-building and other non-controversial yet eminently patriotic activities. [...] Closing their ranks, they marched towards the invader with staves raised high. The foreign hordes faltered and eventually fled in disarray when a squad of genuine tanks, put at the disposal of the organizers of the Rally by courtesy of the Ministry of Defence, headed towards them. [...] Triumphal martial music marked the victori-ous conclusion.[54]

4

Czechs and Germans

IN 1993, A JOURNALIST and author named Robert Kaplan published a book about the looming conflict in Yugoslavia. Kaplan was well intentioned, and *Balkan Ghosts* was both timely and visionary in warning of an impending human catastrophe. Yet far from performing the role of prophylactic, as its author expected, the book ended up a victim of unintended consequences. Serbs, Croats, and Bosnians had begun fighting for the remains of their collapsing federal state. In Bosnia, Serb irredentists supported by the Serbian Republic proper and its president, Slobodan Milošević, had launched a brutal civil war. The Bosnian capital, Sarajevo, was under siege and NATO was debating whether to intervene. *Balkan Ghosts* landed on the American president's bedside table. Kaplan himself writes: 'In 1993, just as President Clinton was contemplating forceful action to halt the war in Bosnia, he and Mrs. Clinton are said to have read *Balkan Ghosts*. The history of ethnic rivalry it detailed reportedly encouraged the President's pessimism about the region, and – so it is said – was a factor in his decision not to launch an overt military response in support of the Bosnian Moslems, who were being besieged by Bosnian Serbs.'[1] The war dragged on as NATO dithered and delivered no more than pinpricks. Bosnia became the scene of the first concentration camps and systematic civilian massacres in Europe since the Second World War. One hundred thousand died and many more were displaced, and the region was left scarred for decades.

How a work of political analysis is written can be just as important as what it says. If two populations are described as having forever been at each other's throats, a certain fatalism will inform the response. If they are defined as one people divided by a fluctuating linguistic or cultural barrier, and who have only really found themselves driven to strife by demagogues from time to time, the suggested remedy is likely to be different. On reading Kaplan's book, one finds that its unintended impact was perhaps not so surprising after all. *Balkan Ghosts* glides over periods of peace to give the relentless impression of a region seething with age-old and unsolvable hatreds. Kaplan, like any good journalist, let his sources speak for themselves, but the result was that his text rarely questioned whether his interlocutors were tailoring what they said to their audience, or making sweeping statements for effect, or disguising ideology as historical fact.

The very vocabulary of a political or historical debate is important. Some historians of Munich or of interwar Czechoslovakia have described the Sudeten Germans as ethnic Germans.[2] At the time, few people employed the word 'ethnic' for the simple reason that they used the even more questionable term 'race'. 'Race' was used by reporters to describe what separated Czechs and Germans; the word was deployed in *The Times*; it was taken up in Foreign Office despatches. The British ambassador in Berlin, Neville Henderson, even called the Czechs a 'pig-headed race'.[3]

Yet even 'ethnic' obscures and misleads far more than it illuminates. The word evokes common ancestry, but this is easily plagued by the illusion that one only has a set of two ancestors going back in time, a nuclear family repeating itself generation after generation; a few hundred years up the family tree, a person's gene pool actually runs into the thousands or tens of thousands of individuals. Germans and Czechs were depicted as if their forebears had all belonged to one or the other national group, without any intermixing or outside addition, each in their own village or cottage looking on balefully at their neighbour. If there were people who called themselves German or Czech in the twentieth century, it must be because they were descended from individuals who had moved in from a place called Germany, or from a Slavic region somewhere into the Sudetenland.

Anthropologists have long debunked this way of thinking.[4] Ethnicity is 'a subjective sense of loyalty based on imagined origins and parentage rather than something to be measured by objectively visible present cultural criteria or historical facts,' write De Vos and Romanucci-Ross. 'A new ethnic loyalty can be created as deliberately as can a fabricated or advanced mythology of origin.'[5] The bond of ethnicity is not common kinship, but rather the accepted myth of shared origins. Such myths easily spill into or are easily recuperated under the banner of nationalism: 'People can retain an intuitive conviction concerning the ethnic purity of their nation whatever the facts, and this conviction is a fundamental factor in ethno-psychology. It is this perceived association between exclusive descent and the nation which accounts for the once popular and still not totally passé practice of interutilizing the terms race and nation.'[6]

Identities fluctuated throughout the Bohemian kingdom's thousand-year history, dependent on factors including locality, class, religion, language, and dynastic allegiance. The Hussites may have been predominantly Czech-speaking, but they were primarily a religious movement. The Habsburgs, after they durably took over the kingdom in the seventeenth century, followed more or less intentional Germanising policies. Under the Counter-Reformation, a 'veritable army of priests' fanned out into the towns and countryside, promoting Catholic education and, incidentally, the German language.[7] Nobles and burghers acclimatised to the monarchy and its administration's increasingly dominant German culture.[8] Eighteenth-century Theresian school reform probably did even more to promote German; in Bohemia, it prohibited the hiring of schoolmasters who were not proficient in the language.[9] More than a century later, as Wenzel Jaksch wrote: 'In Brno, where workers and trades people of both nations lived in close contact, Czech and German almost melted into a single local dialect; the same was true in other Moravian cities.'[10]

A mere glance at people's names confirms that what were described as separate Slavic and Germanic groups were actually an extensively intermixed population. The evidence suggests that people repeatedly intermarried and/or crossed over from one linguistic group to the other. Many Czechs today retain a German family name or are called Němec, the very word for 'German'. An analysis of Czech graves in the border regions performed in the mid-twentieth century throws up numerous names of German origin, ranging from 15 to 40 per cent. Likewise in the two Sudeten towns of Ústí and Lovosice, the percentages of German grave names of Czech origin were 20 and 34 per cent respectively.[11] These are, moreover, likely to be lower limits, as many people probably transcribed their name into Czech or German as they crossed the linguistic barrier.

Even if one looks at the names of the SdP's representatives in parliament, the elite of the supposedly Aryan party, one finds that perhaps a fifth of them were of identifiably Slavic origin.[12] This was the point made by *Přítomnost*, which wrote that if one applied the Nazi criteria for being Aryan, there were no more than a million Germans in Czechoslovakia.[13] 'A proper German must have three German grandparents. The introduction of this principle – that of the Nuremberg Laws so beloved of Sudeten Germans – would decimate Henlein's party. What would the leaders of the SdP do to save themselves who are called Obrlík, Hudeček, Utišil, Pšeníček, Sebekovský, Lukeš, Králiček, Jiříček? [...] What a farce!'[14] Indeed, Henlein himself was partly Czech according to such yardsticks. His mother had been born Hedwig Anna Augusta Dvořáčková, the daughter of a Czech father and German mother, a detail he did his best to keep quiet.[15]

It was only in the nineteenth century that language became, as in many other places, a hard criterion of nationality. Even so, one's language was sometimes hard to pin down. Hubert Masařík writes that in the 1910 census, what nationality people declared themselves as belonging to depended on many circumstances tied to family, place of residence, and workplace. One of his uncles, a Czech, was director of a German school and had a German wife. His son was raised as a Czech and his daughter as a German.[16] The pre-war Austrian criterion for nationality, indeed, was the *Umgangssprache*, or language of everyday use. But 'enormous pressure was exerted upon the Slav inhabitants of Habsburg Austria to register as Germans, more especially since to be German was to rank as socially superior. The census was not a secret vote, and the Czech lignite miner in North Bohemia knew that it might be as much as his job was worth to register as Czech. The lignite mines were German-owned and imposed a German *Umgangssprache*.'[17] This could reach absurd lengths. Wickham Steed, the correspondent for *The Times* in Vienna, had entered himself as British on the census papers. He was visited by an Austrian official, who asked him to write himself down as German; after all, in Vienna his *Umgangssprache* was German.[18]

The Sudetenland Germans whom Henlein and Hitler claimed as theirs were of a very ambiguous German nationality. Ethnic groups, like any imagined community, are prone to recuperation by ideologues and special interests. 'One problem with the primordial is that we know how many of the groups that have engaged in "primordial" conflict are themselves recent historical creations.'[19] The Sudetenland was a recently invented term, attributed to a 1902 magazine article by the right-wing politician and essayist Franz Jesser.[20] In the days of the Weimar Republic, Berlin had actually encouraged activism, and the DNSAP in Czechoslovakia had polled very little. The Nazi paraphernalia of costumes, flags, salutes, and marches was ideally suited to deepening an 'ethnic' boundary between the German and Czech populations that shared the Sudetenland.[21] For Henlein and the pan-Germanists, to claim the Sudetenland as ethnically or racially German was simply to enlist the political backing of the powerful neighbouring Reich.

In Czechoslovakia, Robert Kaplan's role was filled by a courageous, diligent, and equally well-intentioned Cambridge historian named Elizabeth Wiskemann. Wiskemann was familiar with Nazism, having gone to Berlin and written about it as early as 1930–1. She had been banned from Germany for her views. She settled in Prague in 1937 to write a book titled *Czechs and Germans*, which came out in June 1938.[22] Apart from being brave and hard-working, she was a thorough scholar. Yet much like Kaplan's, her book only gave the impression of timeless, intractable conflict. 'Bohemia and Moravia, with Southern Silesia, the Historic Provinces of the Bohemian Crown, lie at the very heart of Europe,' it began. 'Mountains and forests hem in their richness and their beauty. For nature wished well by Bohemia [...]. This lavishness has, however, been constantly counteracted by the destructive forces of racial passion, forces which have become more conscious and therewith more aggressive as the centuries have passed. For Bohemia long ago became the battle-ground *par excellence* between the Germans and the Slavs.'[23]

Wiskemann did not recommend a plebiscite or the dismantlement of Czechoslovakia. She did her best to rely on Czech as well as German sources and interviews. (Czechs could be guilty of the same fictions, such as that the Sudetenland Germans were the descendants of populations invited over by the medieval Přemislyd kings, and Tomáš Masaryk himself had once called the Sudeten Germans 'immigrants and colonists', though this was during the extraordinary time of the revolution.[24]) But while her book offered a wealth of information on such things as agricultural reform or the number of schools and civil servants from each of the two linguistic communities, it also contained a long historical inquiry whose thrust was to portray Czechs and Germans as having been at war with each other since time immemorial. That most of Bohemia's history had arguably been pre-national or that culture, history, symbols were all things Henlein and Hitler had been actively exploiting to ideological ends – these points failed to merit a mention.

The problem with representations of the conflict as national or ethnic in character was that they completely overshadowed key Czechoslovak arguments against carving out the Sudetenland. That Bohemia had enjoyed essentially untouched borders for something like a thousand years ought to have given pause to French and British observers and decision-makers. The brutal and authoritarian nature of the Nazi regime to which it was proposed to transfer the Sudetenland populations ought to have mattered more than exactly how many German schools or civil servants the region counted per capita. But the Nazi description of the conflict as rooted in race, itself interchangeable with national identity, won over and was effectively adopted by the British and French – whether as the result of direct seepage from Nazi discourse, or whether such conceptions fell on fertile ground in an age when social Darwinism and eugenics retained significant cultural clout is a question that lies beyond the scope of this book.

Hitler and Henlein were all too happy to flog Western diplomats with requests for 'self-determination' for the Sudetenland Germans. This played, of course, on residual guilt at the Versailles Treaty – a guilt, it should be noted, that mostly derived from the treaty's controversial reparations clause, for which the Czechoslovaks bore no responsibility. But self-determination, in this context, also drew on the notion of the Sudetenland Germans having a separate ethnic or national character, and no one except for the Czechoslovaks was able to furnish the arguments against it. In the summer, the Foreign Office would despatch a mediator named Walter Runciman to persuade the Czechoslovaks to reach a compromise with Henlein and the SdP. Lord Runciman would be photographed on the train preparing to take him from Victoria Station towards Prague. In the photograph, Wiskemann's book is in his hands. It is not known what he thought of it, but in a letter to Chamberlain on the eve of his departure, he wrote: 'What a cockpit Bohemia has always been! For 800 years they have quarrelled and fought: Only one king kept them at peace, Charles IV, and he was a Frenchman! How can we succeed?'[25]

THE HENLEINISTS QUICKLY RECOVERED from the shock of the May mobilisation. Even as they were opening negotiations on a Sudetenland statute with the government, in the region itself they renewed their campaign of intimidation. The occasion was the set of municipal elections that were held throughout Czechoslovakia on 22 and 29 May and on 12 June.

The stakes were high: if the SdP could increase its majority, it could claim to represent the totality of the Sudetenland Germans. The party periodical *Die Zeit* published every week a list of people 'of German blood' who had betrayed their nation by participating in Czechoslovak cultural activities – writers, musicians, actors, radio speakers – and published apologies and promises that they would cease to do so.[26] Small-town newspapers were even more brazen. 'The way certain persons acted in these recent gravely decisive days – persons who still take upon themselves the honour of being considered Germans – must remain eternally branded in our memory,' wrote the Kraslice *Volksblatt*. 'The gallows are waiting for the traitors and ruffians Schmidt and Vogel, and for the women Krunes, Sobotka, and Vogelin [whose crime had been to send their children to a Czech school],' said a poster in another town. 'We greet our Führer, beloved everywhere, with the oath of fidelity: "Down with the traitors of the Nation! Long live our Führer! *Sieg Heil!*"'[27]

Company bosses friendly to the party were enlisted and told to bus their employees to the polling booths to make the right choice. They threatened staff who were Social-Democrats with the loss of their jobs or actually laid them off. Party members menaced opponents with the confiscation of their house or farm and brawled with them in public places.[28] In many of the smaller localities, SdP intimidation ensured that none but their own candidates were put forward: it required ten signatures to submit a list, and people dared not identify publicly with the opposition to Henlein.[29] The result was that in more than half the municipalities, the only list was an SdP list, and in many others there were only an SdP and a Czech list.[30] Even where an alternative was on offer, rumours spread that the SdP would know who had voted for the Social-Democrats; in several places voters sought to obtain evidence or confirmation that they had duly voted for the SdP. 'At Josefstal, near Gablonz, on polling day uniformed "stewards" surrounded the polling-station, formed a lane of young men shouting "*Sieg Heil!*" to every voter as he, necessarily, passed between the ranks' – and this was but one example.[31]

In May, the SdP had formed a volunteer defence corps, the FS (for *Freiwilliger Schutzdienst*). It was soon to number 40,000 hand-picked men, complete with their own marching song and chief of staff. Astonishingly, the Czechoslovak authorities did not ban it. Nomi-nally formed to protect Henlein, it was not supposed to have access to firearms, but weapon-smuggling enabled it to morph into a veritable private army over the summer. By August, entire platoons would be venturing around the Sudetenland in black riding boots and trousers and the same collared shirts, black ties, and belts as the SS, missing only the eagle and swastika. 'The FS is not a body of troops for parades, but a body of soldiers on duty at all times,' its chief of staff Willy Brand-ner proclaimed. 'We march together with the men of the FS until the victory of our national group for its rights and Lebensraum.'[32] Acts of aggression against opponents, Jews, and Czechs multiplied throughout the spring and summer.[33]

Probably the single biggest grievance of the Sudeten Germans was that they had never been recognised as a state nationality, like the Czechs and Slovaks, but only as a minority. Their share of the popula-tion, roughly on a par with that of the Slovaks, should have entitled them to that status. To political or everyday practice, it made almost no difference; the distinction was essentially psychological, a question of sentiment or pride. But sentiment, when it comes to nationalism, is everything. As the Sudeten Germans saw it, they had once been masters in their own house and they were now relegated to second-class status.[34] Wenzel Jaksch, the Social-Democratic leader, certainly saw this as a crucial issue, and he repeatedly asked for such recognition.[35] By 1938 it was probably too late to grant it: one can only imagine what new claims Henlein would have felt entitled to raise had he been given state nationality status. In 1918 or 1919, it had been too early: key Sudeten German political figures had refused to recognise the republic, and there had been violent clashes leading to deaths in the border towns, making any such gesture meaningless. The ideal time would have been the heyday of activism, the late twenties, or the early thirties. In 1936, indeed, Krofta himself had proposed just that: that the Germans should be officially proclaimed a Czechoslovak 'state nation', but the Czech press had risen up in protest against him.[36]

The Sudetenland, with its heavy coal-and-steel industry and its numerous textile mills, had been hit by the Great Depression more heavily than the rest of the country. Unemployment had risen to 600,000, or 15 per cent of the population, in the predominantly German regions, and though the state provided widespread relief, the temptation was to blame the government.[37] As the Reich's own labour surplus shrank thanks to Hitler's mass enlistment programmes, moreover, a number of unemployed Sudetenland Germans found work over the border. This both fed existing grievances and facilitated Nazi indoctrination.[38] Yet by 1938 unemployment was shrinking fast, and it would continue to fall throughout the year. In 1937 it had declined by a third, and it would halve again by the time of Munich.[39]

Outside observers pored over perceived or actual inequalities – in German schools per capita, the number of German-speaking civil servants, infrastructure budgets, and so on. To the extent these things mattered in interwar Czechoslovakia, it is ultimately for the way they underlined the minority status that the Germans so disliked, or as potential tools for the SdP to embarrass the authorities. By such yardsticks conditions were actually far better in Czechoslovakia than in the German enclaves of Italy or Poland, and even than in some regions of the Reich. There were more German schools per capita in Czechoslovakia than in Prussia, for example. Germans commanded 23 per cent of posts in the judiciary, their exact share of the population, and 25 per cent in the public health services, though less in railways, post, and telecoms.[40] There were even several hundred German-speaking officers in the army, and one general. During the crisis years of 1930–5, the state paid proportionally more unemployment relief, via the trade unions, to Germans than to Czechs, and more statutory aid to those out of work. It spent more on road repair in the German regions.[41] An agricultural reform performed in the 1920s had hit German landowners predominantly, but this was because it mostly hit the tiny group of the aristocratic landed magnates. While Czechoslovaks obtained a disproportionate share of the redistributed arable land, tens of thousands of Sudeten German peasant families also benefited.[42]

Beneš toured the border regions in 1936, making speeches in German and seeking to gauge the situation. Meanwhile Hodža asked the ministers of the three activist parties to make proposals. Based on these, the government had passed a programme in February 1937 consisting of public works to fight unemployment, efforts to improve German representation in the public service, fresh contributions to social and cultural initiatives, and adjustments to the school and language laws. The works were welcome, but the majority ended up going to Czech companies, which bid lowest on price. Putting more German civil servants in place was bound to be slow, and there were already German schools almost everywhere.[43] Jaksch accordingly proposed more ambitious action towards the end of the year: further economic support, initiatives against youth unemployment, and autonomy in education. This would at least have had symbolic value. He incidentally warned that the state's foreign policy was too accommodative of Nazism and its Sudeten crypto-Nazi stooges.[44] Such proposals were in any case overtaken by the emerging crisis at the start of 1938. The greatest sin of the Czechoslovak state was to have overlooked the potential for manipulation of a disgruntled Sudetenland community by a hostile Germany, and never to have grasped that only an excess of deference and solicitude could meet what were essentially psychological grievances.

'Around that time [1938] our everyday lives changed. Suddenly on the streets, men in lederhosen and white stockings appeared, walking in closed groups. They raised their right hands and shouted *Heil* and looked for scrapes with Czechs, especially on the streets where Czechs lived, and I was afraid of them,' remembers Marie Novotná, a schoolgirl at the time. 'My friend Margareta and I visited each other regularly, we did our homework together, and we went together, even though I was not religious, to the devotional ceremonies in May because the church smelled of lilies, they played the organ, and there reigned there a quiet dusk. After the death of my mother, she became the closest person to me. Then one day Margareta told me that we would not be seeing each other anymore. When I asked her why, she said that I am Czech and that her mother forbade it.'[45]

Relationships began to deteriorate at the personal level in the mid- to late 1930s. Ordinary people's testimonials differ as to when exactly this happened, but they identify 1933, or 1935–6, when Hitler's speeches began to filter through, or 1938 itself as the approximate date. Most recall that it was only in 1937 and 1938 that mutual hostility, hitherto confined to narrow, mostly Prague-based political and academic circles, spilled out into daily life in the towns and villages of the Sudetenland. Germans and Czechs each began shopping with their own. Sudeten German men and women took to wearing Tyrolean garb: lederhosen, long peasant dresses, pointy feathered caps, and especially white stockings or socks, a classic case of reinvented tradition helping to cement ideologically inspired ethnic strife.[46]

'The period before Hitler's rise was characterised by good relations between Czechs and Germans,' writes Vratislav Chládek, who lived in a majority-German border town. 'We were friends with many Germans, and we respected each other. From childhood we played together, played sports together, etc., without regard to our different languages. Some Czech kids had the most friends among German children, and vice versa.'[47] 'I was friends with a boy of my age, who lived with his German mother and sister not far from our flat,' recalls Franti- šek Viktora from Rýmařov. 'He was named Kurt Andýsek and his sister

Erna. I learnt German from him and he learnt Czech from me. We were inseparable for almost two years. I was all the more surprised when in the autumn and winter of 1937, he told me that he didn't have time, that he must study, and finally that he could not see me anymore.' Later, Viktora's father was attacked and left unconscious in the street. Then Viktora himself was assaulted by a group of five German youths and left to lie in a field, until he was found by a local factory worker, who took him to the hospital.[48] Numerous testimonials speak of rising hostility after German youths began to go for schooling, or indoctrination, in the Reich. Violence increased in 1937 and especially 1938, whether by these youths or by the FS.[49]

Such changes in cross-community relations were telling. The signs are that the rise in hostility was the product of ideological agitation at least as much as the other way around. This, in turn, makes it all the more difficult to determine to what extent the Sudeten Germans were aiming, as a group, for an *Anschluss*. The results of the municipal elections of May–June 1938 are a poor guide. The SdP's campaign of terror and its ability to impose itself as the sole list on the ballot in most municipalities make the results potentially worthless, or at the very least difficult to assess. Neither were voter statistics collated at the time, which requires compiling and comparing results by national identity across hundreds of towns and villages. The SdP seems to have obtained between 80 and 90 per cent of votes actually cast, but one estimate is that a third of Germans were prevented from casting a free, opposing vote.[50] It is not even clear that all Sudeten Germans understood that a vote for the SdP meant a vote for secession – many members of the activist parties that had merged with it in March may well have thought otherwise – and indeed evidence to the contrary would emerge, as will be seen, in September.

This speaks, of course, to the self-determination demanded by Czechoslovakia's enemies. Aside from the conceptual issues of national identity raised at the beginning of this chapter, there were multiple arguments against holding a plebiscite, even if circumstances had been calm enough to ensure a free and fair vote. Some were practical, such as the difficulty of determining the precise region to which it should apply, or the economic harm a carve-out would cause. Another was strategic: stripping Czechoslovakia of its borders would leave it defenceless. A third concerned the likely fate of anti-Nazi, Jewish, and Czech minorities, whatever the majority might have wanted. Indeed, this applied to the majority itself, as totalitarian Germany was unlikely to allow a reversal of the result should its supporters experience buyer's remorse. If self-determination consists of a democratic choice, it is worth remembering that democracy involves basic rights, not just majority rule. But even ignoring all these arguments, it remains unclear whether a majority existed in the Sudetenland for annexation to the Reich. The SdP obtained around 60 per cent of German ballots cast in the last free and fair vote, the parliamentary elections of 1935.[51] A quarter of the Sudetenland population was Czech. Even supposing that every SdP vote was a vote for secession, this placed the secession vote at between 45 and 50 per cent, less than a majority.

LORD WALTER RUNCIMAN OF DOXFORD arrived in Prague on 3 August. Two groups awaited him on the station platform: a team of government representatives, and a party led by Ambassador Basil Newton, who had come to introduce Ernst Kundt and Wilhelm Sebekowsky. Once these greetings were done with, Runciman headed for the Hotel Alcron, where his team would be based for the duration of his mission.

Lord Runciman's arrival was a major occasion; there was a flurry of media interest when it was announced a couple of days earlier. Two hours after stepping off the train, he received the press, domestic and foreign, in the Alcron's dining room. Runciman being rather short, the staff had put up a platform for him to speak from. They put him at the lobby end of the room to avoid the risk of him being photographed next to a bronze nude of a girl with outstretched arms – the same, presumably, that still stands there today. A curtain allowed for a quick getaway if the journalists turned hostile. The session passed without incident; the line that dominated the press coverage was that the British envoy had come as 'the friend of all and the enemy of none'.[52]

The polite clapping, though, only hid the pressmen's unease. Professions of universal friendship notwithstanding, Runciman looked far more like judge and jury than a benevolent moderator. During the May mobilisation alert, Halifax had finally reminded Ribbentrop that Britain would not let France fight alone were it to become embroiled against Germany.[53] Even this, though, was ambiguous: Chamberlain and Halifax feared a German surprise attack because under the French–Czechoslovak treaty it was sure to bring war. They were prepared to ward the danger off with threats if this was what it took. But this stance was compatible with a policy of forcing concessions on Czechoslovakia to buy peace, and it evinced no intention of defending its integrity against German demands.

Throughout May and June, the British and French had continued to press the Czechoslovaks to come to terms with Henlein. It will be remembered that Henlein had made a timely trip to London in May, during which he presented very different desiderata from what he was insisting on domestically. As negotiations opened in Prague in early June, Hodža had explained that the Carlsbad demands could not form the basis for a Sudetenland or nationalities statute. Henlein reacted by getting a message through to Newton complaining that the government resisted suggestions 'in the spirit of his London proposals'. Newton faithfully went to visit the president to insist that the Czechoslovak government negotiate based on the Carlsbad points. In parallel, Halifax called in Masaryk to express disappointment with the speed of the negotiations and to ask again for major concessions to be made.[54] Shortly thereafter, Lacroix visited Krofta and Beneš to remind them of the SdP's electoral successes and warn them that France could not act militarily without British support.[55]

Around the same time, the Foreign Office had started planning the Runciman mission. Halifax thought the Czechoslovaks guilty of obstruction. In cabinet, Chamberlain had accused Beneš of dragging his feet.[56] Worse, the government had announced the forthcoming publication of an interlocking set of laws – a Language Law, a Nationalities Statute, and an Administrative Reform Law – together forming the Second Plan that was under preparation. This provided for yet more effort on civil servants and schools, but it also included extensive decentralisation measures that would have given a significant degree of autonomy to the majority-German Sudetenland districts. The SdP had rejected these out of hand. The Runciman mission ensured that they could be buried before they were passed.[57]

Ostensibly, the mission was to be independent: Runciman and his team had come to Prague as private individuals and at the supposed request of the Czechoslovak government. Their task was to mediate, to help an agreement come about, not to arbitrate or impose a settlement. The French, who had only been told of the project days before, on the occasion of a royal visit to Paris, had after a moment's hesitation responded enthusiastically. Beneš was appalled. To Victor de Lacroix, the French ambassador, he at first simply declined to accept 'racist' demands for the state's dismemberment.[58] To Newton, he made plain that he was taken aback by what looked suspiciously like interference in his country's internal affairs. The British ambassador rejoined that Runciman was not an envoy of the British government but an independent party. When the Czechoslovak president continued to baulk, Newton declared that if Beneš refused to go along with the plan, Chamberlain would announce that the British government had done all it could, that the Czechoslovaks had declined its help, and that it was now disengaging itself from the crisis.[59]

Walter Runciman was a friendly acquaintance and former cabinet colleague of Chamberlain. Originally a wealthy and successful shipping magnate, he also had a long parliamentary and governmental career behind him. A Methodist, teetotal, impassive, he had a reputation for austerity and, aged sixty-seven, he 'cut a pale diminutive figure'.[60] Runciman came to Prague with his wife Tilda and a team large enough to fill fifteen rooms at the Alcron. This staff included former colleagues both from the business and the administrative worlds, and two diplomats: Ian Leslie Henderson, the British consul in Innsbruck, and Frank Ashton-Gwatkin, the head of the Foreign Office economic relations section. Ashton-Gwatkin, Eton- and Oxford-educated, with experience in the Far East and Moscow, was by far the most senior member of the team. On 'secondment' from the Foreign Office, he would prove the most important member of the mission, possibly more significant than Runciman himself.[61]

On the morning of 4 August, Runciman and his staff, 'attired in top hats and coat tails', took their Rolls-Royce to pay their respects, in turn, to Krofta, Hodža, and Beneš. The next day they were hosted at a luncheon by the president and his wife, followed by, for the English lord, an hour-and-a-half conversation in private. Beneš took his guest through the ideological problem, then through his government's triple initiative. He warned his guest that 'this is a fight between Prague and Berlin and a fight over central Europe itself', and that 'our Germans are simply a tool for Berlin's pan-German policies'. Behind a veneer of affability, Runciman remained inscrutable. In a telegram to London, he complained that the Czechoslovak president had too little understanding or respect for the Germans.[62] The atmosphere was more convivial in meetings with the SdP team, a group of five people centred around Kundt and Sebekowsky. The mission invited them back to their hotel to meet in the afternoon. The Henleinists presented their latest list of demands – another repackaging of the Carlsbad points – and they stayed late into the night for beer and talks.[63]

Runciman's staff spent the first week or so gathering information and hearing the views of the SdP. From 16 August, they switched to government representatives, hosted by the former justice minister and constitutional expert Alfred Meissner in his own home.[64] Runciman, however, remained aloof from these discussions. Indeed, he spent strikingly little time in Prague at all. The day after his arrival, he left town to go shooting on the estate of the aristocratic magnate Zdenko Kinský in

Moravia. A week later, on 13 August, he was invited to the residence of Ulrich Kinský, and on 18 August he paid a visit to the castle of Prince Max von Hohenlohe at Červený Hrádek. Hohenlohe was a high-level SdP activist who was keen to act as intermediary between Henlein and the mission. Prince Ulrich Kinský had been appointed by the SdP to take charge of Runciman's social agenda. On the 13 August visit, Kinský took his visitors on a tour of local German poverty and arranged for a crowd of 150 Germans to come to the castle gates and ask the British lord to help them in their 'distress'.[65]

Though initially it had tried to put a positive gloss on the mission, the Czechoslovak press soon became openly distrustful. Until July, the newspapers had given an almost systematically positive treatment to international doings and pronouncements. Every speech by Chamberlain or Halifax was closely reported on, and likewise what the foreign press wrote about Hitler and Henlein. Interference by the two Entente powers, or what leaked of it, was glossed as proof of interest in and support for Czechoslovakia, failing to convey the ambiguity at the heart of Franco–British policy. As the summer progressed, the cautious welcome turned into palpable nervousness. *Ceský deník* had from the beginning regretted that the intervention placed the matter of Czech–German relations so squarely in the international arena. It sounded the alarm over the false perceptions held by British decision-makers, highlighting the hopelessness of negotiating with Nazis such as Henlein.[66] *Venkov*, the organ of the powerful Agrarian Party, complained for the first time that Chamberlain's aim looked like peace at any price, and Daladier's goal an understanding with Germany.[67] The editor of *Přítomnost*, Ferdinand Peroutka, presciently wrote that the Runciman mission was 'nothing but an illusion', for it required no fact-finding on the ground to understand that pan-Germanism must be stopped.[68]

Czechoslovak officials and other interested parties attempted multiple times to warn the members of the Runciman mission. Vojtěch Mastný from the beginning sought to enlighten Runciman as to the sham of Henlein's professions of loyalty and warn that he took orders from Berlin.[69] While preliminary soundings were still being taken, Hubert Masařík asked Ashton-Gwatkin to his home for lunch in the company of Alfred Meissner and the journalist and presidential confidant Hubert Ripka. The Czechs tried to explain the historical and political background to the German situation. '[Ashton-Gwatkin] took everything with tact, but both his words and attitude gave the impression that the discussion was superfluous and that Runciman's conclusions were foregone.'[70] Representatives of the Sudeten Social-Democrats made the same points as Ashton-Gwatkin received them with 'icy courtesy'.[71] Wenzel Jaksch and Siegfried Taub handed in their own recommendations in the form of a memorandum, including many features of the latest plan but not autonomy, which they warned would only be dangerous, but neither did this make any impression.[72]

Ironically, discussions between the SdP and the government had meanwhile resumed behind the mission's back. Beneš confidentially renewed contact with Kundt via a German law professor, and he and Hodža met again with Kundt and Sebekowsky at the Castle in mid-August. The upshot was a new plan, conditionally vetted as a basis for negotiations by Henlein on 22 August.[73] This so-called 'Third Plan' involved yet bolder proposals on language equality, accelerated provisions for increasing the number of German-speaking officials, and special government loans for the Sudetenland. But its novelty was that it allowed for autonomous cantons, of which three at least would be majority-German: around Česká Lípa, around Carlsbad, and in Silesia. It was, moreover, specific in assigning wide-ranging powers to these cantons, covering education, culture, public works, and social and health policy, plus some economic or financial devolution. With this, the government left little more to demand. Allowing for the patchwork distribution of the Czech and Sudeten German populations, this amounted to a localised version of 'home rule'. The SDP could count on controlling the majority-German cantons, with all the scope for Nazification this offered. When Kundt obtained the proposals in writing, at the end of the month, he told the German chargé d'affaires in Prague,

Andor Hencke, that the plan 'could in fact mean the fulfilment of the eight Karlsbad demands'.[74] The parties were ostensibly inching towards a solution. Henlein disclosed its details to Ashton-Gwatkin in person in Marienbad. Beneš formally handed the text to the Kundt–Sebekowsky pair on 29 August, asking for an answer by 2 September.[75]

Faithful to the strategy that Berlin had set for them from the beginning, however, the Henleinists began to backtrack. Their instructions, as relayed by Karl Hermann Frank, had been that 'His Lordship must take away with him the impression that the situation in this state is so confused and difficult that it cannot be cleared up by negotiation or diplomatic action, that the blame for this lies exclusively with the Czechs, and thus that the Czechs are the real disturbers of peace in Europe.'[76] Kundt told Runciman on 31 August that his party continued to want the full Carlsbad points after all. The British envoy, far from expressing any surprise, allowed himself to be convinced that the Third Plan must be unsatisfactory, and he promptly telegraphed London to raise another alarm over Czechoslovak procrastination.[77]

Henlein had artfully held back during most of the discussions. In a set of meetings with Ashton-Gwatkin, he now persuaded the British diplomat that he, Henlein, should be sent as an emissary to Hitler, with the message that the SdP and the Runciman team supported a negotiated position somewhere between the Third Plan and the Carlsbad demands. This earned more wriggle room, and Henlein was scheduled to go to Berchtesgaden anyway to be updated on Hitler's invasion plans. Henlein also accepted, to Ashton-Gwatkin's delight, to act as an ambassador of goodwill to the Führer and hand over a message to the effect that Great Britain generally desired a peaceful Anglo–German settlement.[78] As a bonus, this gave Henlein carte blanche to turn down any future concessions he might still be handed.

Runciman met again with Beneš on 1–2 September and at last told him that he must accept the Carlsbad demands. The British government would publicly abandon him otherwise. Newton drove the point home in a message from Halifax the next day. Lacroix also chipped in, calling for more concessions, though he stopped short of endorsing the Carlsbad terms.

On the morning of 2 September, Kundt and Sebekowsky officially let it known that the Third Plan failed to fulfil their party's requirements. Instead, they presented a counter-proposal which, for once, was rich in detail and actually built on the Czechoslovak document. This may have encouraged the British mission in the belief that 'moderates' within the SdP were close to an agreement and that one last push would do it. Such hopes were swiftly crushed: Henlein, returning from Berchtesgaden, told Ashton-Gwatkin on 4 September that there were only two possibilities: full autonomy or annexation. Both he and Hitler were for the first solution in the interest of peace, he said, but the history of Czech obstruction meant that they shared considerable scepticism as to its chances.[79]

Ashton-Gwatkin noted of Henlein: 'I like him. He is, I am sure, an absolutely honest fellow.' Runciman did not just spend his first three weekend breaks in company of the Kinský and Hohenlohe, former Habsburg nobility. On the weekend of 20–21 August, he and his wife were on the estate of Prince Adolf Schwarzenberg near Český Krumlov. On 27–28 August, he took his team to the castle of Count Clary-Aldringen near Teplice. On 10–11 September, the Runcimans repaired to the castle of Count Czernín, near Jesenice, in front of which a crowd of SdP supporters gathered to chant Nazi slogans and the 'Horst Wessel' song. They only made an exception to this German-heavy programme on 3–4 September, when they were hosted by Archbishop Karel Kašpar – presumably the Runcimans' idea of socialising with ordinary Czech people. They used the visit to browbeat the prelate into writing to Beneš.[80]

This slanted social agenda, as well as attracting the attention of historians, was noticed at the time already. While some of the aristocratic peers the Runcimans visited were SdP agents, such as Hohenlohe, it must be noted that others would emerge as Czechoslovak patriots during the September days, including Zdenko Kinský, Schwarzenberg, and Czernín.[81] Yet almost all these visits were sited in the Sudetenland, offering excellent agit-prop opportunities to the SdP. Besides, even if they did not necessarily buy into every one of the Sudeten Germans' sob stories, Runciman, Ashton-Gwatkin, and their colleagues saw the old Habsburg nobility as part of their own world. Runciman was a lord; the others, as high-level civil servants and diplomats, gravitated privately or professionally towards the same sort of social notables. It felt natural to trust a Hohenlohe, a Kinský, and their friend Henlein. And hearing the same grievances repeated over and over again was bound to have an effect. As one historian observes: 'Henlein was accorded the consideration due to a sincere, well-intentioned man of honour – suitable to bear messages to Hitler – whereas Beneš, beneath the niceties of official protocol, was treated as a devious and untrustworthy figure requiring to be kept under constant scrutiny.'[82]

Beneš felt he had no choice but to produce yet another, even more accommodative plan, the fourth, which he arranged to have drafted and approved by the inner cabinet by the close of 5 September. This was based closely on the last Kundt–Sebekowsky protocol, the SdP response to the Third Plan. It involved an even more extensively defined autonomy and, for the first time, recognition of a collective Sudeten German identity, the open road to the SdP's sole and total assumption of that identity. Beneš explained, and Runciman acknowledged, that the plan effectively complied with all the Carlsbad demands. The president told Runciman, as he handed it over, that it would result in the establishment within Czechoslovakia of a totalitarian sub-territory that would inevitably become detached.[83]

The SdP negotiators received the plan on 7 September. They concluded they could not reject it without losing face, and could do nothing else but accept it.[84] Luckily for them, however, a trumped-up excuse for breaking off talks emerged in the nick of time: the same day, a policeman keeping order at a demonstration in Moravská Ostrava struck an SdP parliamentarian named Franz May with his riding whip. The near-riot conditions easily justified the action, and no serious harm was done. Nevertheless, the next day, Kundt and another SdP representative visited Hodža to announce a suspension of talks 'until the Moravská Ostrava incidents had been liquidated'.[85] Hodža and the authorities complied and suspended or cashiered the policeman and his superiors. But the SdP had gained the final breathing space it needed. The annual Nazi Party rally in Nuremberg had begun, and everyone's attention was turning to Hitler's 12 September closing speech and what it might bring.

The talks would never resume. On the failure of the 'Fourth Plan', Ashton-Gwatkin embarked on a wild goose chase through the Sudetenland to find Henlein. By then, though, Hitler had spoken, and the mission effectively ended in the backwash of the Moravská Ostrava incident. The Runciman report, filed in London on 21 September, was overtaken by events. Even so, it would provide an important *ex post* validation to Anglo–French policy in the last days before Munich. Though it recognised both that the Fourth Plan effectively fulfilled the Carlsbad demands and that the Moravská Ostrava incident had been an excuse, it recommended that the majority-German areas constituting the Sudetenland 'should be given full right of self-determination at once', without even a plebiscite. In other words, it proposed that they should be handed over to Germany.[86] For Neville Henderson, the 'moral grounds' for such self-determination were 'a principle on which the British Empire itself was founded' – as Messrs Gandhi and Nehru would no doubt have been interested to learn.[87] As a less surprising though equally melancholy justification, Runciman's text offered that: 'It is a hard thing to be ruled by an alien race,' and that therefore 'the resentment of the German population was inevitably moving in the direction of revolt'.[88]

IT WAS A HOT SUMMER that year. In Prague, the Vltava filled with swimmers. Petitions continued to come in at the Castle and Kolowrat Palace. Flyers called the people to arms.[89] A popular song made the rounds of the pubs and bars:

Over the mills, under the mills Hitler winds
Come, Stalin, take a gun and shoot that swine.
[...] Come on, Adolf, we're ready
Come on, Adolf, come ahead.
On our borders the cannons are laid
Corporal Hitler, the Czechs aren't afraid
[...] Come march with us, Adolf, sweet boy
It's something you'll enjoy
When the bombs fall from the sky you'll get one too
On the head, and no one will fix it for you [90]

Demonstrations multiplied. A multi-party event, including the Slovak nationalists, took place in Žilina on 4 September.[91] In Plzeň on the same day, 50,000 people arrived from the border regions to demonstrate in favour of territorial unity.[92] Thousands took to the streets in Jihlava on 5 September, Czechs alongside German Social-Democrats, proclaiming their loyalty to the republic and their hostility to any carve-out, raising the flag and singing the Czech, French, and Soviet national anthems.[93] On 9 September, 50,000 assembled in Moravská Ostrava, shortly after the incident there, raising flags and shouting that the participants were 'ready for any sacrifice for the motherland, but none for its enemies'.[94] In Hlučín, democratic Germans and Czechs ceremonially delivered the flag to the fourth regiment, stationed there, on 11 September.[95]

The *Daily Herald* reporter Geoffrey Cox heard words of defiance from every corner. He was sitting in a riverside pub in the middle of August:

Troops in coarse khaki, men in shiny, tight fitting suits, fair-haired, sunburnt women in bright cotton dresses sat at the long tables roaring out the words of a Slovak peasant song, laughing, drinking the light golden beer of Plzeň, or the sharp red wine of southern Slovakia. The woman accordionist who led the orchestra changed suddenly to another tune, less rollicking, more military. The crowd half sang, half hummed the refrain. It was clear that the words were not yet familiar to them. But when the chorus came, they were all in, with a crash of voices: 'Come on Adolf, we're ready. Come on Adolf, come ahead.'[96]

It was 12 September, the last evening of the Nuremberg rally. That night, the poet Zdeněk Kalista was scheduled to go to the YMCA for his usual swimming session. He had forgotten that everybody would be glued to their radio set or, lacking one, to the closest set at hand. 'I was warned by the cloakroom lady that Hitler was speaking about Beneš, and instead of going into the gym and pool, I went to the room with the radio set, where indeed the "Leader's" wild rants were playing. "It is I or Beneš," shouted Hitler, even more orgiastically than usual. I knew that with this "Antichrist" there was no possible compromise. When the speech ended, I left everything, took my coat back, and instead of sitting in the tram as usual, I ran back home to Spořilov hoping that the physical effort would calm me a little.'[97]

The annual Nazi Party rallies in Nuremberg were always ominous occasions, with their massive, searchlight-lit parades, their fiery speeches in front of battalions of helmeted paramilitaries, the fanatically cheering and saluting crowds. Yet the 1938 rally was the object of exceptional attention. Throughout July and August, the various secret services had been picking up signals that Germany was readying to attack Czechoslovakia, possibly as early as September.[98] To anyone who followed the news, the debacle of the talks with the Henleinists made it obvious that a clash was coming. Goering and Goebbels had primed their Nuremberg audience, Goering famously denouncing 'that little fragment of a nation down there', 'these absurd pygmies', and 'Moscow and the eternal grimacing Jewish-Bolshevist rabble [that] are behind it'.[99] The rally's last day and Hitler's closing speech were widely feared to be the moment when the Nazi leader would launch hostilities.

Yet Hitler stopped short of declaring war. If the speech contained a signal, it was for something else. He gave a fantastical description of Czechoslovakia and conditions in the Sudetenland: 'In economic life these three and a half millions are being systematically ruined and thus devoted to a slow process of extermination. This misery of the Sudeten

Germans is indescribable. It is sought to annihilate them. As human beings they are oppressed and scandalously treated in an intolerable fashion. [...] They are beaten until the blood flows solely because they wear stockings the sight of which offends the Czechs. [...] They are hunted and harried like helpless wild-fowl for every expression of their national sentiment.' Hitler attacked Beneš for war-mongering, taking the May mobilisation for evidence. In response, he had ordered measures to increase again the size of the army and air force. Finally he demanded 'self-determination' for the Sudeten Germans, thundering over the 'serious consequences' that would ensue if it was not granted.[100] This was the first open intimation that the choice for Czechoslovakia was to hand over the Sudetenland or face war. In the Sudetenland, that evening, the FS and the Henleinist foot soldiers took the Führer's words as their cue.

In a string of border towns, the streets filled with people. Whether instigated from the start or merely taken over by the Henleinists, the scenes quickly turned violent. (As Hitler would privately boast: 'I have arranged for these provocations.'[101]) Over the next two days an attempt at a full-scale takeover spread through western Bohemia and as far as Carlsbad. The FS had been drilling and smuggling weapons into the country for the past four months now. Their preparations could be put to use. They attacked border posts, police and gendarmerie stations, and post offices – the last because this was where the telephone exchanges were. They torched Czech and Jewish shops and assaulted police, anti-fascist Germans, and Czechs caught in the open. As local authorities responded, gun fights broke out in a number of locations.[102]

Events in the small, west Bohemian town of Bezdružice offer a good example of what took place in the first phase of events. At 8:40 p.m., shortly after the end of Hitler's speech, around 350 people came out on the streets, chanting anti-state slogans and national songs. A team of gendarmes asked them to disperse, but got driven back to the gendarmerie under a hail of stones. When reinforcements finally arrived in the early afternoon, they had to jump from their cars and enter the town in attack formation. The demonstrators finally dispersed. In the meantime, around 9 p.m., a mob of 100 people had raided the railway station, brutalised the controller and pulled down the Czech signs or covered them with tar, smearing swastikas onto the walls. The demonstrators fell upon a Czech office clerk who was escorting a female teacher home. They flogged him and left him badly injured. The clerk managed to get away. As it happened, he had a gun, and he and his aggressors exchanged shots, though neither side hit their mark. Eventually he reached the gendarmerie and safety.[103]

Růžena Pardusová, a post-office worker in the town of Habartov, was the victim of a more organised attack the next day. There had been SdP demonstrations in the night, and she had cut a call, in German, from the local brewery to the nearby town of Doupov asking for reinforcements of 300 men. In the morning, she and a postman barricaded themselves inside the office. SdP paramilitaries nevertheless managed to force their way in. The employees were shoved to the wall. The phone rang and the caller spoke Czech, though, so Pardusová was called to answer. She lied that it was the Doupov station sending the requested reinforcements, then managed to switch lines and call the gendarmerie in Falknov. When the paramilitaries realised what was going on, Pardusová was grabbed, taken outside, and put up against a fence to be shot. But another group of orderlies arrived, some of whom she knew, someone called 'Halt!', and she was taken instead to her flat, where she locked herself in with her mother and child.

It so happened that Pardusová's husband was a gendarme, and their flat was situated above the local gendarmerie. Shooting broke out below. As SdP men tried to break in, Pardusová jumped out the window with her daughter and escaped. They were caught again, handcuffed, and eventually taken into the cellar of a pub which the SdP used as a meeting place. On the way, she and her child were beaten about the body and face and spat on. Again the SdP orderlies told her she would be executed. She was tied up, carried out, and finally dumped outside the gendarmerie, with the threat that she would be killed if the gendarmes did not surrender. At this point Pardusová's husband and a colleague came out, guns blazing. She was hit on the head and lost consciousness. George Gedye, who wanted to see the events in the Sudetenland at first hand, visited the hospital in Falknov where she was taken.[104]

Such scenes were typical. Elsewhere, full-scale battles took place. In Cheb, a protracted skirmish was fought around improvised SdP head-quarters in the Hotel Viktoria. On the evening of 12 September, a group of FS orderlies with swastika armbands and firearms had taken control of the train station and post office and begun to stop everyone in the streets, telling Czechs to pack their things and leave. They rounded up and imprisoned gendarmes, customs officials, and railwaymen, as well as local Social-Democrats – around fifty people in total. Meanwhile a mob of rowdies went around the town smashing the windows of Czech and Jewish shops. Because Cheb was close to the border, the authorities were afraid of sending in soldiers lest it give an excuse for the German army to march in. On 14 September, they nevertheless despatched two platoons of gendarmes with three armoured cars. These were greeted by machinegun fire from the hotels Walzel and Viktoria, causing six casualties. A stand-off ensued but, in the evening, the police attacked and with the help of hand grenades finally took the Viktoria. They seized a large cache of weapons and liberated the prisoners. A number of Henleinists were caught and one was killed, the rest fleeing through a secret tunnel.[105]

The FS took over Henlein's home town of Aš while a crowd marched through the streets, shouting, tearing down Czech name plates and whitewashing signposts. At Bublava, SdP orderlies captured the gendarmerie station and imprisoned the gendarmes, killing one and wounding three. The stations at Planá, near Marienbad, and at Haselbach were likewise attacked, and at the second place two gendarmes and a customs officer were murdered. In Kraslice, a large mob equipped with automatic weapons and hand grenades took control of the post offices and gendarmerie station, killing three. In Tachov, businesses and schools closed down, and a demonstration led to a stand-off, in front of the town hall, between a group of armed men and soldiers from the local garrison. There ensued a shooting confrontation that left one dead. In Carlsbad, where according to a witness the demonstrators were in a 'murderous and bloodthirsty mood', mobs broke windows and shop fronts everywhere, chanting Nazi slogans through the night.[106]

Loyal civilians took to their own defence in some places. Glass industry workers in Česká Lípa and Haida announced a strike against SdP terror. In Jablonec, Czechs and German democrats together called the military into town. In Teplice, things remained calm in part thanks to the democratic German orderlies of the *Republikanische Wehr*.[107] The border guards and gendarmes had initially been outnumbered in several areas. Local authorities and police had been under instructions to hold back as much as possible, to shoot in the air and try to reason SdP orderlies into cooperation, and to avoid the use of force except in the last extremity. The consequence was that in addition to the casualties, a number of officials were abducted and interned in the Reich.

But martial law was proclaimed in several districts on 13 September. In the following days it was extended to a wider area including Carlsbad and Český Krumlov, though this was still only a part of the Sudetenland. Police and troops poured in large numbers into the affected areas. Even in the places where shooting had erupted, as in Cheb, they quickly overpowered the Henleinists or forced them to flee. By 15 September, the authorities had restored order everywhere. (In response to the declaration of martial law, the Gestapo arrested 150 Czechoslovak nationals resident in Germany and informed the Czechoslovak government via diplomatic channels that these hostages would be killed, or a corresponding number of them, if any Sudeten Germans were ever tried and executed.[108])

The government moved at last to ban the SdP and its paramilitary arm. The SdP's Prague offices were raided. Its periodicals were shut down. The FS was officially dissolved, and the party itself declared illegal. Henlein was charged with treason. The MPs Peters, Kundt, and Neuwirth would soon be arrested. Henlein managed to flee: he was evacuated from Aš by a German armoured column on 15 September.[109] Sydney Morrell witnessed two Czech policemen ringing his doorbell, only to walk away 'with a shrug and a laugh'.[110]

THE REICH'S 'ATROCITY PROPAGANDA', of course, rose to a new pitch. The Nazi newspaper, the *Völkischer Beobachter*, declared: 'Thirteen blood victims for Sudeten German self-determination, fire assaults, murder, martial law, foreign police and army rage against the inhabitants with tanks.' And the next day: 'Thirty more victims of Czech murderers, butchery in Habersbirk [Habartov], with tanks and machineguns against a Sudeten German village.' The German press bureau released pieces such as 'With cannons on the unarmed population', 'The Hussite hordes rage in the Sudetenland', 'We will play football with your heads', and so on.[111]

Yet the most surprising thing about the Sudetenland uprising is how contained its toll actually was. The most reliable casualty list for the events of 12–15 September has the number of dead at twenty-nine, of which eleven were Sudeten Germans, thirteen gendarmes or civil servants, and five Czech civilians.[112] There were perhaps seventy-five wounded. This did not just reflect official restraint in dealing with the disorders. Actually the revolt itself was limited in breadth. Demonstrators and rioters, when all put together, represented a tiny percentage of the total population. The major centres of Teplice, Liberec, Jablonec, Děčín, and Ústí remained quiet. Martial law needed to be imposed in only sixteen out of forty-nine border or Sudetenland districts.[113]

On 15 September, Henlein broadcast, on the radio, a 'back to the Reich' proclamation:

> Fellow-countrymen! As bearer of your confidence and conscious of my responsibility, I state firmly before world opinion, that with the employment of machine guns, armoured cars and tanks against the unarmed Sudeten Germans, the system of oppression by the Czech nation has reached the highest point. By this the

Czech nation has shown to the whole world that it has at last become quite impossible for us to live together with it in one State. [...] All our efforts to bring the Czech nation and those responsible for it to an honest and just compromise have wrecked themselves against their implacable desire to destroy us. In this hour of distress for the Sudeten Germans, I stand before you, the German nation, and before the entire civilised world and proclaim: We wish to live as a free German people! We desire peace and work in our Fatherland! We want to go back to the Reich![114]

Yet the dynamic had now changed. Henlein's attempt at taking over the Sudetenland had miscarried – or, if this was what it was, his wrecking campaign to close discussions with the government and prove Hitler right. The revolt had failed to attract a mass following, save perhaps in the early moments of idle protest, before things turned serious. It had failed to ignite even a very significant portion of the Sudetenland. Far from being shown to be incapable of imposing order, the Czechoslovak authorities had restored calm with almost lightning speed. And far from causing such a large death toll as might make them look like butchers, this had resulted in a mere eleven Sudeten German casualties, fewer than were sustained by the police.

All this could be glossed or lied about, and no doubt resentment among devoted Henleinists still ran deep. What could not be faked, however, was that a large slice of the leadership had left the country, taking many radical elements and the paramilitary FS with them. This did not go down well among those who remained. In Aš, Marienbad, and Broumov, among other towns, local SdP leaders actually welcomed the restoration of order and offered their services to maintain it. In Nýrsko, the local party president issued a joint declaration with the Social-Democrats calling for quiet and order. The rectors and deans of the German University in Prague (usually a hotbed of German nationalism), the heads of the Technical High School, and a large number of Henleinist teachers signed a public declaration repudiating Henlein's radio appeal.[115] The SdP parliamentarians Peters, Rosche, Neuwirth, and Kundt, and the former Christian-Social Mayr-Harting likewise distanced themselves from Henlein's call and expressed their intention to remain in Prague.[116]

The problem with the *Führerprinzip*, the lynchpin of Nazi ideology, was that it did not function well when the Führer was humiliated and forced to flee. Inevitably, the infallibility on which it was meant to rely was exposed. Nor was it at all clear that it was the Czechoslovaks who had made attempts at 'an honest and just compromise' unachievable, or even that they had used 'armoured cars and tanks against the unarmed Sudeten Germans'. Hencke reported back to Berlin that the flight of the SdP leaders had only caused consternation among the population, and a loss of confidence both in Henlein and in the Reich's propaganda.[117]

Even more basically, however, Henlein's leadership, having always involved a significant degree of dissembling, relied on a misapprehension for much of its support. Many of the Sudeten Germans had never been in favour of secession.

As a historian has written of the SdP's 1935 election result: 'The majority had voted for a party that united the Sudeten Germans and aimed to improve their position within the Czechoslovak Republic' – no more and no less.[118] The anecdotal evidence among the foreign reporters who were serious enough to explore the region in those days was that the SdP included plenty of waverers. Morrell interviewed a group of Henleinist youths in a pub in Trutnov: 'We joined Henlein because we thought he was just fighting for self-government,' they told him. 'We never thought he was working for the *Anschluss*. Most of us didn't want that; we would have been better off in this country.' (Admittedly, the reporter also found a man whose wife, the mother of his two children, was Jewish, and who nevertheless proclaimed himself a Nazi because 'I'm a German. It's better that individuals should suffer so that the race may prosper.')[119] Gedye writes of an idle chat shortly before Henlein's flight:

> I stood by the frontier post at Zinnwald looking into Germany
> and talked to a Henleinist mechanic who kept greeting friends

with the Hitler salute. 'Of course we are all for Henlein in Zinn-wald,' he said, 'but I hope it will not mean actually the Anschluss. I have often been at work on the other side, and over there, if you open your mouth about anything you don't like, you just disappear, and one day people learn that you are in a concentration camp. But that they don't believe over here unless they have worked in Germany. I am only afraid they may find it out one day when it is too late.'[120]

Most interesting, though, was the reaction of the mainstream nationalist newspaper *Deutsche Zeitung Bohemia*. The newspaper had consistently expressed trust in Henlein, and even tended to be friendly to Hitler. It wrote of the SdP leader's 'back to the Reich' call:

As to this appeal from Konrad Henlein, we can assure our readers, whose opinions they have made open to us in hundreds upon hundreds of letters, of the following: with this proclamation, Konrad Henlein has not only created a gulf between himself and the State, but also between himself and that part of the Sudeten German people who gave him their votes as *Volksführer* only on the basis of his programme at that time, a programme so wholly different. That programme declared with noteworthy insistence the loyalty and law-abidingness of the Sudeten German people. His present call to irredentism saddles the Sudeten Germans with all the consequences of treason to the State; for such a challenge the electors gave him neither their votes nor their mandate.[121]

There had been attempts, in the summer, to revive German activism. The former Christian-Social Party member Hugo Rokyta had lobbied Franz Spina to that effect, arguing that there was disillusionment with the SdP and that the Christian-Social Party had been absorbed against the wishes of a majority of its members. In July, a group of three former Agrarian and Christian-Social MPs had formally protested to the SdP leadership against its annexationist propaganda.[122] More pointedly, Jaksch, the Social-Democratic leader, now made an appeal 'to all people of goodwill'. A National Council of Sudeten Germans was formed, with a former Christian-Social, a former Agrarian, two German Democrats, and Jaksch at its head, plus the discreet support of prominent SdP sympathisers.[123] The unhoped-for opportunity, indeed, was that there was now available a highly attractive political status for the Sudeten German community: Beneš's Fourth Plan. This promised extensive budgetary aid, unprecedented efforts to redress yet further the linguistic balance at schools and among civil servants, and especially a very broad autonomy – and all this now without the threat of totalitarian recuperation by the SdP.

The SdP was 'beginning to crack', writes Kurt Weisskopf. Weisskopf tells the story of his encounter in a Prague coffeehouse with a party hack called Uebelacker. 'I know that you will be surprised by what I am going to say, but we do not want to return to Germany', said Uebelacker. 'We would not stand a chance, economically at any rate. Look what they, the Prussians, have done in Vienna. Their men are sitting everywhere and the Austrians are playing second fiddle.' When Weisskopf pushed him on supposed Czech atrocities, he replied: 'that's all propaganda and policies, in other words lies', adding that Goebbels was a 'club-footed devil'. Henlein had overreached, and he would be replaced by a moderate.[124]

No doubt all this talk, at least coming from SdP old-timers, was as panicked as it was opportunistic. But the point was that the Henleinist movement relied on momentum for success, and this momentum had been lost. Many, starting with the former activists who had joined in March, had obviously lined up behind Henlein either to be on the safe side if an annexation happened or because he had the wind in his sails and appeared likely to negotiate the best deal with the Czechoslovaks. Still more of his erstwhile supporters probably thought it reckless and absurd to risk war rather than take up the Fourth Plan.[125] Masses can be fickle and prone to flock to whomever the situation appears to show to be in the right. The Czechoslovak state had proved willing to compromise, and the Henleinists revealed themselves to be weaker than they looked. In the face of both significant concessions on the government side and the loss of its ability to enforce its will through fear, the movement was crumbling.

The SdP had finally been liquidated, its leader and kingpin gone, its paramilitary wing broken. With Henlein had fled a number of the most die-hard and violent opponents of the republic. Ironically, this was when a plan had finally been put on the table that met and perhaps went beyond the aspirations of many of the movement's supporters. A national committee of the Sudeten Germans was forming, including directly or indirectly a good number of former SdP members. This team could take advantage of the new plan without the risk of its being perverted to the end of annexation to the Nazi Reich. A resolution of the conflict was in sight. The Sudetenland was on the verge of ceasing to be a ticking time-bomb in the heart of Europe.

Then something extraordinary happened. Chamberlain announced that he would go to Berchtesgaden.

5

In the millions

THE NEWS OF CHAMBERLAIN'S TRIP to visit Hitler caused astonishment and disbelief. When the story broke at the offices of *Lidové noviny*, on 14 September in the evening, it was at first dismissed as a hoax. The telephones rang ceaselessly. The editors called government offices up and got panicked responses that this was 'very bad' and 'extremely dangerous'. Kurt Schuschnigg, the Austrian chancellor, had of course made his own journey there just four weeks before the *Anschluss*. It was clear that Chamberlain's visit would only make Hitler more obstinate in his demands, and the Czechoslovaks would end up paying the price.[1]

Apprehensions were compounded by the 7 September publication of a *Times* editorial that had declared: 'If the Sudetens are not satisfied with the last Czech offer, it can only be inferred that they do not find themselves at ease within the Republic. In that case it might be well for the Czechoslovak Government to consider whether a solution should not be sought on some totally different lines, which would make Czechoslovakia an entirely homogenous State by the secession of that fringe of alien populations who are contiguous to the nations with which they are united by race.'[2] Even if it had prompted denials from the Foreign Office, the piece had been the object of consternation in Czechoslovakia and, indeed, beyond.[3] *Přítomnost*, in a leader entitled 'War by other means', offered that: 'Future historians will one day observe the struggle that the Hitlerite system led over the years against the big European democracies, and they will be tempted to rate the policy of these big democracies as dreadful. Their incomprehension will arise in particular over the second half of 1938 and the "battle for Prague", as they ask themselves: "How did Hitlerite policies manage to hypnotise the world into believing that the Sudeten Germans were the issue on which world peace turned, and that it must be resolved based on Berlin's sole wishes?"'[4]

Krofta primed his ambassadors to the effect that the Nuremberg speech had been a covert call to arms, the plan being to use disorders in the Sudetenland as a pretext for invasion; Hitler's offers to negotiate were for show, the rebels were under Berlin's orders, and the French and British needed to be reminded of it.[5] Jan Masaryk warned that Chamberlain's Berchtesgaden trip meant peace at any price, and he anticipated that the British premier would be 'servile' towards Hitler.[6] The foreign minister gave a speech to the press on 16 September, as Chamberlain returned from the Führer's Alpine retreat. This listed, not for the first time, the reasons against a plebiscite, and warned again that what Hitler wanted was not the Sudetenland but the absorption or reduction into vassalage of Czechoslovakia. Separately, he notified his ambassadors in Paris and London that the Czechoslovaks would not let a solution be imposed upon them.[7]

The first half of September had seen a relative hardening of British cabinet attitudes. The decision-makers in London feared a repeat of 1914, when, as it was believed, the certainty of a British response had not been made sufficiently clear to Germany ahead of its invasion of Belgium. Before Hitler spoke at Nuremberg, Chamberlain had thought it necessary to spell out that an unprovoked attack on Czechoslovakia would be sure to drag Britain in. 'Any attempt to use force after so great an advance towards a solution by peaceful methods would incur universal condemnation throughout the world,' said Chamberlain. 'Undoubtedly it is of the first importance that the German Government should be under no illusion in this matter and that they should not, as it has been suggested they might, count upon it that a brief and successful campaign against Czechoslovakia could be safely embarked upon without the danger of the subsequent intervention first of France and later of this country.'[8] The idea was to foil any potential German adventurism. Again, though, the pursuit of maximum concessions was actually consistent with a firm stance against sudden aggression. British policy may have been based on the wrong analysis, namely the notion that Hitler's ambitions were limited and that one could buy a durable peace from him with reasonable concessions. Nevertheless – leaving aside how much that analysis may have stemmed from wishful thinking and confirmation bias – as a policy it was at least coherent.

The same could not be said of the French. As Osuský reported, the French government was divided, ahead of the Nuremberg speech, ten to seven were against a surrender such as a plebiscite, with Daladier and Bonnet on either side of the vote. As a group, it was only prepared to repeat that France would come to Czechoslovakia's aid if it was attacked.[9] Save perhaps as the consequence of these deep internal divisions, it is difficult to account for French policy as the crisis reached its peak. Both Daladier and Bonnet were war veterans. As in Britain, there prevailed in France a desire to avoid at all costs the terrible butchery of the First World War. The strategic value of Czechoslovakia was far less remote to the French than the British, however. Daladier and even Bonnet had fewer illusions as to Hitler's aims and methods. Yet if, in the French premier's words to the American ambassador William Bullitt, Chamberlain was 'like a high-minded Quaker who had fallen among bandits', the French for their part never grasped or trusted that, had they led, Britain would have been forced to follow.[10] As soon as Chamberlain's public stance appeared to stiffen – as it did based on his latest warning – it was the Quai d'Orsay that drew back. Bonnet had hitherto been happy to let the British look like the weaker partner. Now that it suddenly seemed they might mean business, he summoned the ambassador in Paris, Eric Phipps, to complain of their belligerence. Worse, Bonnet sabotaged Chamberlain's declaration by calling around the diplomatic correspondents of the press corps to dismiss it as insignificant.[11]

Though he had only recently reiterated France's adherence to the Czechoslovak alliance in a speech given in Bordeaux, Bonnet had been playing a murky game all along. He desperately sought to secure a British commitment in case France were pulled into a war as a result of German aggression, but he cared nothing as to Czechoslovakia's own fate. As to Daladier, he appears to have wavered throughout: in principle ready to confront his cross-Channel partners when they went too far, he invariably ended up acceding willy-nilly to whatever they proposed. The divided *Conseil des Ministres* of 13 September had rejected calls for a general mobilisation and decided to wait on Chamberlain instead. The same evening, Daladier addressed a message to his British counterpart proposing the publication and, if possible, the enforcement of Runciman's recommendations (their radical nature was not yet known to the French premier) and, failing that, a three-power conference involving Britain, France, and Germany.

It is in this context that Beneš decided on a backdoor approach to his French problem. The Czechoslovak president had again upbraided Lacroix, reminding him of Hitler's world-dominating aims and stressing that Henlein's radio appeal had been badly received; now was the time to sit down with the resurgent Sudeten German activists, not militate for secession.[12] But the French ambassador in Prague was only doing his master's bidding against his own best judgement, and he was not the issue. Beneš needed to get straight to the decision-makers in Paris.

The task fell to Jaromír Nečas, the minister for social affairs. Nečas was a trusted Beneš confidant, he was not a diplomat and was therefore less likely attract attention, and as a Social-Democrat he was in a position to appeal to other men or women of the left. He was despatched to Paris with secret instructions and the code name 'Kotek' on 15 September. There are contradictory testimonies regarding whom he met with and when exactly, but it is established that he spoke early on with Léon Blum, the French socialist leader, as well as probably with André Blumel, Blum's former cabinet director. Nečas did not meet with Daladier personally, but another intermediary (in all likelihood Blumel) did so and passed on his information just as the French premier was about to leave for fresh talks in London.[13]

Beneš's instructions to Nečas, to be destroyed after use, were to communicate to the French Czechoslovakia's willingness to consider ceding a portion of territory to Germany that would leave its fortified defence line intact while alleviating the minority problem. The terms of this proposal, which included a map, were for between 4,000 and 6,000 km² in Sudetenland territory to be given up (no more than 8 per cent of the Czech lands), lying entirely outside the fortification line. This was to be accompanied by exchanges of population, so that Germany would find itself accruing between one and two million Sudetenland inhabitants, while a corresponding inward transfer of Social-Democrats and Jews would save them from Hitler's depredations. The proposal was to be finalised in secret negotiations between Czechoslovakia, France, and Britain, with a complete veto over delimitations by the Czechoslovaks, and it was to be presented to Hitler as a take-it-or-leave-it offer.[14]

Giving the French the opportunity to accommodate Britain's desire for territorial concessions while preserving Czechoslovakia as a strategic asset was not necessarily a foolish move. Should the idea come together, it promised to buy time. Though Beneš could not know that Hitler was working from a fixed schedule, time was valuable, firstly, in helping an alternative Sudeten German leadership establish itself as a governmental interlocutor domestically, and secondly, with winter approaching, in making conditions for a German invasion more difficult. Nor was the idea entirely novel and original: around the same time, the Quai d'Orsay political director René Massigli separately floated a project for frontier rectifications with population exchanges as an alternative to a plebiscite, warning of the alternative strategic loss to France.[15]

The choice of intermediary or intermediaries, nevertheless, seemed questionable, and the whole mission bordered on the amateurish. Perhaps it simply betrayed incipient exhaustion on Beneš's side. Blum, for all his benevolence towards the Czechoslovak cause and prestige as a former prime minister, was out of office and therefore too far removed from the action. Nečas had neither the experience nor the level of access his mission required. (In an apt irony, *Nečas* means 'no time' or 'out of time'.) Beneš himself could not leave the country while an invasion threatened, of course, and an approach by Krofta could not have been kept confidential. The obvious choices would have been the long-time ambassador in Paris, Štefan Osuský, or perhaps Jan Masaryk, had the president empowered him personally to demand entry to the Anglo–French talks in London. Had Osuský found that diplomatic protocol prevented him from going over Bonnet's head straight to Daladier, he might have privately approached one of the avowed anti-appeasement members of the government, such as Paul Reynaud or Georges Mandel. Broaching such terms with Daladier, in any case, required both diplomatic expertise and firmness, and it was best done while looking him in the eye.

The risk was that the message would end up garbled in a game of Chinese whispers, and that the only point the French premier would retain was the Czechoslovak readiness for territorial surrenders. This is exactly what Osuský warned against when Beneš told Lacroix around the same time that he might accept the loss of regions containing 900,000 Germans. Osuský berated the president for his 'supreme imprudence' and predicted that the French would infer that Czechoslovakia could accept a larger carve-out, as it would have become merely 'a question of quantity'. He went so far as to suggest that Beneš should recall Lacroix and tell him he had misunderstood.[16] Beneš unfortunately did not trust Osuský's judgement, and his instructions to Nečas explicitly mandated that the Paris ambassador be kept in the dark. The result was just as Osuský feared. Daladier left for London primed to accept territorial losses on behalf of the Czechoslovaks.

CHAMBERLAIN HAD FLOWN TO BERCHTESGADEN on 15 September: the first time, at sixty-nine, he had ever travelled in an aeroplane. Landing in Munich at dawn, he then took a three-hour rail journey to the Führer's mountain retreat. Hitler welcomed him at the top of the steps to the villa and, after tea, introduced him into his study, a large chamber with windows overlooking the Alpine scenery and the room in which he had received Schuschnigg seven months before.

Chamberlain talked alone with Hitler, with the Führer's interpreter Paul Schmidt the only additional presence. The discussion began around 4 p.m. and was over before evening. Hitler began with a long harangue about Germany and all he had done for peace, then complained of hundreds dead in the Sudetenland uprising. He demanded the 'return to the Reich' of the Sudeten Germans. He was determined to solve the problem 'one way or another', and professed himself ready for a world war if necessary, though he would be 'sorry' for it. Chamberlain replied that, if this was the case, he needn't have wasted time coming all the way to Berchtesgaden. Hitler changed gears. Declaring himself willing to consider a peaceful settlement, he asked if Britain would agree to 'a secession of the Sudeten region on the basis of the right of self-determination'. The prime minister expressed his qualified assent, warning that he could not commit until he had consulted both his cabinet and the French. After further talk, it was agreed that he should do this, that the meeting should be adjourned, and that Chamberlain should return to Germany at a future date for further consultations. Hitler meanwhile promised that he would take no military action until after this second meeting. Chamberlain left the next day without seeing Hitler again. He nevertheless felt heartened that 'In spite of the hardness and ruthlessness I thought I saw in his face, I got the impression that here was a man who could be relied upon when he had given his word.'[17]

The cabinet did not altogether share Chamberlain's enthusiasm. When it met the next day, Duff Cooper, the first lord of the Admiralty, and several other members argued against bending to Hitler's threats. They thought the premier was all too clearly being blackmailed. Even Runciman, who was asked to report, admitted that Henlein 'had been in much closer touch with Hitler throughout the period of negotiation than he had previously imagined' and that Beneš was 'less dishonest than he appeared to be'. A majority nevertheless remained wedded to Chamberlain's policies, and he managed to rally his colleagues in time for the arrival of the French.[18]

Bonnet and Daladier came to 10 Downing Street the following day, 18 September. The meetings followed a similar pattern to the April talks. Chamberlain began by relating at length his Berchtesgaden conversations, ending with the question of whether the Czechoslovaks should be induced to grant 'self-determination' to the Sudeten Germans. Daladier asked about Runciman's conclusions. The envoy's report was still being drafted, but as Chamberlain summarised it, Beneš was to blame for the failure of negotiations with the Henleinists. Even so, Daladier opposed a plebiscite, which was what 'self-determination' implied, in part because it might give rise to separate demands from the Poles and Hungarians. As he had done in April, he argued the Czechoslovak corner. 'Whilst recognising Lord Runciman's closer personal experience of the problem, [Daladier] did not agree with him that the Sudetens and the Czechs could not live together. They had after all done so for twenty years, without war or menace of war.' The faults were greater on Henlein's side. Hitler's real aims were the destruction of Czechoslovakia and European domination. Familiar arguments were raised on the other side, such as that Czechoslovakia might have to give up its present borders even in the event of a victorious war, again on account of 'self-determination', while Daladier dug in his heels about the sanctity of French commitments.[19]

There the exchange stalled, and the session was adjourned. A second meeting focused on proposed solutions. The alternative to a plebiscite was a plain surrender of territory, which Daladier now accepted as a principle. The French premier, however, wanted the Czechoslovak defences to be preserved, and he proposed a limited handover of territory plus a population exchange – this was what the Nečas plan contained, and it is indeed likely that it played a role in encouraging Daladier to abandon his earlier position so promptly. Chamberlain retorted, however, that ceding only limited border areas would not satisfy Hitler. These would need to be defined as containing an 80 per cent or more German population, whereas a 50 per cent cut-off was required. Again the two premiers failed to agree, and the talks veered into the question of providing a guarantee to Czechoslovakia over its reduced borders as part of a prospective treaty.[20]

It was only at a third session, as it was becoming late in the evening, that Chamberlain at last produced a draft telegram containing in essence the terms he had been proposing. This unexpectedly broke the deadlock and closed the talks, sealing the Anglo–French position and, ultimately, Czechoslovakia's. In a complete volte-face, the French presently agreed to the document with merely stylistic changes. Again, Bonnet and Daladier were content to leave the ugly role of forcing concessions out of the Czechoslovaks to their British partners, but all fight left them the moment this tactic appeared to have run its course. It was as if, having verbally defended the Czechoslovaks, they had done what they could and their work was finished. Astonishingly, indeed, Daladier said that while he would want it endorsed by his council of ministers the next day, he agreed for the telegram to be sent to Prague forthwith.[21]

The British and French ambassadors, Newton and Lacroix, arrived jointly to deliver these terms to Beneš on the following day, 19 September, at 2 p.m. The Anglo–French plan simply proposed to transfer to the Reich all areas with over 50 per cent 'German inhabitants'. It did not specify the timeframe for this transfer, but it left open any border adjustments to the areas concerned as well as the possibility of population exchanges to an international body that was to include a Czechoslovak representative. The telegram demanded an answer within two days, and earlier if possible, as this was when Chamberlain proposed to resume his conversations with Hitler.[22]

The Czechoslovaks were stunned. Beneš, even if he had been preparing for some bad news post-Berchtesgaden, was appalled. Yet again, he attempted to point out to the ambassadors the long-term consequences for Czechoslovakia and for them, but this could of course make no difference.

Beneš called in Krofta and Hodža, followed by another meeting with the full government that lasted late into the night. In the following days, normal work practices at the Castle would become quite disrupted. All-night discussions were common practice. Beneš took to hosting most of his meetings in the presidential apartment, and such was the pressure for time and the need to consult or convey information to multiple parties that it became frequent to run meetings in parallel in the apartments above and the working rooms below. In between sessions, his secretariat busied itself drafting despatches and memoranda. This too needed to be supervised and coordinated with the Czernin Palace, a few hundred metres up the Castle district of Hradčany. The presidential secretariat, including our witness Prokop Drtina, was able to overhear much during its own down time, as government members, army generals, section chiefs, parliamentarians, and sundry visitors pressed into or milled about the 'small library' and other presidential anterooms.[23]

Krofta only handed the Czechoslovak response to the British and French ambassadors on 20 September in the evening. The letter was, under the veneer of diplomatic lingo, quite abrupt, and it spared few words in making clear what was thought of the proposals. The Anglo–French plan was unlikely to further the cause of peace, it began. The Berchtesgaden negotiations had been led 'against Czechoslovakia' and without hearing its case, and it should not come as a surprise that the Czechoslovak government could not accede to demands over whose elaboration it had not been consulted. Many Sudeten Germans did not want to join the Reich, besides which the proposals put before the government would, if executed, destroy the balance of forces in central Europe and in Europe as a whole, having 'far-reaching consequences for all other States and especially for France'. In a polite but barely coded swipe at French faithlessness, the letter further insisted that 'Czecho-slovakia has always remained faithful to her treaties and fulfilled her obligations resulting from them'. Finally, it proposed referring the Sudetenland dispute to the 1925 Locarno arbitration treaty between Germany and Czechoslovakia – the treaty the Nazi bosses had been eager to insist they considered valid when, during the *Anschluss*, they had been so keen to prevent a Czechoslovak mobilisation. This, it was expected, 'would make possible a quick, honourable solution which would be worthy of all interested States'.[24]

Lacroix and Newton told Krofta before they even referred the response to their capitals that resorting to the arbitration treaty was out of the question. This had already been ruled out by the Germans, and Chamberlain was due to meet with Hitler in less than two days and wanted an urgent answer. Lacroix presently notified Beneš that he would receive a reply during the night.

The scenes at the Castle in the next two days, with its fast-paced cycle of conversations at all hours, its panicked gatherings, and the offer of their views by everyone and anyone, all this in the midst of a black-out of government buildings against a surprise air attack, would take on a phantasmagorical hue. Lacroix and Newton, having already consulted with their foreign ministers, returned in the middle of the same night – it was now 2 a.m. on 21 September – staying for more than an hour. Newton handed Beneš a note demanding that the Czechoslovak gov-ernment reconsider its negative response, warning that its publication would trigger an immediate German invasion, and declaring that unless it backtracked, the British government would take no further respon-sibility for or interest in Czechoslovakia's fate.[25] The French response, delivered only verbally, was even worse news: 'If the Czechoslovak gov-ernment will not immediately accept the Anglo–French plan and a war arises as a result of this refusal, Czechoslovakia will be deemed responsible and France will dissociate itself from it.'[26] France was reneging on its treaty obligations, an act unprecedented in its modern history. Beneš was so flabbergasted that he asked for confirmation in writing.[27] He writes that Lacroix broke down in tears as he delivered his message. Drtina was outside the room when the two ambassadors left, and Lacroix came over to shake his hand, muttering something unintelligible, visibly shaken.[28]

Beneš called Hodža, who summoned first the small group of the 'political' ministers at the Castle and then, as dawn broke, the full government at the Kolowrat Palace. Drtina got hold of the president for a while before he went into these meetings and argued for turning down the Anglo–French proposals regardless of the consequences, and fighting come what may. The president, shattered by his session with the ambassadors, was coming to the opposite conclusion: that in the absence of French support, the terms must be accepted.[29] Among the government and coalition representatives, nevertheless, the first instinct was to dig in and make another frank response to the British and French. People refused to believe that the Entente partners understood what their proposal meant. Someone suggested sending a special delegation to Paris and London. At some point, the generals Ludvík Krejčí and Jan Syrový were called in. In their opinion, however, a war in which Czechoslovakia went alone against Germany would be very different from a war at the side of the French, not least because it would pull in Hungary and perhaps Poland. Czechoslovakia could not fight a war on three fronts with no prospect of relief in the west. Meanwhile Lacroix was calling every hour to ask when an answer would come, insisting that his government wanted a definitive, not a conditional, response.[30]

Jan Šrámek, the Christian-Social minister of unification, and František Ježek, the National-Unity minister of public health, led the resistance. Attempting to deflect acceptance, they asked for the plan to be referred to parliament and proposed that the government resign. The government had no mandate to accept such a plan, they argued, and the people did not want it. Only a 60 per cent majority in parliament could endorse such conditions. Beneš wavered. Krofta shared the explicit threats made by the French and British ambassadors. The Social-Democrat Rudolf Bechyně intervened on the side of accepting, and the president joined him in rebutting Ježek's argument.[31] The rebel ministers renewed their efforts in the cabinet meeting. They were now supported by the National-Socialist education minister Emil Franke, and by the minister of public works Jan Dostálek, also a Christian-Social. If one adds the communists, who did not sit in government but would virulently oppose surrender in the coming two weeks, opposition was thus led from both the left and right, though not by the mainstream parties that were the Agrarians and Social-Democrats. Though Hodža expressed his intention to take a positive response to the French, the cabinet session closed abruptly and without consensus.[32]

'The depression which prevailed at all these meetings defies description, and it was only with the greatest self-sacrifice and internal revulsion that the fatal decision was accepted,' writes Ripka.[33] Acceptance, it was felt, was an expedient anyway. In the middle of the ambassadorial talks, Beneš had explained to Drtina that this would not be the last of it. Hitler would up his demands again. 'There will be war,' he said. 'I don't know when or whether now or later. [...] Meanwhile we will have to endure.'[34]

At around 9 a.m., Beneš called in the twenty-member standing committee of the national assembly – parliament itself being in recess – under the joint chairmanship of the presidents of the chamber of deputies and senate. This was necessary not only for political reasons but because the Anglo–French plan, involving as it did extensive surrenders of territory, carried constitutional implications. Again, protests and lengthy discussions arose. Far from acting as a rubber-stamping instrument, this sat until 1 p.m.[35] Meanwhile the French written ultimatum had arrived: though not worded quite as bluntly as Lacroix had been compelled to put it the night before, it spoke quite clearly of the 'conclusions' France would draw if Czechoslovakia did not immediately accept the Anglo–French terms.[36] At last, both a cabinet majority and the parliamentary council having decided that there was no choice but to yield, Beneš drafted a brief reply accepting the Anglo–French plan. Krofta handed it in to the two ambassadors at 5 p.m. It was, of course, hardly enthusiastic. It also remained conditional. The note ran as follows:

> The Czechoslovak Government, forced by circumstances, yielding to unheard of pressure and drawing the consequences from the communication of the French and British Governments of September 21, 1938, in which both Governments expressed their point of view as to help for Czechoslovakia in case she should refuse to accept the Franco–British proposals and should be attacked by Germany, accepts the Anglo–French proposals with feelings of pain, assuming that both Governments will do everything in order to safeguard the vital interests of the Czechoslovak state in their application. It notes with regret that these proposals were elaborated without previous consultation with the Czechoslovak Government. Deeply regretting that their proposal of arbitration has not been accepted, the Czechoslovak Government accept these proposals as a whole from which the principle of a guarantee, as formulated in the note, cannot be detached, and accept them with the further assumption that both Governments will not permit a German invasion of Czechoslovak territory, which will remain Czechoslovak up to the moment when it will be possible to carry out its transfer after the determination of the new frontier by the International Commission referred to in the proposals. In the opinion of the Czechoslovak Government, the Franco–British proposals imply that all details of the practical realisation of the Franco–British proposals will be determined in agreement with the Czechoslovak Government.[37]

In light of future developments, it must be noted that the Anglo–French plan left the door open to population transfers and other adjustments subject to vetting by 'an international body including a Czech representative'; it left the Sudetenland under Czechoslovak control until such vetting had satisfactorily been performed, and it set no deadline. Though Czechoslovakia had accepted the plan, moreover, this remained dependent on a continued right of veto by the government, i.e. if the plan's application failed to safeguard Czechoslovakia's vital interests.

RUMOURS OF WHAT WAS AFOOT had been filtering through the press since 20 September. By the next day, a Wednesday, it had become known what the Anglo–French plan consisted of, though not that the government was about to accept it under duress. In the morning of 21 September, *Venkov* published a leader under the headline 'Betrayed' that described the Czech people as ascending their Golgotha, though the news remained that the government was responding with objections.[38] In the Catholic *Lidové listy* the editor wrote: 'If France does not realise that what is at stake now, is her position as a Great Power, the value of her word, and her prestige among her allies and among the nations of the world who have always regarded her as the hub, the foundation and the main pillar of international law and order, then she is on the downward slope.'[39]

Wenceslas Square was rigged at the time with loudspeakers. By the time Krofta delivered his official response to Newton and Lacroix, a small crowd was beginning to assemble on the thoroughfare. An hour or two later, the news blared out over the sound system that the government had yielded. This, though, was only Prague, or a small part of it, and the information needed to be broadcast nationally.

The person chosen to make the announcement was the well-known actor and director Zdeněk Štěpánek. Štěpánek had starred in a number of movies and was a key figure at Prague's national theatre. He had performed in Shakespearian roles in translation and in Edmond Rostand's *Cyrano de Bergerac*. Aged forty-one, he had also fought in the First

World War, and he was a veteran of the Czechoslovak legion. Štěpánek was fetched from his home in the afternoon, not knowing what was going to be asked of him. A driver took him to the radio studios of the Czechoslovak news agency, ČTK, on Vinohradská, the avenue being called at the time Fochova in honour of Ferdinand Foch, the French First World War generalissimo.

ČTK, as Štěpánek recalls it, was in a state of indescribable chaos, deafening noise everywhere, people running and bumping into each other. In the press room, telephones rang, the journalists vainly asking for quiet, shouting into their mouthpieces, cursing. 'Someone bangs the receiver on the table, sheaves of paper falling to the floor, people stamping on them.' Štěpánek was greeted by the press director, Zdeněk Schmoranz, and taken through this pandemonium into the studio. A group of officials awaited him. 'What is going on?' he asked. Finally he was told what was expected of him and given his text. 'I can't read this, I can't,' protested Štěpánek. 'Don't go crazy,' shouted back Schmoranz. 'I am not going crazy, you can't ask me to do this.' Schmoranz threatened: 'It's an order from the president of the republic. You are a soldier, you must obey. Careful, I am putting you on air.'[40]

The red light bulb glowed, signalling the beginning of transmission. 'I felt like an undertaker,' writes Štěpánek, 'as if tremendously far removed from people and life. I began to read, at the same time with maximum force and a terrible pain and sadness. A proclamation of capitulation, the crippling of our country, the severing of our border regions.' As he read on, the actor began to reminisce about the Chodsko region, where he had spent his youth and which was now destined to be lost, about his mother and childhood days. 'Tears rolled from my eyes, my throat and voice closed, and I could not go on. Schmoranz had to finish reading. They took me out like a condemned man. In the rooms around, there now reigned a graveyard silence. It was as if time itself had stopped over our national tragedy.' Bitter thoughts about Daladier and Chamberlain could not escape his mind, the first associated with a glass of champagne and the other with his ubiquitous umbrella. 'I felt utterly miserable, guilty and insulted at once. Yes, insulted, because I had been shamefully misused. From the waiting room they took me back again into the studio, where I read the text "Prayer" by Karel Čapek. Then I left the radio building through the back door. The crowd outside was already beginning to throw stones at the windows.'[41]

During the summer, a song promoted by the actor-directors of the liberated theatre, Jiří Voskovec and Jan Werich, had found its way to broad popularity. Its title translated as 'Against the wind' or 'Against the storm'. Sung everywhere to a nostalgic yet marching tune, it went as follows:

When we march in the millions
All going against the wind
Each will advance by one metre
And we will add metre to metre
Where is the force of our opponent?
Where is the wind's own force?
Against the current we will advance
By kilometres in the hundreds[42]

Now the millions came out on the street.

On Wenceslas Square, the crowds that had been forming in the late afternoon grew restless. After the announcement came over the loudspeakers, they surged in the direction of Charles Bridge, aiming for Hradčany and the Castle. Though it had been a beautiful autumn day, it was growing dark. Thanks to the black-out, across the river the Castle and hill rose in a sombre bulk against the sky. As people left their workplaces or their homes, or the trams and buses they happened to be sitting in, or as the human current passed them by, they joined the flow of the demonstrators.

On 21 September the PVVZ, the steering council of the 'Faithful we remain!' petition, had declared that 'Things have not been decided yet. [...] We have not lost one rifle, gun, cannon, or fortification. [...] Away with the partisans of capitulation! Away with the internal enemies of the republic!'[43] Gedye was handed a leaflet circulated in 'a hundred thousand copies' urging: 'Long live the Czechoslovak Republic, its splendidly loyal army and the army's commander and founder. Edouard Beneš! Firm stands the President! Firm stands the Army! Firm stands the nation! Let us raise our voices and sweep away the traitors!'[44]

Through the early days of September, the offices of Krofta and Beneš had continued to receive letters, petitions, and resolutions numbering in the thousands, asking for the government to stand up to Henlein, rejecting any further concessions, or proposing to rise to the defence of the republic in various ways.[45] Perhaps the most moving of such appeals was that by the nobility: an open letter which a delegation of twelve titled signatories delivered to Beneš on 17 September in the name of the country's leading landed families – people who had lost far more than they had gained by the dissolution of Austria-Hungary and the creation of Czechoslovakia. The text was the initiative of Zdenko Radslav Kinský and František Karel Schwarzenberg, each hailing from one of the grand old princely families of Bohemia. The signatures included several of the great names of Habsburg times: Kolowrat, Czernín, Colloredo-Mansfeld ... Nor was this without personal risk: several of the signatories would fall prey to Nazi confiscations after Munich. The public address stated:

> Loyalty to the Czech state, which our forebears helped build and preserve for a thousand years, is for us a duty so evident that we thought we should explicitly proclaim it [...]. Our wish that the old borders of the Bohemian crown should remain undisturbed emerges also from a concern for the future of our descendents and a feeling of responsibility for the freedom and prosperity of the Czech Germans. Our ancestors always strove to maintain good relationships between the two peoples settled in the border regions, and so do we hope that our fellow German-speaking countrymen may share our love for our undivided homeland. We are confident that it can be so.[46]

Large crowds now converged from all directions on the seat of power and government; in the evening they would reach hundreds of thousands. Alexander Henderson saw a dense mass of men and women, boys and girls marching past his flat in Hradčany or in Smíchov, on the other side of the Castle from Wenceslas Square, 'a stream of empty trams, golden in the darkness, trailing helplessly behind'.[47] 'There was little fanaticism, only a mixed air of confusion and determination. Here was a man carrying a briefcase, on his way home from work. There a group of students. Behind them factory workers in black leather jackets, their hands still black from the work bench. Women led children by the hand. Well-dressed people came out of cafés to join the march. They all pressed on up the hill, under the blue-shaded street lights – another air raid precaution.'[48] 'I saw a soldier bicycling down a side-street,' writes Morrell. 'A crowd saw him and ran towards him. They lifted him off his bicycle, and I saw him poised uncertainly above their heads. They were cheering. He was laughing and waving his arms.'[49]

At the head of these demonstrations marched small groups carrying the Czechoslovak flag. They sang the national anthem or chanted slogans such as: 'We will not give in. We will keep our frontiers.' Some bore banners with lines taken from Hussite hymns, such as: 'Fear not your enemies, count not their number!' But the main slogan, repeated continuously, carried on banners, and chanted by the crowd, was: 'We made the weapons, let us use them!'[50]

One group had congregated in front of the radio building, near Wenceslas Square. Others seem to have headed towards the defence ministry in Dejvice, on the Castle side of the river but to the north. The main column of demonstrators headed for the Castle itself, though, and their accumulated mass began pushing at its gates late in the evening. Ladislav Feierabend writes that when the crowd reached the square before the gates, the noise could be heard all the way to Ořechovka, more than a kilometre away.[51]

Drtina was in the Castle itself, in the offices overlooking the third courtyard, across from St Vitus Cathedral.[52] The crowds that had been gathering around the city remained outside the gates until late after dark, he wrote. It was a beautiful evening, with not a cloud in sight. What visitors were due to see the president were arriving late, having been detained outside the entrance. Inside, though the large mass of people that had gathered beyond could not be ignored, all was quiet. Then, a short time after 10:30 p.m., the demonstrators overturned the front gates and streamed past the club-wielding stone giants that stand there into the first, then the second and the third courtyard. The police, assigned to push them back, were unable to contain them.

At first, only a few hundred people managed to reach the inner yard, all shouting incomprehensibly or chanting. This went on for half an hour or so while the officials barricaded inside the buildings flailed about for a response. The crowd began shouting 'Long live General Syrový!', unfurled a flag, and sang the national anthem. But the courtyard continued to fill and Drtina, fearing a violent takeover, took the initiative to call the interior minister, Josef Černý.

The nature and aims of the demonstrators could not be ascertained. The next day, the Social-Democratic 'political' minister Rudolf Bechyně, sitting in one of the reception rooms, would keep repeating: 'This is a revolution! This is a revolution!' A violent core might take advantage of the confusion to assassinate the president. Beneš himself was sleeping, having gone the last forty-eight hours without rest. The republic's incapacity to police its own inner sanctum, besides, would drive Czechoslovak prestige on the international scene still lower. This risked forming the excuse for yet more extreme Nazi demands and yet more reprimands from the British and French. The Germans might even seize upon wider disorders, so it could reasonably be feared, as the pretext for an invasion.

Černý replied there was nothing he could do, and when Drtina in turn telephoned Ludvík Krejčí, the commander in chief of the armed forces, the general said the same, though he at least promised to come over. Eventually the demonstrators, having massed in ever greater numbers, turned violent. A vanguard attempted to force its way into the palace rooms and threatened to smash its doors and windows. The guards had affixed bayonets and were about to fire. Drtina decided the president must be woken up, but the first lady turned him back on the threshold, begging that her husband should be allowed some badly needed rest.

At this point Krejčí arrived, in the company of Jan Syrový. Apparently they had had to cross barricades on their way, which had taken them from the Czernin Palace or the defence ministry or both through Hradčany and one of the Castle's multiple entrances. By now, thousands of people were packing the courtyards, backing out from all sides into Hradčany and Dejvice and beyond. Syrový stepped out onto the balcony, with a group of officers standing behind him. The Castle staff had arranged for projectors to be trained on him. He was greeted with a great cry and applause, and the crowd at last fell silent.

Syrový was technically outranked by Krejčí, but his prestige lay elsewhere. During the First World War, a small band of Czech and Slovak émigré volunteers had formed into a brigade to fight on the Russian side, and this had swollen, through the recruitment of prisoners of war, to a fully fledged 'Czechoslovak legion' numbering approximately 40,000. The legion had distinguished itself in a number of battles, in particular the 1917 Battle of Zborov, in which it had broken the line of Austrian trenches. By early 1918, it had been agreed that it would be pulled out of Russia to join the Allies on the Western Front. This could only be done by crossing through Siberia and shipping out of Vladivostok. Just as the legionaries were preparing to do this, though, the Soviets signed the peace of Brest-Litovsk with Wilhelmine Germany. The legionaries first fought their way out of encirclement by the German army at the Battle of Bakhmach, in Ukraine, then they began to march east. From there, they could only pass through Soviet-held territory. The Soviets, mistrustful, wanted them to disarm. The legionaries refused, so Leon Trotsky ordered their neutralisation and arrest. Fighting erupted: the legion prevailed over the Red Army, and in subsequent battles it took control of the entire length of the trans-Siberian railway and, effectively, of Siberia. At its point of maximum control, the legion had been able to threaten, in conjunction with various White Russian movements, the Bolsheviks themselves.

Eventually the legionaries had been evacuated from Russia. Together with a Western Front Czechoslovak legion, they came to form the nucleus of the new republic's army. But the march through Siberia had acquired legendary status. Jan Syrový himself had been among the small band of volunteers who had formed the original Czechoslovak brigade in Russia. He had risen to the rank of general and, by the time of the fight for Siberia, had become the legion's commander. Syrový had returned home a hero. If this were not enough, he had lost an eye at the Battle of Zborov: his eye patch gave him an inescapable resemblance to Jan Žižka, the undefeated fifteenth-century Hussite military leader and terror of Holy Roman German Emperor Sigismund.

Where exactly Syrový addressed the crowds that evening or what he said is not entirely clear from testimonies. Morrell writes that he saw Syrový appear on a balcony at the defence ministry in Dejvice. Though Morrell had to ask someone to translate, the eye patch ensured the speaker's identity could not be mistaken. 'He held up his hand, and the wave of cheering receded and died away. His speech was short, and was more of a command than an appeal. "Keep calm," he said. "Go peacefully to your homes. Everything will be all right." The curtain waved, and he disappeared behind it.'[53] If so, this was before the general made his way to the Castle, where he spoke a second time. The speech to the tumultuous assembly in the Castle courtyard was in the same vein: 'I love our Republic just as much as you do. I am conscious of my responsibility. Have confidence in me. Military dictatorship would be of no help to us. You do not know the causes which forced the Government to take its decisions. We cannot lead the nation to suicide.'[54]

In the ensuing weeks Syrový was to play an important role. For now, though, even his words failed to persuade the demonstrators to disperse. What the people evidently expected was more like the proclamation of a military government, or even a declaration of war. According to

Drtina, it was only the sudden appearance of the well-known singer and right-wing nationalist Karel Hašler, who made a passionate speech ending with the proposal that the crowd go demonstrate by the tomb of the unknown soldier, which prompted it slowly to clear out. Through the courtyards and in surrounding streets, the crowds flowed out into the night. There was a last attempt around midnight to rush back into the inner courtyard, through a mounted police cordon, by another small but determined group. But this too was forced out and evacuated, and the authorities at last resumed control.

As Syrový had pointed out, the public could not yet know the causes of the government's agreement to surrender the Sudetenland. While there had been rumours and much speculation, it was only on 22 September that the press was able to report on the factors having led to the decision, and in particular on Czechoslovakia's stunning abandonment by the French. For the first time, the newspapers informed the public of the nature and flow of recent negotiations, the Anglo–French ultimatum and the reasons for accepting it, the background of the ambassadorial visits, and the risks for Czechoslovakia of finding itself at war alone against Germany. But neither did this discourage further, even more widespread popular agitation in favour of resistance.

The government had produced its own justification, in the form of a radio announcement by the minister of propaganda, Hugo Vavrečka, that came out in the evening of 21 September and was reproduced in the press the next day. While this purported to explain the government's acceptance of the Anglo–French terms, it was peppered with harsh words that could also be interpreted as calls to defiance:

> You have heard the official news of the *démarche* of the Great Powers to our Government, and you have heard how in a manner without parallel in history, our allies and friends are dictating to us those sacrifices, which are imposed on a defeated nation. But we are not defeated, and if nevertheless our Government, headed by its President, has been obliged in the end unanimously to accept these cruel conditions, it has done so only because it wanted to

save the people from vain sacrifices, from useless bloodshed, and from infinite suffering and sorrow. [...] History will pronounce its judgement on the events of these days. [...] Let us have confidence in ourselves; let us believe in the genius of our nation. We shall not surrender, we shall hold the land of our fathers.[55]

Some newspapers appeared with columns blanked out. A 1933 law for the defence of the republic allowed for press censorship, though this was almost never used. The sudden appearance of missing text could only suggest that what had been taken out was blisteringly critical of Germany, or more likely of Britain and France.[56] *Český deník* had declared that though war would bring 'a sea of blood and misery without limits, and even threaten the end of civilisation and the world's Bolshevisation', it was preferable to making any further concessions.[57] The popular *A-Zet* ran as headlines: 'Fateful decision by the government – Dramatic events in the night – English and French ambassadors visit president at 2 in the morning'; and 'Our own allies have dictated to us as to the defeated!', 'The faithful people in the streets', 'Long live our army!'[58]

The demonstrations resumed the following day, 22 September, nationwide. As Milena Jesenská recorded it: 'Throngs from the suburbs flowed into the centre of town, and from the country people went on the march. [...] They sat on the pavement. They stood around our editorial offices. People addressed complete strangers and found that they spoke the same language: we don't want to surrender. We cannot surrender. [...] Factories remained closed. Women didn't cook. The suburbs were empty. Shops silent. The great current of the people united again in demonstrations.'[59]

In the capital, the marchers were now reinforced by contingents of workers and miners from the Kladno region and the suburban factories of Avia and Letov. Others arrived, lunchboxes in hand, from the surrounding villages. Large demonstrations now took place in Bratislava, the Slovak capital, in Plzeň, in Moravkská Ostrava, Brno, Hradec Králové, Turnov, Slaný, Rakovník, Olomouc, Tábor, and other provincial centres.[60] An employee at a law firm recalls that he joined a team of workers from the Orionka biscuit factory, in Prague, which was walking through the suburb of Vršovice for the demonstrations. 'We were shouting slogans such as: "We won't give Prague to the Germans, we would rather destroy it!" and we meant it in dead earnestness. We passed through Národní třída and Karlovy lázně and we were by the Charles Bridge when someone spread the news: "General Krejčí is with us." Some of us did not even know who General Krejčí was, yet we all doffed our caps and hats in respect.'[61] Showing how far they united the Czechoslovak nation, these events were punctuated in the coming days by important proclamations from the Slovak autonomists. Dr Pauliny Toth, the president of the autonomist Protestants, declared that 'for us the Czechoslovak Republic is our only Fatherland and we shall fight for it to our last breath'. *Slovák*, the official organ of the HSĽS, the main autonomist party, would write: 'Let us be ready to defend our Fatherland, to defend the territory given to us by God, and to defend all those moral, material and national values which we have preserved many times by our own efforts, by our own knowledge and by our own blood.'[62]

The calls, on that second day, became more specific, asking for the Hodža government to resign and hand over the reins to Syrový. The target destination of the demonstrations changed. In Prague, their end point became parliament – then seated in the Rudolfinum on the Old Town side of the river – in front of which a quarter of a million people assembled on 22 September. 'Members of all parties and all groups came on to the balcony to speak to the crowd – Catholic, Agrarian, Fascist, Slovak Conservative, Communist. The leader of the Conservative National Union, Dr. Ladislav Rašín, whose father Alois Rašín, the republic's first finance minister, had been murdered by a Communist in 1923, turned to the people and said: "In this hour there is for me no difference between my party and the Communists; we all love Czechoslovakia, we are all willing to die for its independence. I, the younger Rašín, stretch out my hand to the Communists."'[63] Even the retired general Radola Gajda appeared, the leader of the Czechoslovak fascist league.

The writer and academic Zdeněk Kalista recorded his impression of these moments:

> As I watched from a window of the philosophical faculty build-ing [across from the Rudolfinum], I felt the broad wind that rose from this sea of faces, arms, and bodies overpower me, fire me up, and take me away. I leant out of the window and, abandoning all thought of maintaining the dignity of a university professor, I loudly started to call and shout along with the people on the square. I began to applaud when they applauded. I began to call shame on France and England – as the crowd did below me. And finally, banging the window and letting my hat fall off, I hurtled out of the faculty building to merge into the crowd, to whom someone from the parliamentary steps and later from a window was making a 'fiery' speech.[64]

A committee for the defence of the republic had been formed during the night, led by Rašín and composed of members of parliament from all parties, ranging from the communists through the Social-Democrats and others to the National Union. It was the members of this committee who first addressed the assembled people below and around them. The crowds demanded the formation of a government of national defence. The committee hoped to force Hodža's fall. They did not yet know that the Hodža government, having found that it could not go on, had resigned that morning.

AS THIS WENT ON, Chamberlain was flying to the small Rhenish town of Godesberg for his second interview with Hitler. Accompanying the British premier were his adviser, Horace Wilson, and a team of Foreign Office professionals, as well as the ambassador Neville Henderson. In the afternoon, as the Prague demonstrations reached their peak, the British team left the castle-like Hotel Petersberg to catch the ferry across the Rhine to the Dreesen, where Hitler was staying.

In the ceremonial conference room, Chamberlain this time spoke first. He explained how he had by 'laborious negotiations' won over first the French and then the Czechoslovaks to accept the German chancellor's demands. The proposal was to hand the Sudetenland over without a plebiscite. The fate of mixed areas would be fixed by a commission of three members: one German, one Czech, and one neutral. In an interesting twist, Chamberlain offered only territories that were more than 80 per cent German 'without question', with a 65 per cent cut-off to be used by the international commission in 'drawing a frontier which would take political, economic, and military factors into account'. The idea was to 'better the deal from the Czech standpoint'.[65] Twice that September, Chamberlain would develop sudden pangs of conscience – the second time being at Munich. Yet while from the point of view of the country on whose behalf Britain was supposed to be mediating this might appear laudable, as a negotiating tactic the move was surprising. The Anglo–French plan specified the transfer of areas that were over 50 per cent German. The Czechoslovak acceptance of these terms was now public information and almost certainly known to Hitler. Switching suddenly to a different percentage could only cast doubt on the credibility of the British team and bait its German counterpart into moving its own goalposts.

In any case, Hitler had already resolved to turn down whatever the British premier offered and demand more. Chamberlain paused and leant back, looking up either in satisfaction or to confer added gravitas to his report. The ensuing dialogue was recorded by the German interpreter, corroborated by the notes taken by Chamberlain's own translator, first embassy secretary Ivone Kirkpatrick. 'Do I understand that the British, French and Czech governments have agreed to the transfer of the Sudetenland from Czechoslovakia to Germany?' Hitler asked.

'Yes,' replied the prime minister.

'I am terribly sorry,' Hitler replied, 'but after the events of the last few days, this plan is no longer of any use.' The 'events' referred to were the supposed terrorising of Sudeten Germans in Czechoslovakia since the failed Henleinist coup, involving in Hitler's vision hundreds of dead.

Chamberlain sat up, visibly offended. Rather than contest either the dictator's information or his good faith, he chose to complain of his lack of generosity to someone who had 'risked his whole political career' on this peace proposal, mentioning that 'on leaving England that morning he actually had been booed'. Hitler was unmoved. He handed the British premier a map with territories to be ceded by the end of the month, and Chamberlain withdrew with it across the Rhine.

Discussions resumed the next day – through an exchange of notes rather than in person – while the British team attempted, within the limited scope for secrecy their surroundings allowed, to consult London and Paris. Eventually Chamberlain requested that Hitler put his position down in writing, and this formed the basis for a second interview, again at the Dreesen, beginning at 10:30 p.m. on 23 September.

In this meeting, the Führer presented what would become known as the Godesberg Memorandum, a demand that Czechoslovakia hand over an expansively defined Sudetenland, marked out on an accompanying map, by 28 September, or barely five days hence. 'But this is nothing less than an ultimatum!' exclaimed Chamberlain. Hitler famously replied that it was not, pointing at the heading which only said 'Memorandum'. A heated debate ensued. After several hours, all the British managed to achieve was a small delay to the deadline, bringing it to 1 October. Unbeknown to them, this had been the German military launch date all along.

Chamberlain left under a cloud, though both the German interpreter and the CBS journalist William Shirer, who saw the two leaders part, attested to their mutual cordiality as they said their goodbyes. ('Is the position hopeless, sir?' a reporter asked Chamberlain. 'I would not like to say that,' he answered. 'It is up to the Czechs now.')[66]

The Sudeten Germans who, according to the Führer, were groaning under the Czech yoke had meanwhile undertaken, at his direction, to resume their own violent actions. Or this was the new task, rather, of the Henleinist personnel who, having cut themselves off from their home community, had absconded into the Reich. Hitler had ordered the formation of so-called *Freikorps* on the basis of the SdP's disbanded body of orderlies. By 1 October, these would total 41 battalions consisting of 34,500 men, though the Nazis were only able to arm about one-third of them.[67] Their primary mission would be to assist the *Wehrmacht*, especially as irregulars operating behind lines, in the invasion of Czechoslovakia; but they could meanwhile keep the Czechoslovaks under pressure and maintain the impression of a Sudetenland in disarray.

From 20 to 22 September, *Freikorps* units attacked posts on the northern and southern Czech–German borders, killing and wounding several. Czechoslovak border guards remained under orders for restraint, and in most places they accordingly withdrew, though some were taken prisoner. An official report wrote of a border post in the Sokolov region:

> Both the gendarmes Sergeant Eduard Simon and Sergeant Jan Samko (Slovak) have been carried off to Germany, and with them the Customs Inspector František Rerich. The customs-house is burnt to the ground. At the time of the attack a gendarmerie guard was in or near the customs-house, which was attacked from several sides, and shot at from machineguns and rifles. Powerful detonations at the time when the attack began show that the attackers used hand grenades, or that the besieged defended themselves with them. During the attack the Customs Officer Frendrych, who was in the customs-house, managed to escape through the window.[68]

These inroads continued on 22 and 23 September, one going as far as Třeboň, some ten miles inland.[69] The *Daily Telegraph* Prague correspondent reported:

> In Schluckenau, German Black Guards and Storm-troopers crossed the frontier, but withdrew promptly when gendarmerie arrived. In Česke Hamry ten Czechoslovak frontier guards

and eight soldiers were attacked by a band of Nazi raiders from Germany and inflicted casualties the number of which is unknown. At Libenau, a policeman named Jakl was captured and murdered by the Nazis. German Nazis throwing hand grenades and firing revolvers at the frontier post in Weipert killed a Czechoslovak Customs Officer. In similar attacks from Germany, delivered on posts at Jáchymov, Vidnava, Kladruby, Annenthal, and Bromau, there were altogether thirteen persons killed and twenty-four wounded. One of those killed was a Czechoslovak sentry who was shot from behind while on guard.[70]

The greatest coup was the *Freikorps'* takeover of the Aš salient, a slim tongue of territory jutting out from Czechoslovakia's westernmost tip into Germany, on 21 September. There, the Henleinist irregulars pushed in large numbers as far as Hazlov, on the salient's neck, until they were stopped by the combined border guard and army.[71]

On 23 September the defence ministry announced that it was taking charge. A motorised brigade was sent to Cheb, where it put down disorders. The frontiers were secured anew. Pin-prick attacks would continue all around the Czech borders in the following week, some by forces numbering above one hundred men and several involving the seizure of border guards and/or Social-Democrats and communists for abduction into the Reich. The army nevertheless recovered control of its territory everywhere, save for Aš, which was exposed on three sides and not worth defending in the event of a German invasion, and the similarly situated Varnsdorf.[72] The toll was significantly higher than in the failed post-Nuremberg coup attempt, set according to German sources at 52 *Freikorps* dead, 110 Czechoslovaks, plus 2,029 prisoners, many of whom would never return.[73]

The handover of responsibility to the army and the Czechoslovak counter-attack were themselves the result of political events in Prague. In the early morning of 22 September, the Hodža government had resigned. At 11 a.m., a meeting of the 'political' ministers set in motion the formation of a new cabinet.

Visitors and deputations continued to demand access to the president. Miroslav Klinger came to see Beneš around noon to inform him that the Sokol were prepared to rise to the country's defence. His delegation was initially greeted by the first lady, who broke into tears and said that her husband was nervously ill. Wenzel Jaksch, who happened to be recovering from a car accident and spoke in a whisper, likewise asked to meet the president to alert him to *Freikorps* violence against his comrades. The ministers were interrupted by the arrival of the parliamentary delegation led by Rašín and the Communist Party secretary Klement Gottwald. There were meanwhile false rumours of betrayal and approaches to Hitler by right-wing political leaders.[74]

In theory there were two candidates for the leadership: Syrový and the non-party politician and ex-prime minister Jan Černý. In practice the nomination of an emergency government with Syrový at its head was all but guaranteed. The legionary leader had given another calming speech on the radio. Though the demonstrations would continue throughout the country, the crowds in front of parliament had finally begun to thin. By the evening, Syrový was able to form a government in which he combined the posts of premier and defence minister. Cox recounts that when the news was announced, 'the cheering shook the windows of the Ambassador Hotel from which we were watching'.[75]

That evening, Beneš also delivered a speech of his own over the radio. At that point, Czechoslovakia's acquiescence to the Anglo–French plan remained its last word. The nation, however, would clearly not accept it. It was not yet known that the Godesberg talks had been going badly from the perspective of Chamberlain's peacemaking and that they had effectively been broken off. At this stage, Beneš's greatest risk was, therefore, that Hitler would simply accept what Chamberlain had come to offer him. The president needed to leave the door open for this possibility, take advantage of the nation's warlike mood to prepare it for the alternative, and at the same time ensure a return to calm that would enable the country to deal with what came next with firmness.

The Beneš radio speech was important both for what it reveals of the president's strategy and because it would later be badly misunderstood. 'I am watching every development calmly and without fear. [...] I have made plans for all eventualities and cannot be surprised,' said Beneš. 'If it should be necessary to fight, we will know how to do so to the last breath. If it is necessary to negotiate, we will negotiate. [...] I repeat: I see things clearly and I have my plan. I have confidence in our people, in our nation and in our State. Our line of policy is firm, and we are trying to act in a thoughtful manner suited to the circumstances and events, which are now changing so rapidly.'[76] This was an accurate description of the situation and of governmental actions. Beneš would come to be reproached, though, for his statement that 'I have made plans for all eventualities.' This gave the impression that the president was in control, possibly through some secret diplomatic weapon. The speech would be blamed for instilling false hopes until it was too late for popular action to prevent a surrender.

What Beneš meant, according to both Hubert Ripka and his own testimony, was only that time and Hitler's tactics ultimately played into Czechoslovak hands. Beneš's plan was to keep negotiations going for several weeks and in the meantime come to terms with Poland, even at the price of territorial concessions. Hitler was unlikely to accept the Anglo–French proposals, so that the more probable outcome was war. In the unlikely alternative, if the proffered terms were accepted, Czechoslovakia's right of regard over the international commission would help it preserve its military defences. Even in this case, Beneš was convinced, war would only be delayed, and Czechoslovakia would have ensured it stood on the right side when it came.[77]

The problem, of course, was that the British and French did not share this understanding of Hitler's tactics, and they were ready for far more extensive concessions than Beneš imagined. The Czechoslovak president had a better insight into the Nazi regime than into the Franco–British side. Ripka wrote of his physical state at the time: 'Though he was a man accustomed to stand fatigue without showing signs of it, he was quite unrecognisable. For several nights he had not slept, and the events of the previous night had been a most terrible blow for him. [...] We saw before us a man who was physically worn out and morally crucified, and who could only with the greatest difficulty conceal from us his overwhelming despair.'[78]

Good news nevertheless arrived on the afternoon of 23 September. At Godesberg, Hitler had rejected Chamberlain's peace overtures. He actively threatened war and had imposed a short deadline for it. In conferring together, the British and French had concluded it was irresponsible to continue to urge the Czechoslovaks for restraint in their military preparations. At 6:15 p.m. that day, their ambassadors advised the Czechoslovak foreign ministry that they could 'no longer continue to take the responsibility for advising them not to mobilise'.[79] The public mood, the demonstrations, and what was turning into an effective general strike did not leave much choice anyhow. Beneš was immensely relieved. He felt that the country was ready materially and psychologically and that 'London and Paris had finally understood'.[80]

That same afternoon, Ambassador Sergei Alexandrovsky came to reiterate the Soviet Union's support, coupled with a warning to Poland not to line up behind Nazi demands. Drtina writes that when Beneš received the notice that the British and French recommended mobilisation, he registered this with shock, repeated the word 'yes' several times as he paced around the room, then handed the message to Drtina saying: 'Read this! It is to be war!'[81]

Already on 13 September, Krejčí had insisted to Beneš that preparedness against a surprise attack must be raised. It had been agreed to call up various reserve units and put the fortifications on a war footing. The number of men under arms had risen to 380,000. In the following days, the army moved its artillery units into positions from which they could be deployed within three hours, stocked fortifications with munitions, and placed both the alert system and the air force on stand-by for an invasion. On 17 September, Krejčí had requested the mobilisation of another two army classes, going so far as to threaten resignation if this was withheld, and in the end obtained authorisation for raising one more class, bringing numbers to 500,000.[82] At 8 p.m., on 23 September, Beneš called a grand meeting, at the Castle, of the government, coalition party leaders, and general staff.[83]

At 10:30 p.m., Czechoslovak radio broadcast the order for general mobilisation.

6

Preparing for war

THREE DAYS LATER, Beneš convoked General Silvestr Bláha, the director of his military office, and told him:

> This war will be terrible. In the end, every one of us will fight the Germans, uniformed or not uniformed, men and women. Even if powerful allies come to our side, it will neither be fast nor at the beginning decisive enough for us to stop a German invasion of our republic. But we will fight to the last breath and we must go to the end, whatever happens. I will remain by the army with my guard. But you should know this, and so should the commander in chief and prime minister: I will retreat with the army only up to a point. When we must stop, and can give up no more of our territory and fight the enemy to the death, I as president of the republic cannot be taken prisoner. I must stay with those who fight absolutely to the last moment, and fall with them. [1]

Bláha promised that he would do what was necessary.

Both the British and the French military attachés in Prague, Colonel H. C. T. Stronge and General Louis-Eugène Faucher, expected the Czechoslovaks to be able to hold the German army at bay for a substantial length of time, running into months.[2] While the British cabinet tended to be dismissive of Czechoslovak military capabilities, Daladier and the French chief of the general staff Maurice Gamelin were of a different opinion, and both men valued Czechoslovakia as a strategic asset. A retrospective justification of Munich, among the appeasers themselves and among revisionist historians, has been that the agreement bought rearmament time for the Entente powers. This argument, in addition to being questionable in its own right, neither counts the forces which the Czechoslovaks brought to the fight nor the contribution their armaments made to Hitler's armies, after they were bloodlessly conquered.

As Beneš's words hinted, the Czechoslovak strategy was to pull back as gradually as possible into the last redoubt that was Slovakia. Prague was to be sacrificed. The various military plans, culminating in Plan VII of July 1938, envisaged a gradual withdrawal eastward relying on three natural bulwarks: the rivers Elbe and Vltava, the Bohemian-Moravian highlands, and the Slovak Carpathians. An initial stand was to be made on the fortified line which, where it held, was to facilitate this withdrawal. The aim was meanwhile to give France maximum time to push against Germany's western flank. If the enemy could be fended off long enough for Soviet help to arrive and/or the Allies to make serious inroads into Germany, a counter-attack was to be launched from the Slovak redoubt. If not, the goal was to inflict maximum casualties, then blow up all domestic military assets.[3] The strategy had been agreed with the French, who, though they could not relieve the Czechoslovaks directly, planned to advance into the Rhineland.[4]

Leaving France aside, of prime concern to Czechoslovakia were its immediate neighbours, especially Hungary, Poland, and the Soviet Union. The Soviet Union was a great power and a Czechoslovak ally. Hungary, on the other hand, was friendly to the Axis and could threaten the Czechoslovak position on its southern, Slovak flank. That would draw forces away from defence against Germany and make it difficult to use Slovakia as a last bastion. Poland was in the ambiguous position of being at once hostile to Czechoslovakia and a French ally. If Poland joined the Allies, it could vitiate the Nazi invasion into Czechoslovakia by attacking the northern German army in the rear. Even the poorly equipped Polish army, moreover, was capable of overcoming the German holding force in East Prussia, whose loss would have presented the Reich with a major embarrassment and tactical defeat. Conversely, if Poland fought on the side of Germany, it threatened to make the Czechoslovak strategic situation untenable.

Hungary, while likely to partake in a German descent on Czechoslovakia alone, could be expected to remain neutral in a general war. The Hungarians were a revisionist power. Like the Poles, they would famously partake in the division of the spoils post-Munich. They were far more timid beforehand, however, and their actions revealed a degree of caution in committing themselves. Hitler met Béla Imrédy, the Hungarian prime minister, and Koloman de Kanya, the foreign minister, on 20 September in Berchtesgaden. The Nazi leader exhorted them to be more forward in making demands from the Czechoslovaks. He warned his interlocutors that they must take more risks if they expected rewards. Even so, the Hungarians made only a token military deployment on their border, in the last days of September, and they continued to refrain from specifying any territorial demands.[5]

The Hungarians were loath to risk war with the Western powers, and concerned besides at the implications of German hegemony in central Europe. The spring and summer saw the initiation of bilateral talks and conferences attempting a rapprochement between Hungary and the Little Entente.[6] The main reason Hungary was a prospective neutral, however, was that it was held in check by the Little Entente itself – the alliance that united Yugoslavia, Romania, and Czechoslovakia against Hungarian revisionism. On 25 September, the Yugoslav government warned the Hungarians that it was ready to fulfil its treaty obligations against them.[7] Both the Romanians and Yugoslavs confirmed in Prague that they would stand by their Little Entente commitments in case of a Hungarian attack.[8] (The Romanians went so far as to warn Germany that they would stop supplying it with oil.[9]) The Hungarians thus faced potential attacks from the south and east, plus the ultimate prospect of a Soviet thrust towards Budapest. They could be counted on to stand aside.

The authoritarian Józef Beck, Poland's foreign minister and de facto leader, was no friend of Czechoslovakia. Poland had long considered the Silesian district of Teschen and other minor border enclaves containing Polish-speaking minorities disputed territory. In May, the Polish ambassador in Paris had refused to commit to join France, were it to declare war on Germany on behalf of the Czechoslovaks.[10] On 21 September, on the back of the release of the Anglo–French plan, the Polish ambassador in Prague, Kazimierz Papée, notified Krofta that Poland was revoking the treaty of April 1925 arbitrating its border with Czechoslovakia. Beneš understood that now was not the time to be having it out with the Poles. Indeed, it was militarily well worth bringing them on side, if this could be done, even at the cost of territorial sacrifices. Beneš wrote directly to the Polish president Ignacy Mościcki in the night of 23–24 September, appealing to the common danger and the common cause while hinting at territorial compromises. Mościcki replied encouragingly on 27 September, but on the back of his response came a letter from Beck asking for the immediate surrender of a section of Teschen and a plebiscite for the remainder. Admittedly this was not extremely encouraging, but Beneš now took a step towards meeting Polish demands more squarely: he promised, on 30 September, to establish within five days a Polish–Czechoslovak commission for agreeing, on another very short deadline, on border adjustments.[11] This was tantamount to accepting Beck's terms, as Beneš was prepared to do if war started.

Meanwhile the French were putting pressure on the Poles, both through the diplomatic service and privately via Gamelin, and warning them not to aggravate Czechoslovakia's position unless they wanted to be the wrong side of a conflict involving France.[12] Nor was Polish decision-making quite as purblind as it first appears. The Poles only handed in their first demands on the heels of the Anglo–French plan. They only resorted to threats, in the form of an ultimatum, after the outcome of the Munich conference was actually known, on the evening of 30 September. The *Kurier Warzsawski* wrote: 'Does France not understand that it is not in her interest to strengthen Germany at the expense of Czechoslovakia, unless Poland is strengthened at the same time? She reproaches us in her press for taking advantage of a time when Czechoslovakia is deserted, in order to present our claims. We may say in answer, however, that our claim for frontier rectification is being made only after we have ascertained that France and England have considered such rectification in favour of Germany to be possible.'[13]

The Poles had been friends of France for two hundred years. Poland, resurrected in 1919, owed its very existence to the Versailles order which Hitler was busy demolishing. Its alliance required Poland to come to France's assistance in the case of an unprovoked attack by Germany. Poland could invoke its 1934 non-aggression treaty with the Reich as an excuse to do nothing if it was France that declared war. Yet the pact's technicalities could surely be finessed if the Poles decided they must fight on the Allied side. According to Michal Lubienski, Beck's subaltern and a person who had no reason to lie after the fact to protect a chief he disliked, Beck called in the general staff on the evening of 30 September and asked what should be done – should they mobilise in defence of Czechoslovakia in case of war? The Poles decided that 'this could have been done if there had been certainty that the Czechs wanted to fight'.[14]

As to the Soviets, they were even more threatening than the French. On 21 September, the Soviet vice-commissar for foreign affairs, Vladimir Potemkin, presented a strongly worded note to the Polish chargé d'affaires in Moscow, warning that any incursion into Czechoslovakia would lead Russia to denounce the Polish–Soviet non-aggression pact.[15] The forces mobilised by the Soviet Union in September 1938 stood mostly on the Polish border, making any Polish intervention on the side of Germany, even with the limited aim of grabbing Teschen, inconceivable.[16]

As a recent study indeed establishes, the USSR had by the end of September mobilised very significant forces: one army group by Bessarabia, two along the Polish border, and two in the corner formed by the Polish and Lithuanian borders. 'The total scale of these preparations included thirty infantry and ten cavalry divisions, seven tank and motorized infantry brigades, twelve brigades of fighter planes and bombers. [...] Further orders were issued on 29 September to the Kiev, Belorussian, Leningrad, and Kalinin military districts to call up from reserves and form seventeen additional infantry divisions, the staffs of three tank corps, twenty-two tank and three motorized infantry brigades, and thirty-four air bases.' This was without counting 'a considerable second echelon of forces' formed in the interior of the country.[17]

The Soviet Union was committed to fight on the side of Czechoslovakia under a 1935 mutual-assistance treaty, this commitment containing the precondition that France honour its own obligations towards Prague. Stalin's ways could sometimes be inscrutable and narrowly aggrandising, but in September 1938 the Soviet preparedness to join Czechoslovakia against the Reich, were France also to do so, was plain enough. The USSR had approached France and Britain several times during the year, privately and publicly, with proposals for cooperation in the defence of Czechoslovakia.[18] Mikhail Kalinin, the USSR's Supreme Council president, had stated on 11 May his country's intention to fulfil its treaty obligations. Aleksandr Troyanovsky, the ambassador to the United Sates, did so on 25 May, and Maxim Litvinov, the foreign minister, on 23 June.[19] Litvinov affirmed very publicly on 21 September, at the League of Nations in Geneva: 'We intend to fulfil our obligations under the pact and, together with France, to afford assistance to Czechoslovakia.'[20]

The question was more how effective and swift Soviet participation was likely to prove. The Soviet Union's military forces had been the scene, from 1936 onwards, of sweeping purges, with 35,000 out of 70,000 officers either shot or packed away to the Gulag, including 80 per cent of colonels and generals.[21] The USSR lacked a common border with Czechoslovakia, and access ran through either Poland or Romania. The easiest route by far ran through Polish open country, but it was likely to be resolutely denied.

Yet though the Romanians never issued a formal authorisation to the Soviets, by September they had several times assured the French that they would allow Russian land or air forces through.[22] On 7 September, the Romanian general staff drafted a mobilisation plan designed for a war on the side of the French, Czechoslovaks, and Soviets, and its annual plans of campaign had since 1936 foreseen the facilitation of Red Army transit.[23] Land troops could pass through the north-western corner of Romania or transit through by rail. Neither the Soviet nor the Romanian rail networks were designed to move large quantities of equipment into Czechoslovakia, but one to two divisions might have been expected to cross over by that route per week.[24] Nor was flying war planes over Romania easy, as it involved a long, high-altitude route over mountains. The Czechoslovaks had collected fuel at Slovak airfields and gathered specialists in preparation for Soviet arrivals, but Soviet aircraft required, except for their engines, different spare parts and they used different ammunition, all of which would have to be imported.[25] The Czechoslovaks could expect no Russian steamroller. In the context of their strategy of holding off the Germans for as long as possible, however, then pulling back into Slovakia in preparation for a counter-attack, the Soviets could make a significant contribution.

THE FRENCH, while the Czechoslovaks pulled the bulk of the enemy against themselves, were for their part planning to march into Germany via the Rhineland.

Contemporaries at once labelled the French army the victor of the Great War and the greatest army in the world, and wrung their hands over French inferiority to Germany. This, though, reflected shorthand comparisons of relative demographics – and what mattered ultimately was armaments, not population. Retrospectively, the potential role of France in a conflict beginning in 1938 has been completely overshadowed by the collapse of May 1940 and the irresistible urge to account for it. (Surprisingly, none of the historians of Munich offers a complete tally of the forces involved as of September 1938.) But Germany's stunning set of early Second World War victories lay in the future, and they built on the very gains achieved at Munich. The balance of forces between France and Germany, and even more so France and Czechoslovakia together against Germany, was completely different in 1938 than in 1939, let alone 1940.

The French strategy was not to relieve the Czechoslovaks directly – this had been considered, but the terrain was judged too difficult. The idea was rather to take advantage of Germany's concentration in the east to advance towards the Rhine and eventually into the Ruhr: Plan R.[26] Hitler had allocated only five active infantry divisions and four reserve to his western front under General Guillaume Adam, the rest being assigned for use against Czechoslovakia or on duty on Germany's north-eastern frontier.[27] There was supposed to be a Siegfried Line or West Wall, but construction on this had barely begun, and the concrete was not even dry on what shelters did exist: a 'Potemkin' defence that offered little to no obstacle to an attacker.[28]

The plan for the Rhineland invasion involved a massive force that counted four armies: the French second, third, fourth, and fifth, with another two standing in reserve based in Rheims and Strasbourg. These four armies counted upwards of forty infantry divisions, or not very far from a million men, including five motorised divisions. It was intended to commit the overwhelming majority of France's tank force, centred in the eastern town of Nancy, in addition to substantial light and heavy artillery support. Adam was very badly outnumbered and outgunned. The bulk of the invading armies, moreover, consisted of regular divisions: standing units composed of a core of professionals supplemented at mobilisation, a fighting elite which also happened to be available immediately.[29]

Preliminary operations were to involve breaking into the Saar on a broad front and preparing to attack the Siegfried Line, such as it was. These initial moves were expected, together with troop concentration, to take two weeks – and by the end of September, the French army had partially mobilised and was ahead of schedule. Phase one of operations proper would consist in taking possession of the Saar. Timing was not specified, but later studies calculated that it would take eighteen days to break through the Siegfried Line.[30] Phase two of Plan R involved a broad sweep across the Rhineland in the direction of Trier and Mainz, on the Rhine. This could broadly be expected to take place in the second month of war.

Gamelin made his intention explicit to carry through Plan R on multiple occasions: for example, at meetings with Daladier on 12 and 23 September.[31] The French offensive strategy was slow, admittedly, based on doctrine developed during the First World War. It involved the deployment of artillery, intensive shelling, then the advance of infantry accompanied by tanks, and it was no *Blitzkrieg*. The French intelligence bureau overestimated German strength, which dissuaded the general staff from bold, swift thrusts. But this conversely stood to deliver a positive surprise when it was realised how few divisions the Germans could deploy in the west. Success in the Rhineland, indeed, was liable to encourage the French to adopt more mobile tactics as they discovered that the speeds of advance were no longer those of the First World War but something akin to the faster, tank-assisted sweep of the closing months of 1918.

Yet the French army stood to prevail over the Germans for one very simple reason: significant superiority in numbers, even more so when combined with the Czechoslovaks. Once General Adam was defeated, there was nothing or almost nothing left to oppose the French. France and Czechoslovakia together could align almost twice as many army divisions, after general mobilisation, as Germany. France alone could deploy larger forces than the Reich.

Germany remained, in 1938, only halfway through its rearmament

Table 6.1 Total army strength (divisions) [32]

	France	Czechoslovakia	France + Czechoslovakia	Germany
Infantry – regular	35	20	55	36
Infantry – reserve	21	14	35	8
Infantry – motorised	7	1	8	4
Armoured or rapid	2	4	6	8
Fortress troops	15	3	18	12
Cavalry	5	—	5	1
Total	85	42	127	69

effort, and it was bumping against significant physical limits. The Versailles Treaty army limitation clauses had long cast their shadow over German military power. The treaty had restricted army size to a total of 100,000 men, of which 4,000 could be officers. It had stringently curtailed weapon and ammunition levels. Hitler had reintroduced conscription in 1935 and declared rearmament limitations null and void, and there had always been a degree of cheating. The Nazis had undertaken the army's reconstruction under a breakneck system of mass mobilisation geared towards war. Yet this took place in a context of a world economic crisis, with the attending foreign-exchange constraints on raw material imports. Germany sought to build a large air force at the same time, and the beginnings of a fleet. Factories and arsenals needed to be constructed, and weapons stockpiled. All this demanded time and imposed calculated choices. An even greater constraint was that modern warfare required trained officers, NCOs, and men. This was difficult and time-consuming to build from a base of a mere few thousand cadres. In 1938, Germany's military remained far short of what its demographic and industrial potential allowed in the long run.[33] Three years of rearmament (compared to five by 1940) did not suffice to close the gap.

The story of 1930s rearmament is too easily misconstrued if the fundamental difference is ignored that France, or indeed Czechoslovakia, faced no such limitations. (Britain, lacking conscription or a sizeable standing army, was in yet another position.) Czechoslovakia possessed a world-class armaments industry that was a significant exporter.[34] The Škoda works alone nearly matched in output the whole of the British armament industry.[35] For France, rearming meant modernising its stock of weapons, not building one from scratch or training multiple new classes of officers. A good share of stockpiles retained from the First World War – for example, field artillery and machineguns – remained perfectly serviceable.[36] While the situation was different in the air force, where obsolescence rates were much higher, on land the French army possessed plentiful weapons, in many areas superior to their German equivalents. Neither the French nor the Czechoslovak armies faced any difficulty equipping all the units they could train.

The balance remained the same with army tallies narrowed down to what was strictly available for campaigns in Czechoslovakia and on a Western Front. France would be leaving some troops in its colonies and interior. Four German divisions were stuck in East Prussia. French fortress troops, most of which were assigned to the *Ligne Maginot*, could

Table 6.2 Available army strength (divisions)

	France	Czechoslovakia	France + Czechoslovakia	Germany
Infantry – regular	26	20	46	33
Infantry – reserve	17	14	31	8
Infantry – motorised	7	1	8	4
Armoured or rapid	2	4	6	8
Fortress troops	—	3	3	5
Cavalry	3	—	3	—
Total	55	42	97	58

be counted out. Likewise, some German fortress troops were stationed in the east, where they would not be doing any fighting. Even then, the German land forces were significantly outnumbered before one considered any British, Polish, or Soviet help.

The only area where Germany enjoyed a relative preponderance was in armoured divisions, yet even this is deceptive. Panzer divisions were pure tank units, German or French 'light' divisions combined motorised infantry and tanks, and Czechoslovak 'rapid' divisions mixed a tank brigade, a cavalry brigade, and a motorised artillery brigade. (Cavalry brigades and divisions, incidentally, did not consist of heroically old-fashioned, sabre-wielding troops but of what were effectively mounted riflemen.) Then again, most French and Czechoslovak tanks were not allocated to specific divisions but directly to army corps and are therefore not counted in the divisional tally. France had around 2,800 tanks, most of them heavy and gun-mounted.[37] Czechoslovakia had more than 400 tanks and Germany around 2,200.[38]

Even more seriously, there was a notable German inferiority in materiel. The German panzers of 1938 were all Mark I and II. The German tanks that punched through the French front at Sedan in 1940 were the much heavier, gun-mounted Mark III and IV – a third of them of Czechoslovak provenance and confiscated or manufactured by the Germans after Munich and the March 1939 annexation.[39] The Mark I panzer was not even mounted with a cannon but merely a machinegun. Mark I and II panzers suffered from inferior thickness of armour and gun power, and neither could be expected to perform well against the heavy French tanks or the Czechoslovak LT-35.[40] Panzers were meanwhile vulnerable to French anti-tank guns, but French tanks were resistant to fire from German anti-tank weapons.[41] The Czechoslovak 34-model anti-tank gun, the weaker of two models in use, could hit and puncture a German tank in movement at a rate of 12–25 times per minute at a distance of up to 2,000 metres.[42] The German panzer arm that was to spearhead the stunningly successful campaigns of 1939 and 1940 was yet to come into existence, and it would only be built with the help of Czechoslovak factories and stockpiles.

Nor did the *Luftwaffe* have the ability to mount the devastating bombing raids of which the British and French were afraid. Arguments that France and Britain were not militarily ready in 1938 sometimes relate specifically to air defence. Yet the contending air forces were merely in diverse stages of unreadiness, and none had reached such strength as to alter the course of a land war. Even in 1940, with a larger, modernised air fleet, the Germans were only able to attack Britain through control of Belgium and northern France. In 1938, German bombers lacked the range to carry anything like a useful bomb load over Britain. By the estimates of the high command itself, they could achieve no more than 'pin pricks'.[43] Nor were Messerschmitt fighters able to reach London from Germany, and any bomber that did make it over British soil, deprived of fighter protection, would have been shot down.[44]

By the best estimates, the *Luftwaffe* possessed 643 first-line fighters against 406 for Britain, 429 for France, and 240 for Czechoslovakia, for a total of 1,075.[45] Reliable Soviet aircraft numbers are hard to come by, but a contemporary French source had them at 840 fighters, of which 400 were the modern and effective I-16, trialled in the Spanish Civil War.[46] In bombers, Germany had a first-line strength of 1,157 aircraft, plus 207 dive bombers.[47] Opposite, Britain had 650 first-line bombers, France 444, and Czechoslovakia 104, totalling 1,198.[48] According to the same official French source, the Soviet Union had 1,366 bombers.[49]

Most British and French aircraft were early to mid-1930s models, and their fighting characteristics, such as speed and manoeuvrability, were inferior to the newest German aircraft. In Britain, deliveries of Hurricanes and Spitfires were just commencing. But if several of the French and British models were obsolescent, so were many of the German aircraft. 'For most of 1938 the Luftwaffe was involved in exchanging its first generation aircraft for those with which it would fight most of the Second World War. Fighter squadrons replaced their

Arado Ar-68s, which were bi-planes, for Me-109s, but by the autumn of 1938 there were no more than 500 Me-109s in the regular fighter squadrons.'[50] The British and French 1938 air fleets moreover contained models that saw service in the early years of the Second World War and performed well, even against the Messerschmitt. 'With its Juno engine, the Bf 109 [Messerschmitt] was not the fighter it would become. [...] Fighters like the British Gladiator, French Dewoitine D 500 and Czech Avia B534 were some 30 mph slower, but their more powerful engines meant they had better acceleration and climb and were capable of patrolling altitudes the Bf 109 could not reach,' writes one historian. 'In terms of quality there was still not much dividing the fighter forces.'[51]

Britain's aerial defences may have remained a work in progress, but more pertinently the Czechoslovak anti-aircraft defences were strong and considered by the Germans themselves capable of causing them 'serious difficulties'.[52] There had been a lot of propaganda and scare-mongering by Goering or tendentious observers such as Charles Lindbergh, often eagerly accepted by French and British air officials. But the *Luftwaffe* actually suffered from spare-part shortages and incomplete crew training. Its aircraft reserves were a mere 25 per cent of the total, lower than the British levels that were judged so inadequate.[53]

The question of air defences, especially British air defences, was in any case only important to a hypothetical Battle of Britain. If the war took place in Czechoslovakia and the Rhineland, and the Germans lacked the armour to tear through Belgium and northern France, as they would do in 1940, the question of British air preparedness became completely irrelevant. Churchill made this very point in his memoirs:

> The German armies were not capable of defeating the French in 1938 or 1939. The vast tank production with which they broke the French front did not come into existence until 1940, and, in the face of French superiority in the West and an unconquered Poland in the East, they could certainly not have concentrated the whole of their air-power against England as they were able to do when France had been forced to surrender. This takes no

account either of the attitude of Russia or of whatever resistance Czechoslovakia might have made. I have thought it right to set out the figures of relative air-power in the period concerned, but they do not in any way alter the conclusions which I have recorded. For all the above reasons, the year's breathing-space said to be 'gained' by Munich left Britain and France in a much worse position compared with Hitler's Germany than they had been at the Munich crisis.[54]

OBSERVERS, FOREIGN AND DOMESTIC, would report that the Czechoslovak general mobilisation was performed with speed and determination. The chief of the German army general staff himself recognised that 'The Czech will fight to the bitter end, because his [national] survival depends on it. The Slovak will within Czech units probably fight also.'[55] Nor would the existence of a German minority among mobilisable men turn out to be a problem. The officer corps and elite units occupying key positions were predominantly Czech or Slovak.[56] The percentage of Sudeten Germans who answered the call to arms varied regionally between 30 and 70 per cent, but there was no revolt against mobilisation.[57] The SdP's paramilitary and other extreme

Table 6.3 Czechoslovak campaign (divisions) [58]

	Czechoslovakia (total)	Germany (total)	Czechoslovakia (Czech lands)	Germany (Plan Green)
Infantry – regular	20	28	16	27
Infantry – reserve	14	4	12	—
Infantry – motorised	1	4	1	4
Armoured or rapid	4	8	3	6
Fortress troops	3	—	3	—
Total	42	44	35	37

elements had already fled to the Reich. Some German conscripts even asked to be put in shooting roles, and 'many Sudeten Germans in khaki did their duty obediently and unprotestingly'.[59]

Meanwhile, far from being hopelessly outmatched, numerically the Czechoslovaks faced an approximately even force, with only a relative German superiority in armour and regular divisions. Subtracting General Adam's army, the divisions stranded in East Prussia, and fortress troops left a total of forty-four divisions for the Nazis to throw at Czechoslovakia. But the German distribution of forces also allowed for a small back-up or strategic reserve to be kept in the interior; accordingly, Plan Green counted on a slightly smaller contingent than the available total. Likewise, Czechoslovak reserves stationed in Slovakia would not have been involved in combat, at least not initially. In either case, as the comparative tallies show, Germany enjoyed an advantage of only two divisions.

Just as France's defeat of 1940 looms over assessments of its pre-Munich capabilities, so does the Polish defeat of 1939 retrospectively distort estimates of the Czechoslovaks' own chances. There were major differences between the 1939 German Polish campaign and a potential 1938 Czechoslovak campaign. First, the terrain was completely different: the Poles were slaughtered in flat and open country; the Czechoslovaks benefited from mountain borders for defence. Second, Plan Green did not concentrate the as yet inferior German tank force – that tactic would only be tried against the Poles a year later. Third, Czechoslovakia possessed an extensive fortification line. Fourth, its army was better equipped, its units rivalling German units. Fifth, while the Poles were surprised in the middle of mobilisation, were only able to put together two-thirds of their army, and lost their air force within hours, the Czechoslovaks had fully mobilised. Sixth, the ratio of forces against the Poles was roughly two to one in favour of Germany in 1939 whereas it was closer to one to one against the Czechoslovaks in 1938. Seventh, the Soviets were an enemy of Poland in 1939 and they participated in its invasion, whereas in 1938 they were a Czechoslovak ally.

Plan Green involved five armies. Three of these were to attack Bohemia and converge on Prague along a north-west, west, and south-west angle: the eighth army, with four divisions, the tenth army, with six infantry divisions plus one panzer and one light, and the twelfth army, with nine infantry divisions. The key to the plan, though, was a pincer movement set to cut Czechoslovakia in two at the 'waist' between Moravia and Slovakia: this involved the second army striking south from German Silesia towards Olomouc and the fourteenth going north from Vienna towards Brno. The second army, under General Gerd von Rundstedt, was composed of eight infantry divisions, one panzer, and one light. The fourteenth, under Wilhelm List, comprised four infantry divisions, one panzer, and one light.[60] If successful, the German pincer movement stood to prevent the Czechoslovak retreat into Slovakia and force instead a desperate and probably short-lived last stand around Prague.

Everywhere, however, the invading Germans faced the hurdle that was the Czechoslovak fortifications. The fortified line, in most places a single but in some areas a double line, stood at a variable distance behind the borders encircling Bohemia and Moravia. The fortifications were of three main types. First came light works protecting machine-gun nests. Second came larger pillboxes built to withstand artillery fire, containing anti-tank guns and howitzers, and designed to hold up to twenty men. Third came fortresses built to withstand heavy artillery and bombs, and which were capable of housing from thirty up to, in a few cases, hundreds of men equipped with machineguns, mortars, anti-tank guns, and flame-throwers. These different units were situated for mutual support and cover, and the network was completed by anti-tank obstacles and mines.[61]

Begun in 1934, the works remained unfinished in places, and a number of emplacements still awaited their complete array of weapons, especially on the section facing annexed Austria. By September 1938, there were nevertheless 6 completed fortresses in southern Moravia, and 250 on the north-eastern segment – in the path of the Rundstedt army.

Of the smaller and medium pillboxes, 3,800+ were distributed around western and southern Bohemia (across the German thrust towards Prague), 1,800+ in northern Bohemia (somewhat uselessly against Plan Green), 1,000 in southern Moravia (before List's Vienna army), and 1,200 in northern Moravia (again before Rundstedt).[62] Air power was unlikely to facilitate the job of storming these defences very much. German dive-bombing attacks were only likely to prove ineffective – on the Maginot Line, in 1940, they wasted significant ammunition taking out only light structures.[63] The Germans had begun training a glider-and-parachute unit, but this remained embryonic and was not envisaged for use against the fortifications.[64] German post-Munich reports suggest that the larger fortresses 'would have been difficult to capture', while destroying other works would have required using heavy artillery or driving tanks between them (assuming these tanks were not taken out first).[65] Bringing up heavy artillery took time. Breaking through the Czechoslovak line was going to involve high-casualty, hand-to-hand fighting.

The Czechoslovak chances nevertheless ultimately depended on foiling the German 'pincer' strategy. Under Plan VII, the Czechoslovak forces were distributed among four armies. The first army, commanded by Sergei Vojcechovský and based in central Bohemia, comprised twelve divisions in infantry and frontier troops – this would defend against the German thrust towards Prague. The third army, under Josef Votruba, was spread across Slovakia, with six infantry divisions and one rapid. The fourth army, under Lev Prchala and based in Brno, comprised seven infantry divisions and two rapid – this stood opposite List's army. The second army, under Vojtěch Luža, comprised four infantry divisions plus frontier units – this stood against Rundstedt.[66]

Prchala's fourth army had a strong chance against List's. List's fourteenth army was mostly composed of converted Austrian divisions that were of low quality.[67] Prchala's forces, moreover, outnumbered it, and while this was where the fortifications were the weakest, the routes through south Moravia were poor and would hinder List's progress.

Rundstedt's army was stronger than Luža's, but it faced by far the toughest part of the fortified line. There was also a strategic reserve, moreover, under Commander in Chief Ludvík Krejčí, likewise based in Moravia. This comprised eight infantry divisions and one rapid and could move to bolster Luža if necessary. The pincer movement therefore faced a major hurdle. Opposed to it was the largest concentration of the Czechoslovak forces. List faced a superior force, and Rundstedt, though he led the strongest of the invading armies, was tasked with breaking through heavily fortified and partly mountainous terrain only to face thirteen divisions, including one rapid, if one counted Krejčí's reserve, to his ten.

Hitler himself was sceptical. At the last minute, he attempted to revise Plan Green at a series of meetings with the general staff. Hitler rightly distrusted German information that the Czechoslovaks had left the line almost undefended in Rundstedt's quarter, or that the fortifications were unfinished. 'Prospects for 2d Army (O.S.) are smallest. Strongest Czech fortifications here. Waste of troops. [...] Possible repetition of Verdun with the 2d Army. Attack there would mean bleeding to death for a task which cannot be accomplished.'[68] He wanted to reinforce the tenth army instead, striking from Bavaria straight towards Prague. His instinct, almost certainly wrong in light of the Czechoslovak preparedness to abandon the capital, was that this would force the decision before the Allies could intervene. The generals insisted, and in the end the pincer movement was kept with only small modifications.

In a final twist, Krejčí himself decided Bohemia was worth defending more strongly, and he moved two infantry and one rapid division westward – where they could also facilitate a withdrawal over the highlands separating Bohemia and Moravia.[69] This weakened slightly the Czechoslovak ability to resist the German 'pincer'. Six strategic-reserve divisions remained available, however, to relieve Luža if need be. Even after these changes, the bulk of the Czechoslovak forces remained concentrated in Moravia, the section of their country through which they were planning to retreat. Rundstedt, in addition to facing by far the strongest segment in the fortified line, would have to contend with ten divisions at the least – and this was without counting any potential relief from Votruba's army in Slovakia.

Even taking Prague, with its concentric fortified lines, was going to take time. German memoranda estimated the length of a Czech campaign (i.e. the conquest of the Czech lands of Bohemia and Moravia, not the whole of Czechoslovakia) as a minimum of three to four weeks, assuming it benefitted both from surprise and Hungarian participation: as of September 1938, it could count on enjoying neither.[70] The moment Poland entered the war, incidentally, Rundstedt was doomed, since he would be surrounded: his attack was to drive through a salient between Czech and Polish territory.[71] If the Czechoslovaks managed to retreat in reasonable order, the *Wehrmacht*, even after having taken Prague, faced a second campaign eastward, then mopping-up operations in Slovakia. And unless this was all done under eight weeks, the French were likely to be in the Ruhr.

GENERAL LUDWIG BECK, the chief of the general staff of the German army, fired between May and August a volley of warnings to his colleagues and to the Führer against an invasion of Czechoslovakia. An attack on its south-eastern neighbour would place Germany at war with a coalition of stronger powers, Beck argued. The resulting strategic position, both in terms of economic resources and army strength, made the conflict unwinnable. Nor should a lightning victory be expected against the Czechoslovaks. While they were sure to be defeated eventually, this would take time and extract a heavy toll in men and materiel. 'If France enters the war,' he wrote, 'even in the case of a successful campaign against the Czechs, any war begun before September 1939 at the earliest must be expected to end unsuccessfully for the German army.'[72] Hitler, faced with this bad cheer and the sniping it entailed among the officer corps, eventually accepted Beck's resignation and replaced him with General Franz Halder. Halder took office on 1 September 1938.

His first initiative was to put in motion a plot to overthrow Hitler, should he make good on his war threats.[73]

The chief of the general staff was the person in charge of army planning and strategy. Clearly, neither Beck nor Halder believed in a winning strategy. Germany simply did not have the firepower, in 1938, to ensure victory. It was outnumbered and, except in the air (and even there only marginally so), it was outgunned. Everything needed to go right for Hitler if he was to succeed and, indeed, survive. Poland needed to remain neutral. The Soviets needed to be too slow to move more than a division or two into Slovakia. The French needed to prove too incompetent to push past the Saar in time, regardless of their vast numerical superiority in that corner. Rundstedt needed to pierce the Czechoslovak bunker system, then defeat an army equal or superior in numbers to his. Even then, the prospect was only for grabbing, possibly at great cost, a Czechoslovak military industry devastated by scorched-earth tactics.

Nor were German forces likely to be replenished much, let alone expanded, based on domestic resources. Ammunition was short: a December 1937 estimate had put it at a mere two weeks of fighting.[74] Stockpiles were good for no more than six weeks on the eve of Munich, and German industry was not ready to replace them sufficiently fast.[75] German oil in storage sufficed for three months at most. There were worse shortages in essential aviation lubricants and in the non-ferrous metals used for everything from aircraft to shells. Iron in storage sufficed for three months of wartime production.[76] Though something could be scavenged from civilian structures, Germany imported most of its ore from France and Sweden. But the Reich suffered from a crushing naval inferiority. German naval reconstruction had barely begun, with neither the *Sharnhorst* nor *Gneisenau* ready for action and Bismarck-class battleships two years from completion, no aircraft carriers, and only twelve submarines capable of operating in the Atlantic.[77] The Russians alone were capable of blocking the vital Swedish ore. In 1939 and 1940 all this was remedied with Soviet economic help – which became available after the signature of the Molotov–Ribbentrop pact of August 1939 – and the Narvik operation, but there could be no prospect of either in 1938. On the contrary, every passing month of hostilities involved depleting reserves and a struggle to keep army and air force at capacity, all this against the perspective of mounting British and/or Soviet involvement. The German generals knew they lacked the tools for their assigned task, and this was why they baulked.

The Halder plot against Hitler, it was alleged, involved the commanders of the Berlin and Potsdam garrisons and the official in charge of the Berlin police, and it had at its disposal a panzer division stationed just south of the capital. Whether the generals would actually have carried it out, let alone have succeeded, may be doubted, though Churchill rated the plan as genuine. On 27 September, a further group of German officers submitted yet another memorandum to Hitler complaining of low morale among the population, deficiencies in armaments, and shortages in officers and NCOs numbering in the tens of thousands. This predicted that the Czechoslovaks could hold out for three months.[78]

The Czechoslovaks, the French, and the British were meanwhile all informed both of Hitler's plans and of this internal opposition. The Czechoslovaks were at the very least tipped off by Otto Strasser about the generals' intended attempt against Hitler.[79] The French secret services knew both of Beck's resignation and of a planned coup by German generals.[80] The plotters around Halder, at considerable risk to themselves, contacted the British directly. A first emissary visited the Foreign Office under-secretary of state Robert Vansittart in August, in parallel to an approach through the military attaché in Berlin. In September, the plotters enlisted the cooperation of the chargé d'affaires at the German embassy, Theodor Kordt, who saw Chamberlain's confidential adviser, Horace Wilson, and Halifax himself in an urgent meeting at Downing Street. The first approaches attracted Chamberlain's attention, but they were deflected by Neville Henderson as 'biased' and 'propaganda', and the last approach was seemingly ignored.[81]

On the evening of 27 September, Hitler ordered a parade of motorised troops through Berlin at dusk, at rush hour, when it was expected to receive active crowd support. It found a sullen reception, proof, as some saw it, of a lack of enthusiasm for a war over the Sudetenland and of low morale among the German population.[82] Over the summer, the Nazi leader had been putting the finishing touches to a general mobilisation carried out covertly, though in practice with the knowledge of enemy intelligence services. Large manoeuvres had been performed in Bavaria, Saxony, and Silesia, all three provinces adjacent to Czechoslovakia, where several age groups were recalled for exercises, then kept under arms and used to complete regular divisions or to form reserve units.[83] Conscripts were now advised that they would not be released, but that their military service was extended until March 1939. Though this also meant that there would be no new increase in the reserve, the German army was ready to march.[84]

France had meanwhile carried out its own precautionary measures. By late August, already, it had summoned reservists to a number of military regions, then in the first week of September recalled recently discharged fortress troops, curtailed leave, and moved key artillery and anti-aircraft units into place. This would continue throughout the month, with the recall of more technicians and army classes and the placement on alert of a number of divisions and regiments. By 28 September, France had 1,100,000 men under arms, of which almost half were in regular divisions, bringing its regular army contingent very close to strength. Aerial defences were placed on a war footing and troops moved into their forward positions, especially in the north-east.[85]

With Czechoslovakia's own general mobilisation, the Second World War, or probably something much shorter, was ready to begin.

7

Last orders

THE ARTILLERY CAPTAIN VILÉM SACHER was assigned to the third rapid division, stationed outside Bratislava. Sacher was a career officer. During the Second World War, he would become a resister, then flee Czechoslovakia to fight under British and Soviet command and participate in the liberation of his country. After the war, he would continue to pursue a military career, later to become a writer and a political dissident. His book *Pod rozstříleným praporem* ('Under the torn banner') records his impressions of September 1938:

> On the Slovak border.
>
> It cannot quite be called an advanced observation post, more a simple shelter hurriedly dug in the night. In it, the commander of the third rapid division, General Jaroslav Eminger, awaits an attack so that his unit may participate in the fight. I stand behind him, binoculars in hand. On the other side of the narrow shelter, still fragrant with the smell of freshly dug earth, squats the telephone operator. The captain in charge of the division's intelligence unit, evidently nervous, repeatedly asks him

to connect him with headquarters or with this or that observation post. According to information from the high command, the expectation is that Hitler's divisions will launch hostilities that day at 14:00. Our whole rapid division has for this reason been on combat alert since the early hours of 28 September in the Nové Zámky-Štúrovo segment.

After a look at my watch, I have become convinced that only a few minutes are left until the start of war. I raise the binoculars to my eyes again: the south Slovak country extends before me all the way to the Danube. The fields already harvested, clear, clad with only a few bare cornstalks. On the left, on the river bank, rolls a wild overgrowth, and on the right, around the village where our infantry is entrenched, lie green meadows. The blue sky opens without a cloud, not even the trail of an enemy surveillance aircraft.

I lay down my binoculars and wipe my brow. The sun, almost a summer sun, burns straight into my face. But the tension, the determination to fight, to knock back the enemy, contributes just as much to the sultry feeling. At last our government has shown the necessary decisiveness!

General Eminger, next to me, does not seem very calm either. Every few minutes, he pulls out his monocle (as a former cavalry officer he has never done away with it) and wipes it conscientiously with his handkerchief. Even his perfectly shaved face exhibits a faint gloss of sweat. He takes out his pocket watch, looks at me, and turns to the operator: 'Call Goliath and ask if there is any news!' As is his habit, he enunciates that slowly, as if he feared not being understood.

The telephone rings. The operator introduces himself as 'David' and asks for information. He takes the time to listen to the reply and once more out of so many times announces: 'General, the message is: nothing new!'[1]

Sacher's description almost reads like a scene from Dino Buzzati's *The Tartar Steppe*. The horizon, the enemy line, was destined to remain forever empty. As in the Italian novel, the enemy would never launch hostilities, or rather they would do so too late for the Czechoslovaks. And like the novel's hero, Sacher's comrades would be forced into the humiliation of seeing others do the fighting in their place.

Yet the general mobilisation had gone well, and all the testimonials are that it was performed with alacrity. 'I have no doubt whatsoever that later in the month when general mobilization took place, the army as a whole, officers and other ranks alike, was not only prepared to fight but inclined to want to fight and settle the affair once and for all,' would write H. C. T. Stronge, the British military attaché in Prague.[2] Earlier in the month, the general staff had notified the president: 'Germany's goal is the Black Sea. There will be no mercy for our people. If it does not defend itself, it will be wiped out in the vilest and the most inhuman manner. If we are to die, then at least die with honour!'[3]

Geoffrey Cox, the reporter, witnessed the scenes in Prague when the call to arms came through on the radio:

The proclamation of the mobilization was broadcast in Czech, then in Slovak, then in German, then in Hungarian, in Ruthenian, and finally in Polish. [...] It precipitated an extraordinary spectacle. Men rushed wildly through the blacked-out streets to get to their homes for their equipment. Waiters in restaurants took off their aprons, late-night shop-keepers closed their premises, cars in the streets were halted by the police and asked to take men to their assembly points. Soon the streets were full of men, each with his small suitcase, hurrying towards barracks or the railway stations. One man walked with at his side his ten-year-old son proudly carrying his suitcase. With little traffic in the streets, the dominant sound was of hurrying feet, insistent in darkness. At every corner, in hotel lobbies, on station platforms, men and women were taking their swift farewells. Guards appeared in front of every public building, and in the Alcron hotel the management produced a gas mask for each guest. [...] Three years later, when I found myself with a Free Czech battalion on the outskirts of Tobruk, I met two men who had been mobilized that night. Their faces lit up when they recalled it. 'We only wanted to fight,' they said. 'Why couldn't you have let us do so?'[4]

German-language reservists were issued with equipment but not weapons and in a majority stationed in Slovakia or Ruthenia. Though some Sudetenland Germans fled or sought to hide, the more recalcitrant of the Henleinists had already left for the Reich, from which they were indeed sniping at the border posts. Many others obediently followed their orders. The executive of the German democratic youth movement, composed not just of Social-Democrats but of Catholics and centre-right members, proclaimed to Beneš that it was ready to fight: 'We welcome the military measures which have been taken [...] We want to prevent our life in the future from having to be spent in mental and social slavery such as German Fascism tries to impose on our nation. We desire to continue to live and to work as free people in the Fatherland in which we were born and in which we have grown up. [...] Upon us, dear President, you can unconditionally rely!'[5] On 25 September, a training centre at Špičák was attacked by Henlein's *Freikorps*, yet it was a local unit of eighteen Sudeten German soldiers, some of whose relatives had gone over into Germany, that repulsed the attack and drove the invaders back over the frontier.[6]

Official reports were that mobilisation was proceeding just as speedily and without disorder in the major centres of Brno and Bratislava.[7] The army received an ovation as it passed through Mladá Boleslav and through Olomouc. A witness describes the scenes in Litoměřice: 'I look out the window and the street is full of people. Our border-region people, who were waiting for the mobilisation most ardently, are laughing, crying, embracing each other, shouting. From a distance one could hear the song "In our barracks stands the Czech guard", and when they got to the words: "Come on Adolf, the time has come, the Czech gates will open and we will march," they were not singing anymore but shouting to the point of losing their voices.'[8] In Turnov, according to Sydney

Morrell: 'Pandemonium broke. The crowd dissolved into individuals running here and there, paying bills, drinking up beer hastily, grabbing hats and coats and running out. My chauffeur went wild. He told me in excited German he had six hours to get back to Prague and offer his car to the army.'[9] The region was soon crawling with soldiers, roads mined, railway lines blown up, barricades coming up everywhere. Villages were being blacked out. A long line of troops, three miles long, had soldiers cheering and shouting '*Nazdar!*' ('hello' or 'salute'), and young men ran to paste blue paper on the car's headlights. When Morrell arrived in Prague, it was 'much darker than on the country road where the open sky gave some reflection', with Wenceslas Square looking like a black pit.[10]

Within five days, the general mobilisation and army deployment were complete. The Czechoslovak Republic had approximately 1,250,000 men under arms.[11] The air force had dispersed, robbing the *Luftwaffe* of the chance to catch its aircraft with a sudden strike.[12] Krejčí had moved, with a section of the general staff, to his battle headquarters and command centre in Vyškov. The lieutenant-colonel and future general Ludvík Svoboda was based in the Moravian town of Kroměříž at the time. Morale was extremely high, he recalls, both among the soldiers and the families who came to part with them at the railway station, crying: '*Nazdar!* Don't surrender!' His men arrived on foot, bikes, trucks, train, motorcycles, and by the end of the first day his regiment of 8,000 men had been sorted and put together. It would be combat-ready by 27 September. Moving at night and through darkened towns, it reached its forward position, on the fortifications under Prchala's fourth army, in the night between 28 and 29 September.[13]

The army leadership could be satisfied that it had done all it could to prepare. The dreaded scenario of a German attack undertaken before Czechoslovakia had been able to mobilise and move its forces into place had been avoided. Now the generals were confident. Krejčí and Syrový spoke on the telephone on 29 September, just before Hitler's latest ultimatum was due to expire. 'Our forces and the enemy's are evenly balanced,' they agreed, 'and our side benefits from a level of morale such as no army ordinarily enjoys. Yesterday our situation was still troubling, by tomorrow it will be very good. Our forces are arranged so that we can face threats from all sides. [...] We can see that Hitler cannot go to war and indeed fears doing so.'[14]

Another heartening piece of news arrived shortly after the mobilisation order. France had called up further reserves, bringing its own forces that much closer to their full, wartime level. And Daladier had proclaimed on the radio: 'France has gone to the extreme limit of her concessions ... If Germany makes an attack on Czechoslovakia France will fulfil her commitments.'[15]

THE FEW DAYS AFTER Chamberlain's return from Godesberg found Europe hurtling towards war.

Back in London, the British premier summoned first an inner circle of advisers, then the full cabinet to Downing Street in the afternoon of 24 September. In the intervening time since the composition of the Anglo–French plan, his estimate of what was acceptable had been downgraded again, and his recommendation was now to accept the Godesberg terms, which he described as involving concessions from Hitler. Chamberlain was 'satisfied that Herr Hitler was speaking the truth when he said he regarded this question as a racial question', and that the Sudetenland was the limit of his territorial ambitions. 'Hitler had certain standards. [...] He would not deliberately deceive a man whom he respected.'[16]

This time the premier had miscalculated. Alexander Cadogan, the under-secretary for foreign affairs, was 'completely horrified'. Leslie Hore-Belisha, the secretary of state for war, simply called for the army to be mobilised. Cadogan thought of Chamberlain that 'Hitler has evidently hypnotised him to a point', and Duff Cooper that 'Hitler has cast a spell over Neville'. When Chamberlain insisted that 'we should accept those terms and that we should advise the Czechs to do so', Duff

Cooper and several others nearly resigned. Even Chamberlain's unconditional partisans were unusually silent. The meeting, when it ended
that evening, was followed by a rush of backdoor discussions. Another
important reversal took place when Halifax was persuaded to switch
sides overnight, seemingly by Cadogan and on the private intervention
of Anthony Eden. As a result, when the cabinet reconvened the next
morning, the session was even stormier. Halifax unexpectedly led by
confessing that he had 'found his opinion changing somewhat in the
last day or so'. He thought that Hitler was dictating terms and that the
Czechoslovaks should not be pressured to accept. Lord Hailsham, nor-
mally also a Chamberlain stalwart, produced a press cutting listing the
many occasions when Hitler had broken his word. Only two ministers
supported the premier. It was all he could do to convince his colleagues
to leave the matter to the Czechoslovaks – even if in the private interview that followed he remained prepared to browbeat Jan Masaryk over
the consequences of turning down Hitler's conditions.[17]

The foreign secretary may have been aided in his conversion by
a conversation with Masaryk. The Czechoslovak ambassador, finally
provoked beyond the niceties of diplomatic etiquette, did not hesitate
to use the words to which he was sometimes accustomed in private:
'Halifax insisted we should consider whether it is not better to give in
to Hitler than to be crushed. I responded negatively. He announced
that the prime minister remains convinced that Hitler is *bona fide* and
that, if he received the Sudetenland, he will forever leave Europe in
peace. At my expression of astonishment at such criminal naiveness,
he repeated what he had said. Chamberlain was but the messenger,
he insisted. When I explained how amazed and appalled I was that
the English premier should have become the errand-boy of gangsters,
Halifax, deeply affected, repeated: "Unfortunately, so it is."'[18]

Lacroix, in Prague, was likewise losing all restraint, writing to
Bonnet to pass on Beneš's description of the Godesberg proposal as
an 'enormity' and the 'assassination of Czechoslovakia'. 'I implore the
President of the Republic and the French government to come to their

senses. I appeal to the Prime Minister and to Your Excellency [Bonnet] to declare in London that France will not commit such an abominable crime,' the Czechoslovak president had said. Lacroix added: 'What if it were France's turn next? We should ask ourselves whether we had not better face the trials imposed on us with the help of the Czechoslovak army, which remains solid.'[19]

Reich press organs were themselves becoming ever more brazen. The *Westdeutscher Beobachter* declared that: 'The Czechs do not understand that the question at issue is not the solution of the Sudeten-German problem, but whether Europe shall be relieved of their bloodthirsty existence.' The *Westfälische Landeszeitung* demanded the removal of the Czechoslovak political leaders and the country's foreign policy neutralisation. Both were quoted in *Le Temps*, a newspaper friendly to Bonnet, which revealed that in German quarters it was 'stated openly [...] that the new Czechoslovakia must pass into the orbit of Germany'.[20]

Chamberlain again managed to defuse opposition within his cabinet by referring the matter to the next set of Anglo–French meetings, which were scheduled for 25 September. The talks themselves followed a well-rehearsed pattern of chipping at French sullenness, with the difference, however, that this time Daladier refused to back down.

Chamberlain opened with a summary account of his Godesberg negotiation with Hitler. Daladier, when his turn came to speak, opined that 'we were confronted with a plan of Herr Hitler and his regime, not so much to take over 3½ million Germans as to destroy Czechoslovakia by force, enslaving her, and afterwards realising the domination of Europe, which was his object'. The French council of ministers had unanimously rejected the Godesberg terms, and they could not form a basis for further negotiations. There ensued lengthy clarifications over the map adjoining Hitler's memorandum and an argument over whether German troops would be entering the areas marked on it by force or 'for the purpose of preserving law and order'. Finally Daladier proposed that Chamberlain, in his next despatch to the Führer, merely return to the Anglo–French proposals. If these were rejected, 'each of us would have to do his duty'. This, though, could only cause the British premier horror. Chamberlain enjoined that 'we should have to go a little further than that', warning that all should get down to the 'stern realities of the situation'. A counter-proposal should be made, accompanied by an offer of a conference. But Daladier, the son of a Carpentras baker, was rediscovering the peasant-stock stubbornness of his native region. Not for nothing was he nicknamed the 'bull of the Vaucluse' after all. At first he pretended not to understand. Probed over his refusal and asked point-blank 'What then?', he repeated that 'each of us would do what was incumbent upon him'. Pressed for a third time, he confirmed this meant France would go to war. One million Frenchmen had already gone to the frontier, he reminded everyone, 'calmly and with dignity, conscious of the justice of their cause'.[21]

John Simon, the chancellor of the exchequer and a committed appeaser, next began to press Daladier on military plans. There ensued a discussion about air forces and French plans for an attack on Germany, with Simon trying to bait Daladier into saying that the French would not fight. The French premier became so worked up that he felt compelled to point out that the Czechs 'were human beings', that they already 'thought that their country had been abandoned and regarded the French as traitors', complaining that France was having to pay a heavy price for the peace. Attempting to find a compromise, he proposed setting up an international commission immediately, as a peace gesture, for delimiting the territory outlined in the Anglo–French plan. Chamberlain thought this would make no impression on Hitler. He switched to the familiar tactic of expatiating on the horrors of aerial bombardment. Daladier's last word, however, was to ask point-blank whether the British cabinet was prepared to accept the Godesberg proposals or to force them on the Czechoslovaks: at this point Chamberlain had to admit that it was not.[22]

Since so much of the debate had revolved around French military preparedness, and since war seemed so close besides, the decision was made to invite over General Gamelin. He arrived in London the next day. Gamelin first spoke with Chamberlain in a small committee. What the British premier thought of the interview is not known, but he recorded that the French general thought the German line weak and that he intended to attack within five days of war. As to Czechoslovakia: 'General Gamelin thought that the Czechoslovak army would give a good account of themselves. [...] They would try to keep open the bottle-neck at all costs, so that even if they were forced to retire their army would still be able to pass out from the western frontier to the eastern part of the country, and they would be able to maintain a fighting force.' France's own offensive action would concern particularly the industrial districts near the Rhine border.[23] Later, in discussions involving a variable-geometry group drawn from British military and cabinet personnel, Gamelin explained that the Czechoslovaks enjoyed close to numerical parity with Germany and should be able to resist around a Moravian redoubt. Minor delays were to be expected both on the German side, because it had lost the benefit of surprise, and on the French side if it became necessary to evacuate major towns against air attack, but land operations would otherwise commence 'without delay'.[24] Gamelin, then, was sticking to Plan R and to the strategy agreed with the Czechoslovaks, even if all this was new to the British.

The last set of Anglo–French meetings thus ended on a firm note. France and Britain were not prepared to accept the Godesberg terms. As an afterthought, it was agreed that they should address yet another appeal to Hitler via Horace Wilson. Meanwhile Masaryk had already called at Downing Street to deliver his government's reply to the Godesberg memorandum. This contrasted 'the unique discipline and self-restraint' of Czechoslovakia with the 'unbelievably coarse and vulgar campaign of the controlled German press and radio'. Pointing out that the Anglo–French plan had only been accepted 'under extreme duress', it labelled Hitler's latest proposal an 'ultimatum of the sort usually presented to a vanquished nation' and declared it 'absolutely and unconditionally unacceptable'. 'The nation of St Wenceslas, John Hus and Thomas Masaryk will not be a nation of slaves.'[25]

APOLOGISTS OF APPEASEMENT have argued that public opinion, whether on the British or the French side, was unprepared for war. This, as recent studies have shown, is debatable. Chamberlain received 20,000 letters and telegrams thanking him for averting war at Munich. The delirious scenes of welcome to Chamberlain and Daladier on their return bear witness to the preparedness of many to salute a peace that sacrificed Czechoslovakia. Yet sheer relief at not having to fight or endure the dangers and hardships of war, especially after it had appeared so close, must account for much of this enthusiasm. When the statesmen returned, the full details of the Munich Agreement were not yet known, and it looked as though they had extracted actual concessions out of Hitler and at least saved face. That public support for Chamberlain after Munich owed as much to a relief reflex than to confidence in his policies is borne out by the comprehensive analysis by historian Daniel Hucker, whose conclusion is that 'In many ways the "turning point" for public opinion was not the Prague coup [the German invasion of March 1939], but the Munich Agreement itself.'[26]

In 1938, opinion polls were taking their first, baby steps. A British poll taken in the Munich conference's immediate aftermath had 57 per cent satisfied with Chamberlain, 33 per cent dissatisfied, and 10 per cent undecided.[27] When questioned about rearmament, however, or about future dealings with Nazi Germany, respondents were more bellicose, suggesting far more doubt about the justice or durability of the peace: 72 per cent favoured increased defence spending.[28] Nor was 57 per cent perhaps such a large majority once account is taken of the propaganda value of Chamberlain's shuttle diplomacy and its ostensibly triumphant conclusion. An admittedly less statistically robust survey by the so-called Mass-Observation system gave 40 per cent as 'indignantly anti-Chamberlain' and only 22 per cent in support as of 20 September.[29]

A French opinion poll carried out in early October 1938 had 57 per cent in favour of Daladier's policy, 37 per cent against, and 6 per cent undecided, very similar to Britain's post-Munich numbers. But, likewise, 70 per cent also replied that any further demands from Hitler must be resisted.[30] The shadow of the Great War meant that panic took over in September. During the crisis, however, French opinion was only fluid. In both countries, pro- and anti-appeasers straddled the left–right divide. As in Britain, an incomplete understanding of Czechoslovakia's national and strategic issues jostled with sympathy for an ally that was also an underdog, dislike of Nazism, and the urge to stave war off – though in Britain negative opinions of the Versailles settlement also helped make appeasement look more respectable.

Another factor specific to Britain was that the Dominions, whose participation was regarded as essential in any future war, were highly reluctant to fight on behalf of Czechoslovakia. South Africa and Canada were keen to avoid any sort of European commitment. The New Zealand high commissioner in London was more hawkish, but his Australian counterpart emerged as supportive of the *Anschluss* and of ceding the Sudetenland. When Chamberlain returned from Berchtesgaden, 'applause was heard from every corner of the Commonwealth'.[31] Yet domestically at least there was room for a more decisive leadership to mould an ambivalent opinion in favour of resistance to Hitler. The historian Yvon Lacaze writes of France: 'A preference for slavery over war did not form the basis of public opinion. [...] To hold French pacifism as an insurmountable obstacle to a firm attitude is to indulge in political rhetoric; the desire for peace, a normal aspiration of the masses, must not be confused with the defeatism of a few.'[32] The same could have been said of Britain.

It is to this international opinion that the Czechoslovaks now frantically tried to appeal. In the last days of June, the PEN Club, a London-based writers' association founded for the defence of free speech and mutual understanding across cultures, had held its annual congress in Prague. Taking place over several days, this overlapped with the Sokol festivities and involved various lectures and receptions, most of which were convened at the philosophical faculty, and one in the Castle gardens, where the club had been hosted by the president and first lady. Hodža himself came to speak on the congress's second day, 27 June, to a packed audience.

At this conference, the French novelist Jules Romains, the club president, felt it necessary to denounce complaints that the PEN Club was engaging in politics, labelling these complaints 'naïve' and 'hypocritical'. 'The PEN Club as an association of writers does not wish to engage in politics,' he said, 'but it cannot stand idly by when the most basic individual rights are being threatened. It cannot agree when a completely apolitical author such as the president of the Vienna PEN Club, Raoul Auerheimer, is deported to a concentration camp and when Sigmund Freud is forced to follow Thomas Mann into exile.'[33] At the time, this had given rise to controversy, particularly with Romains's predecessor as president, H. G. Wells. Wells, who was a committed pacifist (it was Wells who had coined the phrase 'the war to end war' in 1914), 'defended the radical opinion that the PEN Club should not turn against specific political movements, but that it could at most protest against conditions that threatened artistic creation'.[34] There followed a lively debate in which Wells stood his ground against the French novelist, and in the end the club had confined itself to adopting a general resolution against racism, anti-Semitism, and the repression of freedom.

This made it all the more noteworthy, and perhaps poignant, that Wells now joined, in September and as war actually threatened, the ranks of literary personalities to speak out publicly in favour of Czechoslovakia. On 10 September 1938, a congregation of Czechoslovak authors led by Karel Čapek, the poet Josef Hora, and the essayist Jaroslav Kratochvíl and involving a total of 195 writers in the Czech, Slovak, and German languages had addressed an appeal to their colleagues in Britain and France through the daily press, radio, and writers' associations. The one-page address ended with the words:

> We invite you to explain to the publics of your countries that
> if a small and peaceful nation such as ours, situated in the most
> exposed part of Europe, is forced to fight, we will fight not just

for ourselves, but for you and for the common moral and spiritual property of the free and peace-loving peoples of the world. No one should close their eyes to the fact that after us would come other nations and countries. We ask all writers and all people engaged in cultural work to publicise this letter among the peoples of the world through all possible means.[35]

The text attracted responses from writers' groups in Britain and France and from German writers in exile. Bertolt Brecht sent a telegram to the president of the republic with the single sentence: 'Fight, and those who dither will join the fight with you.'[36] The British writers, whose most prominent names included H. G. Wells, W. H. Auden, Eric Ambler, and A. A. Milne, offered that 'It is not just Czechoslovakia, but democracy, peace, and civilisation throughout the world that are being attacked. These are the very basis for culture. That is why we writers feel justified in publishing this appeal for the defence of these values and their endangered representatives, and for the defence of the Czechoslovak people.'[37]

There would be numerous more such appeals from Czechoslovak personalities, and the responses came as many as they were varied. A meeting at Friends House in London chaired by the Labour politician John Strachey sent in a note of solidarity on 20 September. From New York, a Dr Rudolf Brandl issued a telegram in the name of the association of Americans of German origin, claiming a membership of 100,000, urging the Czechoslovak president to 'remain firm'.[38] As September neared its end, similar messages arrived from Montevideo, Glasgow, Bucharest, and South Africa.[39] The Yugoslav Sokol issued its own declaration of solidarity, and young Yugoslavs appeared at the embassy to volunteer in Czechoslovakia. There were demonstrations in Ljubljana, Belgrade, and Zagreb.[40]

Thomas Mann took to both pen and pulpit in defence of his surrogate homeland, proclaiming his pride at being a Czechoslovak citizen and praising the republic's achievements. He attacked a 'Europe ready for slavery', writing that 'the Czechoslovak people is ready to take up a fight for liberty that transcends its own fate'.[41] The Nobel laureate addressed an enthusiastic public in New York's Madison Square Garden on 26 September: 'It is too late for the British government to save the peace. They have lost too many opportunities. Now it is the peoples' turn. Hitler must fall! That alone can preserve the peace!'[42]

Between Chamberlain's Berchtesgaden and Godesberg trips, both the leaders of the British Liberal Party, Sir Archibald Sinclair, and the Labour Party, Clement Attlee, came out publicly against any further appeasement of Hitler. Churchill issued his own simultaneous warning. 'The partition of Czechoslovakia under pressure from England and France amounts to the complete surrender of the Western democracies to the Nazi threat of force,' he said. 'It is not Czechoslovakia alone which is menaced, but also the freedom and the democracy of all nations.'[43]

A week later, as the war scare was peaking, Chamberlain would speak on the radio and pronounce, as part of a brief harangue taking stock of the situation, the lines that would become notorious: 'How horrible, fantastic, incredible it is that we should be digging trenches and trying on gas-masks here because of a quarrel in a far-away country between people of whom we know nothing.'[44] In fairness, Chamberlain also said that he understood the reasons why the Czechoslovak government had turned down Hitler's last demands and spoke of the sympathy of the British people for 'a small nation confronted by a big and powerful neighbour'. In Czechoslovakia, nevertheless, the contempt for these people of whom Chamberlain claimed to know so little struck home, as well as disbelief that the British premier would still not acknowledge what was at stake.[45] Under the headline 'A small nation?' the daily *Národní politika* attempted a reply:

> On a moral, cultural, economic, or social level we are as well placed as the world's great democracies, and we are proud of it. The defence of our state should accordingly be worthy of this moral and cultural level, this all the more that we form a dam against the violence and lawlessness that is threatening the world's moral and legal order. The size of a country is not decisive: on

the scales are truth and justice, ideals of which the British prime minister should think first and foremost, if he is to speak of the democratic duties of his renowned country.[46]

ON THE EVENING OF 26 SEPTEMBER, Hitler spoke out again to the ranks of his assembled followers, at the Berlin *Sportpalast*, in a speech designed to respond to the rejection of his Godesberg terms. Calculatingly, Hitler declared the Sudetenland to be 'the last territorial claim which I have to make in Europe'. He singled out Czechoslovakia, and he singled out Beneš personally. The Czechoslovak president had always been 'determined slowly to exterminate the German element', he had 'hurled countless people into the profoundest misery', and 'through the continuous employment of his methods of terrorism' he had reduced millions to silence. ('To the scaffold! To the scaffold!' the crowd responded.[47]) Beneš was protected by the French and by the Bolsheviks only because they planned to use Czechoslovakia as a platform for bombing Germany. Finally, Hitler issued his first specific, public ultimatum. Czechoslovakia must comply with his terms or face imminent war. The Führer exulted: 'I have made Mr. Beneš an offer which is nothing but the carrying into effect of what he himself has promised. The decision now lies in his hands: Peace or War! He will either accept this offer and now at last give to the Germans their freedom or we will go and fetch this freedom for ourselves.'[48]

On the night of 23 September, the French cabinet and general staff had decreed a new raft of measures to complete the creeping mobilisation that had been taking place since August and bring the number of men under arms over a million. This included the calling up of new categories of reserves among various classes, moving into place fortress troops and units covering the north-eastern frontier, and placing on alert a number of divisions already at strength. Within another three days, the territorial air defence system would be ready to operate.[49] On 'black Wednesday', 28 September, Parisian concierges calmly distributed sand to be used to fight the fires anticipated from German incendiary bombs. The streets became choked with traffic as thousands of Parisians desperately sought to leave the city.[50]

On the other side of the Channel, ever since Chamberlain's return from Godesberg, the British people had been 'grimly, but quietly and soberly, making up their minds to face war'. Sunday, 25 September had been 'gas mask Sunday', as people queued at Air Raid Precaution stations to get theirs. Famously, there was frenzied digging of trenches in Hyde Park and London's other green spaces. Anti-aircraft batteries were deployed around the capital, and food prices were frozen for fourteen days.[51]

'If in spite of all efforts made by the British Prime Minister, a German attack is made upon Czechoslovakia, the immediate result must be that France will be bound to come to her assistance, and Great Britain and Russia will certainly stand by France,' an official British statement announced on 26 September.[52] The statement was the most bellicose to date, the first to state that Britain's assistance to France should be considered certain, and the first to call for Russian participation. Backstage, however, the leadership was fast becoming far less hawkish. Anglo–French readiness to oppose Hitler, actually, had reached its high-water mark.

On the same day, Horace Wilson had flown to Berlin to deliver Chamberlain's latest appeal to the Führer. This contained a proposal for a bilateral Czechoslovak–German conference under British supervision designed to 'discuss immediately the situation by which we are confronted with a view to settling by agreement the way in which the territory is to be handed over'.[53] Hitler had refused to listen, violently rejecting any compromises. Wilson had struggled even to keep the Nazi leader in the room while he finished speaking. He could only read through the two- to three-page document in between 'insane interruptions', and with Hitler 'vociferating in staccato accents' that the Sudeten Germans were being treated like 'niggers' and 'Turks'. In the end, Hitler had insisted that he would only speak to the Czechoslovaks after they had accepted his Godesberg terms. The deadline for acceptance, as specified in the German spa town, was 28 September. When Wilson, finally, asked if that meant midnight that day, Hitler had replied: 'No, 2 p.m.' (That was, the Czechoslovaks had until 2 p.m. on 28 September to accept an occupation that was to begin on 1 October.)[54]

After a second and equally ineffectual interview, Chamberlain's envoy returned in the afternoon of 27 September to London. Wilson's recommendation, after this debacle, was simply to advise the Czechoslovaks to surrender and open the areas demanded by Hitler to an immediate German occupation. As the cabinet met, for the last time before Munich, at 9:30 p.m., Chamberlain endorsed the proposal. Again, this encountered unforeseen opposition. Cooper spoke at length against the premier, and he was supported by Halifax and even the arch-appeaser Simon. The session turned stormy. Cooper exclaimed: 'If we were now to desert the Czechs, or even advise them to surrender, we should be guilty of one of the basest betrayals in history.'[55] It had meanwhile been decided, in the afternoon, to mobilise the Royal Navy. Yet Halifax had in parallel come up with a fresh project, a 'timetable' providing for an accelerated implementation of the Anglo–French plan. This proposed the transfer of the Aš and Cheb areas on 1 October, a meeting of Czechoslovak and German representatives within an international commission on 3 October, the entry of German troops into a first set of agreed zones on 10 October, and finally the handover of remaining areas as determined by the commission by 31 October. The same evening, this was sent simultaneously to Hitler via Neville Henderson, to the French, and to the Czechoslovaks.[56]

The panicked, last-minute firing of proposals that was to lead at short notice to the Munich conference had begun. As Wilson was returning from Berlin, the French ambassador André François-Poncet telegrammed Bonnet with his own solution: the immediate cession of Aš and Cheb to Germany and the occupation of the rest of the Sudetenland by an international force, with a deadline for further surrenders to the Reich of 1 November.[57] Then, the same day, 27 September, the

French *Conseil des Ministres* met. This set in motion a sequence of events revealing again the deep dysfunction at the top levels of French decision-making.

Daladier reviewed the *Sportpalast* speech, which, from a narrow French perspective, was not as bad as feared since Hitler had explicitly eschewed claims to Alsace-Lorraine. The French premier was prepared to endorse the immediate surrender by Czechoslovakia of limited salients such as Aš or Cheb. In the same breath, nevertheless, he called for a general mobilisation. This was a complete shock to Bonnet, who argued for negotiating further and for letting parliament decide on mobilisation. The cabinet lined up against the foreign minister. Even defeatists such as Camille Chautemps and Guy La Chambre failed to speak up for Bonnet. Paul Reynaud went on the offensive, and Daladier categorically refused to give up the executive prerogative that was the right to order mobilisation. The cabinet in the end only opted for yet more partial military measures. Bonnet, though, had felt compelled to leave in the middle of the meeting. He seemed on the brink of resignation.[58]

Yet, later that afternoon, Bonnet managed to persuade Daladier to keep him on board in spite of the mutual disavowal their cabinet performances signified. This accomplished, the French foreign minister proceeded to take matters into his own hands. Having now seen Halifax's 'timetable', he decided to venture his own proposal. Bonnet's rationale is laid out in a note on his activities that day. After recording that France, in his opinion, had only ever told the Czechoslovaks they would be supported diplomatically but never militarily, he wrote:

> Never has the diplomatic situation been so bad, and we have no aviation. Britain can bring no serious assistance on land; its air force is only beginning to be built. [...] It is impossible to wage war. I am against general mobilisation. At any price, an arrange-ment must be found. I face strong opposition from my cabinet colleagues. The question of my resignation is undeniably put forward. The communication issued by the *Conseil des Ministres* will not even bear my name, but only Daladier's.

[...] In the evening, after Sir Eric Phipps's visit, I decide to send a telegram to François-Poncet to make a proposal to Chancellor Hitler, whom he will ask for an appointment the next morning. This proposal is drafted by me on a broader basis than the proposal by the British government. It seems to me completely acceptable. I insist with François-Poncet that he request an urgent meeting.[59]

This last proposal was not, contrary to what Bonnet writes, actually 'on a broader basis' than the Halifax 'timetable'. It did involve the sacrifice of a wider swathe of territory on 1 October but, inspired by an analysis by the Second Bureau, France's military intelligence agency, this left all or almost all early surrenders of territory outside the Czech fortification line. Its philosophy thus remained to keep Czechoslovakia a defensible unit, at least while talks continued.[60] French diplomacy nevertheless remained on a slippery slope: from the Anglo–French plan to Daladier's proposal, in London, for the immediate convocation of an international commission, to François-Poncet's and now Bonnet's own initiatives. Munich was not far off.

AS SOON AS THE GENERAL MOBILISATION had been announced, Prague had been placed under a comprehensive black-out, a measure soon extended to other major cities. Horses, cars, aeroplanes, and boats were requisitioned for military purposes. All civil flying was forbidden. Telephone calls and telegrams for abroad were stopped. The authorities distributed gas masks. The whole country cut itself off and began hunkering down for war.[61] People bought black and blue paper for pasting on glass to mask the light, and 'across the windows of one private house after another appeared the criss-crossed strips of gummed paper which in Spain had done such good service in arresting the huge pieces of whirling glass which within half a mile radius of a really good high-explosive bomb could take your head off as efficiently as a knife or a guillotine.'[62]

'Many cars drove through town, leaving. They carried bedding, children, food parcels. No one hindered them. No one told them that they would clog the roads,' writes Milena Jesenská.[63] Arrangements were made to evacuate women and children, while some women took the men's places as tram conductors and older men controlled the traffic or dug trenches in the parks. 'Many civilians also left by train. These too departed in an orderly fashion; there was room for them. In the midst of this heavy traffic came the black-out. [...] The city changed. The parks were churned up, the windows taped over with dark paper. Soldiers moved into the schools. The night began at sundown, the city looking like a scene from the apocalypse. And yet by day there shone a bright, late-summer sun, and the night was full of stars. Bomber aircraft were supposed to come out of that sky? Many of us had not left. We waited.'[64]

Turčiansky Svätý Martin, in the central Slovak mountains, was declared to be the new capital: Prague would fall, to exact the highest possible cost in materiel, time, and men from the enemy. Around it, the army deployed troops, including columns of armoured vehicles, mortar and other heavy gun batteries, fifty-five fighter aircraft, and the same number of anti-aircraft batteries. Bridges and tunnels were mined. The Sokol and Orel (the Sokol's Catholic counterpart) took the initiative of gathering civilian units to defend against air raids.[65] The guards at the Castle put on field uniforms, technicians moved in to install new telephone lines, and the staff was given gas masks, camp beds, and pocket lamps. 'In the courtyard of the Hradčany Castle, a great pile of sand had been placed, to be used against incendiary bombs. Children played on it in the sunshine, laughing as they shaped it into sand castles.'[66]

The public mood had turned both more optimistic and more stubborn. 'We are ready and we will defend ourselves,' ended the 26 September editorial of *Lidové noviny*, whose thick headline ran: 'We will fight.'[67] 'The nation is united and enthusiastic,' wrote the right-wing *Venkov*.[68] By now, the British and French willingness to demand extreme sacrifices from the Czechoslovaks to avoid war had been made public. But at least the government's own actions had been elucidated, and under Syrový and after the general mobilisation order its preparedness to fight had been made plain enough.

Besides, the Entente powers were taking their own warlike measures. 'England is resolved on war,' announced *Lidové noviny* on 28 September – one day before the Munich conference – writing that 'an attack on us would mean the destruction of Germany'.[69] The French partial mobilisation aroused similar enthusiasm. 'Gamelin's plan – France will not stay on the Maginot Line, but will launch an offensive,' proclaimed *Český deník*.[70] 'We are not going in alone,' wrote *Právo lidu*. 'In the last two days, the international situation has changed decisively. Chamberlain's negotiation with Hitler has not brought the expected success. Daladier has proclaimed very firmly that France will come to Czechoslovakia's aid. The Soviet Union has likewise announced that it will support us if we are attacked. Besides this, the Soviet Union has warned Poland against any adventures on Czechoslovak soil.'[71]

The fifth day after mobilisation, 28 September, was St Wenceslas day, the day of Bohemia's patron saint, the king martyred in the tenth century. For the first time in years, 'all day crowds gathered round his statue in [Wenceslas Square], crowds of women and children and soldiers. Flowers covered the steps of the statue, were hung on the figure itself, flowers in opulent bouquets and wreaths, flowers in tight bunches, flowers in a handful tied with string, single flowers scattered.'[72] In churches, special services were held. 'At St Vitus's Cathedral, in the Hradčany, the skull of St Wenceslas, his golden crown, and his sword and armour were brought out from the treasure chests and displayed to thousands of worshippers. [...] All day long crowds stood in silent contemplation round the image of their king of a thousand years ago.'[73] Whether the devotees were praying for war or for its worst horrors to spare them is unknowable. Perhaps it was both.

The preparations meant the country was increasingly shut out. Even the *Sportpalast* speech did not get the attention of earlier pronouncements by Hitler. Many of the Sudeten Germans had had their radio sets confiscated, so that it was not widely followed in the Sude-tenland.[74] Beneš himself missed the broadcast. In a strange episode, the military men in charge of the president's security decided there was a risk of a surprise air raid on the capital and the Castle that evening, and they decided to remove him and his entourage to an anonymous subur-ban villa. A cortège of cars left the Castle, under cover of night, weaving through the streets of Malá Strana. Progress through Prague was slow and traffic unusually heavy, the result of vehicle movements from requi-sitioning and the black-out, which had the effect of channelling more traffic in the night-time. Eventually they reached the private residence where the president was expected to stay. Beneš crashed in a chair and slept, then only woke up as the security men changed their minds and it was decided to bring everyone back to the Castle at the same, winding pace. When the president woke up, he asked if Hitler's speech had taken place. General Bláha said that it had, and that Hitler had made it a per-sonal matter against him. 'What an honour,' smiled Beneš.[75]

Though the Nazi leader had made explicit threats at the *Sportpalast*, it was left to Newton to inform the Czechoslovaks of the exact dead-line for his ultimatum. This was done in the evening of 27 September: Czechoslovakia had less than a day to accept. (In practice, German orders were for the attack to commence at 6:15 a.m. on 30 September, unless the terms were accepted.)[76] Newton returned later the same evening with the 'timetable' proposal. This contained the by now worn but still threatening language to the effect that even in the case of a victorious war, Czecho-slovakia's borders as they stood would not be restored. As Ripka notes, British statesmen were becoming 'somewhat disturbed when they saw that this argument (which in their opinion contained so much of human interest for the Czechoslovak nation) did not impress Prague'.[77] Was the point that this conflict was not about borders and minorities but about sheer survival at last coming through? Beneš consulted with Krofta, and in the night they elaborated an answer: this buried acceptance under so many conditions that it amounted to a polite refusal.[78] While the initiative itself was not encouraging, both the latest French and British military measures and the looming deadline announced war, and all had to be done, without sacrificing anything serious, to keep Czechoslovakia's partners, however tenuously, on side.

The hectic cycle of meetings, consultations, and despatches to draft had not abated – on the contrary. In addition to fresh demands from the Poles, the Castle received multiple visits from the Soviet and the American ambassadors, which came in addition to those by Newton and Lacroix and the daily cabinet meetings. After it was all over, the foreign ministry press attaché František Kubka would catch a glimpse of the president through a palace window: 'I never saw a man so shattered! He could scarcely stand on his legs. He wore a soft hat, a bright raincoat and, in his right hand and thrown back over his shoulder, he held a pair of oversized yellow leather gloves. Round-shouldered, walking with downcast eyes, he looked utterly broken.'[79]

Beneš himself writes that the last blow, paradoxically, was a message from Franklin D. Roosevelt.[80] The isolationist US, though it was a friendly power, had so far hung back from the entire crisis, and this came out of the blue. Roosevelt's message, issued in the form of a press release on 26 September, asked that war be avoided at all costs and that negotiations continue. 'Whatever may be the differences in the controversies at issue and however difficult of pacific settlement they may be, I am persuaded that there is no problem so difficult or so pressing for solution that it cannot be justly solved by the resort to reason rather than by the resort to force. [...] So long as these negotiations continue so long will there remain the hope that reason and the spirit of equity may prevail and that the world may thereby escape the madness of a new resort to war.'[81] Roosevelt's appeal, of course, sprang only from good intentions. After Munich, the American president would presciently comment: 'That may have saved many, many lives now, but that may ultimately result in the loss of many times that number of lives later.'[82] His intent was not for the great powers to get together behind the Czechoslovaks' backs. Roosevelt's appeal, though, was unhelpful in that it failed to note the context of interference, bullying, and war ultimatums by a powerful and aggressive state against a weaker, demo-cratic neighbour. It asked all participants, whether Hitler or Beneš, to make an effort for peace, placing them on the same plane and disregard-ing the reasons why the problem had arisen in the first place.

The Roosevelt message attracted immediate replies from Cham-berlain, Daladier, Beneš, and Hitler. Beneš thanked the American president and tried to unearth Czechoslovakia's arbitration pact with Germany. Hitler gave a long-winded answer listing his grievances and the crimes supposedly committed against the Sudeten Germans. This in turn gave rise to a telegram response from Roosevelt calling for a 'fair and constructive solution' and proposing a conference at a neutral European place. As to Chamberlain and Daladier, they both made short replies to the effect that they were grateful to the American presi-dent for his intervention, had done their best to preserve peace, and intended to continue to do so.[83] And this was the second problem with Roosevelt's appeal: it only offered an excuse to the French and British to renew their pursuit of peace at any price.

Both Halifax's 'timetable' and Bonnet's new scheme were submit-ted to Hitler in the morning of 28 September. Henderson had handed in the timetable during the night, and François-Poncet met with the German dictator shortly before midday. Hitler objected to the reten-tion of their fortifications by the Czechoslovaks under the latest French plan. He nevertheless promised to consider the proposal and respond shortly in writing.[84] There were two hours left on the ultimatum.

In parallel with the 'timetable' trial balloon, Chamberlain had penned a private appeal to Hitler and, crucially, another to the Italian dictator Benito Mussolini. 'I am ready to come to Berlin myself at once to discuss arrangements for transfer with you and representatives of [the] Czech Government, together with representatives of France and Italy if you desire,' the first letter said.[85] This last missive, almost a suppli-cation in its style, thus contained the idea of a third one-on-one summit or a broader high-level meeting. The Foreign Office had prepared the ground in Rome by communicating the 'timetable' to the Italians and asking, through ambassadorial channels, that Mussolini 'use his influence' to convince Hitler to consider it.[86] Chamberlain's private message to Mussolini now asked that he persuade his fellow dictator to accept the idea of a conference.

The Italians reacted promptly. All this converged on the Berlin chancellery in the late morning on 28 September: the 'timetable', Bonnet's proposal as delivered by François-Poncet, and Mussolini's endorsement of a conference.[87] Hitler had every indication that his opponents were ready for surrender, and he could deploy the face-saving excuse that was Mussolini's friendly intervention to lift his ultimatum. Invitations to Munich were sent out that afternoon. None, of course, was sent to Prague.

8

An unbearable choice

THE MUNICH CONFERENCE was scheduled for the next day, 29 September. In the confusion, the Czechoslovaks do not appear to have been told that they were not expected to participate or even attend. Beneš made a final appeal to Czechoslovak interests but he only received a terse reply, delivered through Newton: 'His Majesty's Government wishes to express their firm hope that the Czechoslovak Government will not obstruct the already difficult task of the Prime Minister by the formulation of objections [...] and by insistence on them.'[1] It was only the next day, after the conference had begun, that Chamberlain relented and invited the Czechoslovaks as part of his own delegation.

Even then, their role remained unclear. Masaryk and Osuský had at first been considered as envoys, but both rightly expected they would only be left outside the door, and they declined.[2] The choice fell on Hubert Masařík, counsellor at the foreign ministry, and Vojtěch Mastný, the ambassador in Berlin. Masařík, who left a key eyewitness account of his team's experience in Munich, writes that when he was asked to go it was on the notion that he and his colleague would have their word, and that their government would in the last resort be able to withhold its assent. When Masařík returned to his room after it was all over, he would find the code-writer busy decrypting a telegram from Beneš: 'Hold firm!' this said.[3]

Masařík and Mastný left Prague at 3 p.m. in a hurry, accompanied by the code-writer and an administrative assistant. At the airport, they were sped on their way by a 'deeply moved' Max Lobkowicz, a legation councillor in London but also the scion of one of the old noble families, who beseeched them 'not to abandon Bohemia's thousand-year-old frontiers'.[4] Little did this reflect what awaited them. The Czechoslovaks had only been invited in as observers, or rather as recipients. Requests to give them admittance to the conference room would be flatly rejected. Whereas the French and British leaders were feted, and even serenaded, by the Bavarian crowds as they arrived, Masařík and Mastný were welcomed by the police and Gestapo, to cries of '*Die Tschechen kommen!*' Driven to the hotel where they were to stay in between assault vehicles bearing the tag *Polizeiwagen*, they were then escorted to their rooms, before which yet more guards awaited. It was as if they were already German prisoners.[5]

The Czechoslovak team found the Hotel Regina, where the British were also staying, empty. All the diplomats were away at the *Führerbau*, Hitler's drab and squat Munich reception centre, a mere ten-minute walk away but off limits to them. Even getting in touch with anyone by phone was difficult, though eventually they managed to get Ashton-Gwatkin on the line, who said he would come to speak to them at the hotel. The diplomat only arrived at 7 p.m., with the conference already well under way, looking 'very moved and not very talkative'. The news was bad, he hinted, and the agreement that was being discussed was not an improvement on earlier Anglo–French proposals. Masařík brought up the question of the vital areas which the Czechoslovaks wished to preserve. But Ashton-Gwatkin showed only a cursory interest, volunteering that 'We did not appreciate how delicate the situation was for the Western powers, and how difficult it could be to negotiate with Hitler.'[6]

The Czechoslovak envoys were left to cool their heels. At 10 p.m. they were called in a second time, this time into Horace Wilson's room. Reflecting the drift of the *Führerbau* talks, the terms had worsened again. Wilson gave an outline of the plan under discussion and, producing a map, he pointed at the border districts to be immediately occupied under this plan. Masařík asked for more information as to what was going on in the conference room, but Wilson replied that he must leave and had nothing to add. Left once more with Ashton-Gwatkin, the Czechoslovaks pleaded again for taking into account the country's vital needs in deciding on border adjustments. The British delegation was favourable to the German plan, replied Ashton-Gwatkin with sudden formality. 'If you do not accept, you will find yourselves facing Germany alone. The French may sugar-coat this with fine phrases but, believe me, they are of the same view and have lost interest in your fate.'[7]

Meanwhile the proceedings themselves, according to witnesses, were a chaotic affair. Everything had to be translated into multiple languages, and progress was slow. There was no agenda, no chairman, and no one to take notes. At first, discussions were confined to a small committee of the four leaders – Hitler, Mussolini, Daladier, and Chamberlain – plus their close advisers or interpreters, who assembled in Hitler's private study. The draft that formed the original basis for the negotiations was brought to the table by the Italian dictator: this was presented as a compromise, but the document had actually been prepared by the Germans the day before, and its only difference with the Godesberg memorandum was that it extended the occupation phase by a few days. Everyone promptly agreed that the Sudetenland should be evacuated beginning on 1 October, the very first item on the memorandum, so that the fundamental matter at dispute was given away from the outset. Daladier and Chamberlain did object to the very short period for completion, and it was at this point that the British premier had asked for the Czechoslovaks to be invited. This, though, had only prompted a brutal tirade from Hitler, and in the end it had only been agreed that a Czechoslovak representative 'should be made available', incidentally letting the point about the handover period be conceded.[8]

The conference adjourned twice, in the afternoon and for a dinner break. After the first interruption, a number of hangers-on, ambassadors, generals, legal advisers, and aides impatient at the slow progress drifted into the room, making interaction between the participants even more shambolic. Maps were unfolded and strewn over coffee tables and desks. Though there was some bargaining over the extent and shape of the territory to be handed over, peripheral matters such as the guarantee to be granted the rump Czechoslovakia occupied much of the negotiations. The conference fragmented into smaller discussion groups. The voluble Mussolini, who was the only one able to converse in all four languages, played host and strove to ensure that Hitler's terms were swallowed without excessive bitterness. A surly and discomfited Daladier followed along. Chamberlain vainly attempted to obtain mitigation on such minor points as compensation for Czechoslovak state property and, when this was turned down, confiscated private property, only prompting another explosion from the Führer over the futility of his requests. The second break had been intended for a celebratory dinner, but the treaty was not ready yet, and the British and French, none of whom found themselves in a festive mood, managed to skirt the event and go their separate ways.[9]

When the conference resumed again, at 10 p.m., it was for drafting. Even this was slow, but eventually the document, 'no more than a few typewritten sheets clipped together', was made ready for signing at 1:30 a.m. on 30 September.[10] The four leaders affixed their names in turn to the document, under the eyes of the assorted participants. As the Italian foreign minister records, the French ambassador François-Poncet felt compelled to observe: 'So this is how France treats the only allies who had remained faithful to her.'[11]

The Sudetenland, broadly defined, was to be handed over to the Reich. Occupation was to begin on 1 October and it was to extend, zone by zone, over ten days. Hitler had obtained everything he had asked for. Within little more than a week, Czechoslovakia would cease to be defensible.

The two dictators and their teams left, but a small group of the French and British remained – Chamberlain, Daladier, Wilson, the consular official Alexis Léger, François-Poncet, Ashton-Gwatkin – in order to disclose these terms to the Czechoslovaks. This group asked Masařík and Mastný into a conference room.[12] It was explained to them what had been agreed, and they were allowed to ask for a few clarifications. Masařík was able to record his impressions:

> I had ample chance to observe the actors in this historical moment. First and foremost Chamberlain: yawning, that asparagus with a long neck and bird head felt no shame in showing openly that he was tired and that he found this last formality unpleasant. He was visibly intoxicated with the idea of having prevented war in these last hours. [...] At first sight, Sir Horace Wilson, Chamberlain's grey eminence, exceeded his chief intellectually by far and was able to impose his conceptions without scruple. F. T. A. Ashton-Gwatkin, who was a professional diplomat, was the only Western delegate not to hide his reservations over the negotiations with Hitler. He alone spoke with us openly and humanly.[13]

As to Daladier: 'The French premier obviously grasped what this meant for his country's prestige. He seemed to me, among all present – I sat next to him – the only one to appreciate the stakes. Though I was the representative of the Munich victims, I even caught myself in a moment of compassion for this sweating and obstinately silent man. [...] He was ashamed of his country's weakness and he appeared despondent at the role he was made to play. Red-faced, he said nothing.'[14] Masařík was right. The French premier expected to be booed on his return and, before landing at Le Bourget, he would ask the pilot to delay their landing to down a few goblets of champagne for courage. 'The fools! If only they knew what they are cheering,' he is known to have muttered when he was instead met by delirious rejoicing.[15] But it was too late for regrets.

To the Czech envoys, the atmosphere in the conference room was leaden. The treaty read like a guilty verdict. Neither Chamberlain's disdain nor Daladier's mortification made the pill any easier to swallow. When he heard the news, Mastný at first burst into tears.[16] Masařík found that, while he had been filled with anger in anticipation, the awful result only left him calm and lucid. Both managed to gather themselves sufficiently to request clarification on the treaty's mechanics, points on which they knew they would have to report back in Prague. Finally Masařík writes: 'I asked Daladier and Léger if a response or stance was expected from our government to the accord that was being presented to us. Visibly embarrassed, Daladier answered nothing, while Léger, noting that the four powers had little time, told me explicitly that nothing was expected from us, that the accord was considered as accepted. [...] The text was read to us, we were handed a second, slightly modified map, then we separated and that was it. The Czechoslovak Republic as con- stituted within the frontiers of 1918 had ceased to exist.'[17]

IN *THE UNBEARABLE LIGHTNESS OF BEING*, Milan Kundera muses that after having fought and lost to the German empire at the Battle of the White Mountain in 1620, the Czechs surrendered bloodlessly in 1938 only to find they were again at threat of obliteration by their larger neighbour. Should they have fought this time also, he asks? But as is the key to the novel, human lightness resides in our being condemned to face each of life's choices only once, without the benefit of foreknowl- edge. 'If Czech history could be repeated, we should of course find it desirable to test the other possibility each time and compare the results. Without such an experiment, all considerations of this kind remain a game of hypotheses. *Einmal ist keinmal.* What happens but once might as well not have happened at all. The history of the Czechs will not be repeated, nor will the history of Europe. [...] History is as light as indi- vidual human life, unbearably light, light as a feather, as dust swirling into the air, as whatever will no longer exist tomorrow.'[18]

Like Kundera, Czech political actors and commentators would invoke the feats of 1620 to urge resistance to the Munich verdict. Defeat back then had forced a long winter on the Czech nation, they contended, but it emerged again triumphant in the eighteenth- to nineteenth-century National Revival. The comparison, though, was always approximate. The Habsburgs had never directly sought to Germanise the Czechs, and what Germanisation had taken place was the by-product of other policies, such as the Counter-Reformation or Enlightenment attempts to extend the state's administrative reach. In its last decades, especially, the Habsburg Empire had arguably been friendly to the Czech nation, even if the Slovaks had groaned under a viciously hostile Magyarising regime in the empire's other half. Under Hitler, the Czechs risked annihilation, especially if they attempted to resist.

Beneš and Krofta were handed their report cards by a gleeful Andor Hencke, the German chargé d'affaires, in the early morning, before Masařík and Mastný had even had time to fly back. Hencke called at the foreign ministry at 5 a.m. and was received by Krofta and the president an hour or so later. Beneš promptly convoked the coalition party leaders at the Castle, who gathered at 9:30 that morning. In parallel, time being so short, the government was called in to sit, at the Kolowrat Palace, beginning at 9:45.[19]

'This is the end. This is a piece of perfidy that will bring its own punishment upon itself,' Beneš told Drtina. 'It is unbelievable, they think they can save themselves from war or from revolution at our expense. They are wrong.' The president's first instinct was to give up, and in the presence of several witnesses he dictated a letter of resignation. Beneš's departure, leaving no one in charge, would have amounted to a de facto refusal to accept the Munich terms. But the coalition leaders were waiting.[20]

At the Castle meeting, the atmosphere was charged with anger. In a voluntary slight to the president, no one rose as he entered. Just as during the discussions of the Anglo–French plan, the voices of the National

Unity Party and the Christian-Social Party were the first to speak against accepting the Munich terms.[21] Beneš, having forced himself to sober up, explained that the Nazis would wipe out the Czechoslovaks if they were given the excuse of resistance. 'If we refused to accept, we would fight an honourable war, but we would lose our independence and the people would suffer mass murder.'[22] Yet to accept, to take the responsibility for agreeing to the Munich terms, was equally agonising. The discussion dragged on miserably. Drtina, who did not wish to wait outside, left to visit the first lady, Mrs Benešová, who was in the company of Alice Masaryková, the late president Masaryk's daughter. The two ladies asked whether he thought Czechoslovakia should fight alone. He answered in the affirmative; no people should surrender their freedom without a fight, he said, and the Czechs had always defended themselves historically. The first lady thereupon asked him to pull her husband out of the meeting and to argue for fighting alone, as he had just done to her, which he proceeded to do. Beneš only listened, repeating 'yes, yes', not arguing back, then returned to the coalition leaders.[23]

The government session was bitter and contested. Syrový opened by announcing the result of the Munich conference: it left the Czechoslovaks the choice between murder, which was what the Munich Treaty amounted to, and suicide, which was what refusing to abide by it would mean. Krofta said that this message was the hardest he had ever had to deliver. The worst expectations had been exceeded. The great powers had agreed without Czechoslovakia based on a German diktat. It was a painful but revelatory detail that it was Hencke who had brought the text of the agreement to them, he noted. One possibility was a war against Germany, alone, and also likely against Poland, without any Soviet help or at best with ineffective help. Acceptance meant obtaining border guarantees and perhaps the cooperation of the international commission which the treaty provided for. At the same time, there was the risk that the *Wehrmacht* would find an excuse to continue marching beyond the agreed borders. 'Either choice is terrible,' Krofta concluded.[24]

Several voices promptly arose against acceptance. Stanislav Bukovský, who was leader of the Sokol as well as minister without portfolio, said that 'We have historical and strategic borders for which the people will give their lives. If we concede, we become powerless, we lose our unity and our very reason for being. There will be a popular upheaval, and Germany will invoke security reasons to occupy us.' Petr Zenkl, who was a member of Beneš's party and, as such, an important voice, complained that the principle of self-determination has been misused throughout. Criticising the cabinet for its actions in the past week, he asked to hear what the army had to say. 'This cabinet cannot under any account accept the Munich Agreement,' he argued. 'Only an organ answering directly to the people can do so,' by which he meant the national assembly. Imrich Karvaš conceded that a war, waged with modern weapons, would be a war of extermination, whereas the alternative was only creeping Germanisation. Even so, he thought that while convening parliament was unrealistic, a decision so heavy could not be taken by the government. Only the representatives of all parties – including the communists, who were certain to refuse – could claim to represent the nation in such a matter. Because Munich mandated the evacuation of the Sudetenland starting the next day, such objections amounted to an effective rejection of the treaty and a clash with the German army within twenty-four hours.[25]

At some point, Syrový left to visit Beneš. As the interior minister Josef Černý took the chair, the session, which lasted for two hours, threatened to turn inconclusive. Justice minister Vladimír Fajnor concurred with Karváš, and so did Stanislav Mentl. 'The nation was never prepared for this capitulation,' said Mentl, 'and it cannot be forced to swallow an occupation by the German army within twenty-four hours and without a conflict. The demonstrations showed what the people want, with their cry of "Long live the army! Long live Syrový!" We are in a similar situation to General Syrový and the legionaries, who decided to fight even though they were isolated [in the First World War]. We must also uphold the nation's honour.' František Nosál added:

'Perhaps a war would mean the destruction of a part of the nation, but its spirit will endure. Freedom can only be bought with blood.' Josef Černý intervened lest this turn into a full-scale rebellion. Referrals to the people were all very well, he said, but an answer on the treaty was due this very day. The cabinet members worried over popular reactions. Several of them were concerned that the German army would not stop at the new treaty border, especially if popular disorders provided an excuse for driving on all the way to Prague. There were requests to hear the generals, and some speculation as to the Soviet position. Eventually, though, everyone paused as they considered the implications of their position and Černý's words sunk in. To take responsibility for accepting the Munich terms was awful, but so was the prospect of an unwinnable war, alone, against Nazi Germany. Perhaps if the people were properly informed, internal order could be preserved, proposed Bukovský. 'We have already been defeated without a war, and we have the choice between murder and amputation with a chance of further survival,' relented Hugo Vavrečka. Černý stepped into the breach: 'He admitted that the situation was atrocious, but it must be addressed not just with the heart, but with reason. He had heard the fine voice of the heart, but also that of reason, to which he affixed his name.' The rebels yielded, with the exception of Zenkl. Vavrečka read out a proposal for a declaration thanking the army. It was 11:30 and the clock was ticking. Černý closed the meeting with a resolution to take the government's acceptance to the president.[26]

There followed another discussion among the full cabinet, less Zenkl, plus Beneš, at the Castle beginning at 11:45 a.m. As the news of the Munich conference emerged, meanwhile, Krejčí had decided to return to Prague, and he arrived around that time. Shortly after the convening of this extended cabinet meeting, a group of generals accordingly demanded an audience at the Castle, including Krejčí, Vojcechovský, Luža, Prchala, and Syrový. They were led into the small or 'Masaryk' library, and they spoke one after the other in angry and agitated tones. Some of the generals had tears in their eyes, others mixed veiled threats with their pleas. 'Whatever the great powers have decided, the army, mobilised and encamped on the border and in our fortifications, will not bear that we should give in to pressure and make whatever concessions to Hitler. We must go to war, whatever the consequences may be. The Western powers will anyway be forced to follow. The nation is united, the army is firm and determined. And even if we were to remain alone, we cannot give in. The army has its own duty to defend the territory of the republic, and it intends to and will fight.'[27]

Yet even the generals could not tip what were heavily loaded scales. As Krejčí recognised, not without anger, Poland and Hungary were sure to intervene if Czechoslovakia found itself without allies, and this made the republic's position hopeless. War would come eventually, Beneš reassured them. The French and British would indeed be punished in that this would involve a far harder fight than if they had stood firm now. But he did not believe that they would follow Czechoslovakia into a conflict it had embarked upon alone.[28] (This obviously belongs to the realm of speculation. Perhaps, moved by the spectacle of the brave but doomed Czechoslovak resistance and revolted at the sight of Nazi atrocities, the French and British publics would have risen in favour of war and carried their governments with them. This hardly seemed something to be counted on, however. In any case, both the time lost and the risk that Stalin, made ever more distrustful of the Western powers, would at that stage have held his forces back, implied significant strategic cost.) The prospect before everyone's eyes was that, given the ideal opportunity that was a Czechoslovak refusal to abide by the Munich Treaty, Hitler and the Nazis would decimate the Czech people. No one abroad would understand why the Czechoslovaks were prepared to fight to keep the Sudeten Germans within their state, failing to see that the issue was entirely elsewhere. The Czechoslovaks would be condemned as the aggressor. The generals left, some of them to join the extended cabinet meeting that was still going on, all of them in a bitter, desperate mood.

The second government session lasted well past midday, but it came to the same conclusion. Beneš said that the decision everyone faced was terrible and that honour was only kept because it was imposed by the very people who, only yesterday, had told the Czechoslovaks to mobilise. Syrový added that after a long debate, the government had decided to accept the Munich terms. Bukovský only asked that the Allies be told that the Agreement was accepted under duress. Time was running out, with Czechoslovak representatives expected in Berlin on an implementation commission that same afternoon. 'History will judge,' concluded the president, cutting short any remaining objections.[29]

Newton and Lacroix presented themselves at the Czernin Palace shortly thereafter, at 1:30 p.m., to ask for the Czechoslovak response. The government had accepted, Krofta told them laconically. Lacroix attempted to offer an apology, but the foreign minister only flared: 'We have been forced into this situation. Now everything is at an end. Today it is our turn, tomorrow it will be the turn of others.'[30]

AS THE DAWN OF 30 SEPTEMBER had broken over Czechoslovakia, the results of the conference remained as yet unknown. The morning issue of *Venkov* announced that 'the great powers have found agreement on the Sudeten German issues', but it still expressed the hope that Munich was only the first step towards another conference, as proposed by Roosevelt, and that Czechoslovakia would now be heard.[31] As the afternoon progressed, the news began to spread by word of mouth. Soon it would come out, in Prague at least, on the loudspeakers.

'I stood on the Wenceslas Square and watched people weep as the news of the disaster at Munich came in,' remembers an American attaché who had just arrived.[32] At a brewery in the small southern town of Písek there was a meeting during the lunch break, and a clerk came and announced the news, which he had heard on Austrian radio. His co-workers accused him of being a traitor and, amid complete incredulity, beat him so badly that he had to be taken into hospital.[33] Morrell was stunned to see, for the first time in his life, adult men and women crying in public, people walking blindly along the pavement with tears streaming down their faces. The former minister of justice Ivan Dérer himself wept and could not go on as he spoke on the radio that evening.[34] The agronomist and future minister in exile Ladislav Feierabend writes of pure pain, of being barely able to breathe, of the feeling of having been 'shot in the head'. His first thought was that his mother was lucky to have died earlier that year, and his brother in an avalanche in the Alps in 1933.[35] All theatres were soon closed, all concerts were cancelled, the bands ceased playing in cafés, and all radio broadcasts other than news bulletins were halted.[36]

The pain and consternation were greatest in the army, at the border, where men and officers had been waiting for the war to start. The humiliation was hardest on soldiers who were now forced to evacuate before an enemy they had not been allowed to fight. Some would attempt to disobey orders, which were to leave the fortifications intact, or throw their weapons away in disgust. Some would resort to suicide rather than retreat, like the young artillery officer charged with giving the news to his men who preferred to shoot himself.[37] 'Men of all ages stood with tense, white faces and the tears came into their eyes as the surrender order was read out. Then, for a while at least, discipline broke down. Men flung away their arms, blindly cursing, and sought to drown their shame and misery in deep intoxication.'[38]

The printed evening news remained inconclusive, but it would not be long before the recriminations and denunciations began. 'We gave in to greater force,' tersely wrote *Lidové noviny*.[39] For *České slovo*: 'Our own allies threatened a war against us,' a theoretical though unlikely consequence of a refusal to abide by the treaty.[40] 'Around us, faith in the world's values is being extinguished,' lamented *Venkov*. 'Everyone abandoned us and submitted us to an unexampled humiliation. Right and justice, trust in honour and commitments have been crushed. Shadow engulfs the lands of Czechoslovakia, our homeland.'[41]

Nor would the rejoicing in Paris and London go unnoticed. The press was keen to quote the lone voices of a Duff Cooper, who the next day tendered his resignation in protest, or a Churchill, but it also remarked on the widespread celebrating. At Heston, people had climbed onto the roof of the airport buildings in expectation of Chamberlain's homecoming. The British prime minister had been feted by delirious crowds all the way to Buckingham Palace and, after night had fallen, to the very door of 10 Downing Street. '*Vive Daladier, vive la paix, vive Bonnet!*' the massed Parisians had chanted as Daladier made his own way home. The buildings had sprouted French and British flags along his route, and someone commented that it looked like the arrival of the Tour de France.[42] Chamberlain would carry the House of Commons by 366 to 144 votes, with some 30 abstentions.[43] In the Palais Bourbon the score was even more crushing, with 535 votes in favour against 75.[44] 'No conqueror returning from a victory on the battlefield has come adorned with nobler laurels,' exclaimed *The Times*.[45] The popular newspaper *Paris Soir* launched a public subscription to purchase a villa by a stream for the British premier to come fishing.[46]

'Think of it, they are actually having champagne parties in celebration of their Munich peace,' a Czech journalist commented privately. 'They thought they were drinking champagne, the fools! They didn't know they were drinking the blood of their future generations.'[47] *České slovo* speculated bitterly that Chamberlain's popular worship would go so far as to earn him the Nobel Prize or the garter.[48] A professor at Charles University told the visiting writer Maurice Hindus: 'A half-defeated dictator with one foot in the abyss, lifted by the democracies, our friends, to a position of supremacy in Europe, and over our dead body. [...] Don't imagine this thing is finished. It's just beginning ... The blood will come later – perhaps sooner than Chamberlain and Daladier anticipate.'[49]

This was not, though, or not yet quite the end of it. In the afternoon of 30 September, still, a committee of fifty members of parliament representing the coalition majority had come together to discuss the matter: this too concluded that there was no alternative to surrender.[50] Meanwhile a cross-party group of parliamentarians presented itself at the Castle, from the hard left to the right, including the nationalist

Ladislav Rašín, the Communist Party leader Klement Gottwald, and the centre-left Josef Tykál and Jaroslav Stránský, to be received by Beneš at 2 p.m.[51] The meeting took place in the same room where Beneš had met the government that morning, its tables covered in green baize and two maps of Czechoslovakia hanging over them. The parliamentarians wanted to fight. 'We cannot believe that the state, which has such a disciplined and self-sacrificing people, such a fine army, can voluntarily surrender,' said Stránský. 'We should fight. Perhaps it would not be in vain. At least the world could not quietly ignore it.' 'As President Masaryk taught us, death is preferable to slavery,' continued Josef David. 'The people would not understand it if we gave away our territory without a fight.' Beneš had reached a point of complete exhaustion and was barely coherent – 'President Beneš looked pale, his features drawn, red eyes suggesting that he had not slept,' states the record.

> This has no parallel in history, such behaviour towards an independent state. You cannot imagine what I have been through in the last few days. It is indescribable. We are abandoned and betrayed, they are cowards, and the most revolting is that they told us we could mobilise. That we would be going into this. [...] It was an impossible choice between accepting their conditions and saving the nation, and letting ourselves be massacred. [...] The Western democracies are in a desolate state. [...] A well-known French lady came to visit my wife and on her knees begged her not to damn the French nation for it. General Faucher came to me and said that he was ashamed to be French.

Gottwald pointed at the heroic resistance of the Ethiopians, in 1935, against the better-armed Italians. Were the Czechoslovaks not capable of what the 'bare-footed' Ethiopians could do? He appealed to the example of the republican Spanish. 'It is not too late. We should reject the Munich demands.' As Beneš got lost again, Rašín interrupted him: 'Excuse me, Mr President, but I disagree. In this very castle once ruled the Czech kings of an independent state, and often they decided the course of European affairs. Here, in this castle, though, they never gave in. We should defend ourselves. We are giving in. Future generations will condemn us for surrendering our lands without a fight. [...] To the cowardice of foreigners, we are associating our own. It is true that they betrayed us, but we are betraying ourselves.' Nothing, though, could be done. The prospect that France and Britain would eventually join in a struggle begun by Czechoslovakia was remote, explained Beneš. A war alone would mean the extermination of the Czechoslovak people. For the second time that day, the president began speaking of his resignation. Moved by the terrible weight that seemed to oppress him, the parliamentarians departed; they could achieve nothing, or at least nothing along constitutional lines.[52]

Appeals to overturn the Munich Agreement continued to emerge in the following days, even as the German troops had begun to move in. A petition was sent to the government from the Prague suburb of Suchdol as late as 12 October.[53] The presidents of the two houses, the parliament and senate, Jan Malypetr and František Soukup, issued on 1 October a radio and press appeal directly to their French and British counterparts, denouncing their short-sightedness and asking them to force a reconsideration.[54] There were more petitions from various groups, beginning with a denunciation of the Munich conference itself, as it was about to take place, by the 'Faithful we remain' steering committee and ending with an open letter to the president by another group of parliamentarians calling the surrender 'high treason'.[55]

There could not arise, however, the type of popular mass movement that had overthrown the Hodža government and led to mobilisation in mid-September. Prague did see some disorder, mostly instigated by the extreme left and right, but the crowds were missing.[56] Too many men remained away in the army, and yet more had left the capital in anticipation of invasion. The news was too vague, besides, on the day itself, and after that the German troops had already begun to march in.

The only serious attempt to overturn the capitulation was made by a group of politicians and officers in the first days of October. Even here, it is hard to separate rumour from reality, but it seems that Zenkl joined up with some of the parliamentarians who had gone to visit Beneš, including Rašín, David, Stránský, and possibly Gottwald. The conspiracy, however tentative, would also have involved Ripka and a few other parliamentarians, journalists, and officers of the general staff. The group pursued the possibility of a military coup or government overthrow, to be followed by army moves to stop any further seizures of territory by the advancing Germans. Rašín would have approached Krejčí and asked him to take power, without success. Syrový was equally reluctant, causing the conspirators to fall back on a second tier of generals. Action was planned for 3 October, and it ostensibly involved senior officers based both in Prague and in Moravia, where the high command remained centred.[57]

In the end, however, the plot petered out. It was too late anyway. The Czechoslovak borders had already become impossible to hold against the advancing Germans. In a bitter irony, the last words had been left to be pronounced by a soldier, the legionary legend Jan Syrový, who had spoken to the nation to announce the decision to concede:

> Citizens and soldiers! [...] I am living through the hardest hour of my life; I am carrying out the most painful task ever imposed on me, a task in comparison to which death would be easy. But precisely because I have fought, and because I know under what conditions a war is won, I must tell you frankly and as my conscience as your army chief dictates, that the forces opposed to us at this moment compel us to recognise their superior strength and act accordingly. My first aim, and that of every one of you, must be to preserve the life of our people. [...] In Munich the four great powers met and decided to demand of us the acceptance of new frontiers, according to which the German areas of our state would be taken away. We had the choice between a desperate and hopeless defence, which would have meant the sacrifice not only of an entire adult generation, but of women and children, and the acceptance of conditions which in their ruthlessness and

in being imposed under duress and without a war are unprecedented in history. We desired to make a contribution to peace. We would rather have made it in a different manner than that imposed on us. We were abandoned. We stood alone.[58]

9

After Munich

ASK MOST CZECHS WHAT MUNICH meant for their country and
they will reply: 'Fifty years of totalitarianism.' In March 1939, less than
six months after the powers had put their names to the treaty, Nazi
Germany annexed the remainder of the Czech lands: exactly what
Prague had predicted would follow from the surrender of the Sudetenland. Six years of Nazi rule followed. After a brief, post-war attempt at a
democratic restoration under the Red Army's watchful gaze came forty
years of Soviet vassalage. The Nazis virtually obliterated Czechoslovakia's Jewish community. Through executions and deportations, they
also did their best to destroy the Czech political and intellectual elites.
The coup of 1948, in which the communists took power, likewise had
the effect of purging the country of many of its best men and women
from the political, cultural, and business spheres. So did the repression
that followed the end of the liberalisation experiment known as the
'Prague Spring' and the Warsaw Pact invasion of 1968. This may have
involved fewer physical eliminations than the German occupation or
the aftermath of the 1948 coup, but it forced hundreds of thousands

into menial positions or exile. Indeed, the effects of Munich may be said to remain with the Czech Republic today, a land that belonged among the world's most advanced in the interwar period yet presently remains a country both economically and politically in transition.

The war and the Yalta settlement of 1945 no doubt played a role in enforcing this protracted eclipse. Nevertheless, as of 30 September, when the Czechoslovak leaders chose to accept the Munich verdict, they knew their country faced a long time in darkness. Just as striking, at the same time, was the speed with which events unfolded on the ground. The treaty left the Czechoslovaks a mere ten days to evacuate an area that had been part of the state or crown of Bohemia for the best part of a thousand years. Because the evacuation was to be realised zone by zone, they were in fact asked to clear out some areas even earlier, as early as 1 October, the very day after the treaty had been handed to them. This was bound to cause chaos. It required impeccable military coordination. But beyond the diplomatic and military ramifications, it involved innumerable private tragedies, as tens of thousands suddenly found themselves trying to flee Nazi violence.

In Prague, the sporadic demonstrations abating, the mood remained more sullen than angry. The mass of mobilised men remained away, and the numerous women and children who had taken themselves to safety had yet to return. Removing the last traces of war preparedness would take several days at least. Meanwhile the air had become uncomfortable to breathe for visiting British and French citizens, whose prestige fell to zero. Their hosts had become openly contemptuous, if not hostile. The once popular French and English names for shop fronts, e.g. 'Coiffeur' or 'English Tailor', were erased and an effort made to strip foreign expressions from the language.[1] As he was walking outside with his wife, who was a foreigner and with whom he spoke French, the new foreign minister František Chvalkovský was spat at by a student.[2] Czechoslovak veterans of the Western Front returned their First World War decorations to France en masse. The *Daily Herald* journalist Alexander Henderson writes that two of his friends were refused admission in a restaurant, and that official British residents had been advised to remove the flags from their cars.[3]

The eerie quiet, however, was broken by a flood of desperate and often destitute refugees. Wilson Station teemed with washed-up people. For several weeks the railway terminals filled with men, women, and children with suitcases, packages, or whatever they had been able to take with them. Hotel lounges thronged with 'new faces, those of taut, grey-visaged men and women, political refugees or Jews who had fled from the Sudetenland'.[4] Official tallies place the number of refugees from the regions annexed to Germany at 152,000 from October to December 1938.[5] Because some had already fled in September and more would keep leaving in 1939, the overall number displaced was higher. Many or most did not flee to Prague itself but spread out into innumerable towns, villages, and temporary shelters all over the country. 'On the roads I saw uninterrupted lines of people fleeing the border regions,' a witness writes, 'some pulling small carts, others with no more than the rucksacks on their backs.' Train stations all around the country were packed and full of distressed, screaming people, with retreating trains and even motorcars being occasionally shot at by the Germans.[6]

In many cases, these departures were the result of actual or threatened violence. Entire Czech villages were seized and the men taken away, the Germans returning with machineguns to make their point. Relatives and parents, usually but not always male, were taken in and interrogated, and sent to prisons and camps from which they never returned or came out fatally injured. Some people were made to run the gauntlet of hostile German neighbours, and there was the uncontrolled violence of the crowd and *Freikorps* orderlies to contend with.[7] 'A horde of several tens of Germans attacked the shop and house,' writes a shopkeeper from the small town of Ledvice. 'The Henleinists, that is Nazis, unhinged the solid doors and to the cry of "Out with the Czech dog, out!" dragged my brother and beat him up on the stairs, and threw him out on the street to their kinsmen. The most ferocious was a woman from a neighbouring house, who arrived with an axe. [...]

My brother lay on the pavement, bloodied, while they plundered the shop. Doctor Havlíček from Kostelec had to attend to him for several weeks afterwards.'[8]

Some people were tipped off by friendly Germans that they were 'on the list' and managed to escape. Especially in the first days, there was confusion everywhere and nobody knew exactly which areas were to be annexed and which were not. People might only learn of the German takeover or arrival by chance, through word of mouth or from a last-minute warning from local officials. One witness reports leaving in the middle of doing the dishes. Another writes that he saw a group of German Social-Democrats boarding his train in their underwear.[9]

There was in any case a variety of situations and reasons for leaving.[10] Some already had been intimidated or attacked by neighbours and/or the FS or *Freikorps* in September. The situation in the southern town of Český Krumlov, for example, appears to have been extremely tense. Some knew themselves to be in exposed positions as border guards, railway officials, civil servants, post-office employees, and so on, or as nationalists, such as members of the Sokol or former legionaries. They faced joblessness or Nazi violence or both. Others were simply told that the German army was coming and fled, leaving entire villages or towns empty. 'We left by the last train, taking only basic necessities with us,' was a common refrain.[11] Finally, a number were threatened or physically forced out, either with the aim of seizing their homes or businesses, or as part of a policy to expunge minorities, especially in areas where the Germans were less numerically preponderant. Those who left under police pressure or under the weight of Germanisation measures tended to be the last to go. Then there were the Jews and the democratic Germans, who could expect no pity.

Most refugees left everything behind, whether because there was no time to collect their belongings or because the Germans coveted their property. They lost houses but also workshops, factories, hotels, farms.[12] They left their working tools, their animals, and furniture behind. 'I lost everything I had.' 'We and our mother left for Prague, each with a small suitcase.' 'My parents left, empty-handed, the property they had just finished paying for in 1938.' 'It touched my childish soul that I could not even take my toys with me.'[13] Much plundering may have been improvised, the work of SdP men, but the SS and even the army were involved too, often because they were looking for housing for their own staff.

Some last-minute departure stories were quite hair-raising, like nightmares in which one can never escape from some unseen pursuer. Hubert Hoger, the son of a gamekeeper in the area of Plzeň, writes that his family, having been threatened with deportation to the camps, decided to grab their documents and flee. They were under surveillance, though, and they only slipped out of their home through a back alley. They crossed through open country, wading twice through the local river. But to reach unoccupied territory, they needed to cross an asphalt road, and because the road was guarded by German soldiers, this had to be done under cover of darkness. Finally they crept through field and meadow up to the road, only to be fired at with machineguns. No one was hit, and they made it onto free territory. Two weeks later, Hoger's mother was bold enough to return to see if she could collect some of their belongings. Not only had the house been looted, but she was seized, taken to the town hall, beaten up, and imprisoned in a cellar without food or water for two days, until she signed an acknowledgement that she had found everything in order.[14]

Willy Kapusta, a democratic German, was waiting with his voluntary defence unit to evacuate from the town of Mikulov by bus. They were waiting for the driver – perhaps they were missing the keys or the famed German discipline prevailed even among democrats – when the Nazis arrived. First the SdP orderlies banged on the bus, hurling insults and baying for one of its passengers, a Jew named Nissel. Then they attacked and began grabbing the men, dragging them off the bus and through the square into the town hall jail, where they were tortured. Several were gravely hurt, until finally they were allowed to leave and join the retreating Czechoslovak army. The Nazis kept Nissel, who was sent to a concentration camp.[15] In another story, a democratic Sudeten German journalist only managed to escape through the shafts of a coal mine into Poland. Another 'crept for hours on hands and knees, seeking cover in woods of the hilly country round Karlsbad, desperately anxious to escape the Nazis. For two days he ate nothing.'[16]

Squares called Náměstí T. G. Masaryk were renamed Adolf Hitler-Platz. Sokol buildings were made over to the SdP. The Nazi salute was promptly enforced, and signs on the windows of many shops appeared with 'Czechs and Jews not admitted'. The Czech language was banned in writing everywhere, even on garlands and ribbons at funerals.[17] Josef Bublík, a Czech from the small town of Želenky, had worked for thirty-eight years for the German machine-tool firm Berndt, first as a worker, then as foreman, and his daughter had served there for fourteen years as a secretary. When the Nazis arrived, they told him to hang the swastika flag from his home on pain of being shot. He hung it from his toilet window. They came back in the night with sub-machineguns and hand weapons, but he had already fled and was on his way to Prague.[18]

The Czechoslovak army was in the main humiliated and cowed, in no mood for resistance. Geoffrey Cox observed: 'There were lines of field guns drawn by the roadside, cavalry in village squares, lorry upon lorry filled with dejected men. [...] A brilliant rim of flame broke from the windows and doorway of a concrete pillbox, whose wooden fittings had been set on fire. At the rear was a young officer, map case under one arm, field telephone under another. Tears coursed down his sunburnt cheeks.'[19] Witnesses describe the men as stolid and silent. There was no talk, no laughter, no singing, though some retreating soldiers had sprayed in large letters on their bunkers: 'We will return in 1939.'[20]

The veteran British officer R. G. Coulson was appointed by the Foreign Office as one of thirty-eight observers to witness the handover's peaceful implementation. Coulson arrived in Prague on 2 October and, paired with another of the delegates and a Czech officer, he was sent to the southern town of České Budějovice, the home of Budvar beer. A Union Jack armband on his sleeve, his main task was to prevent fighting between Czechs and Germans. Though a number of the officers at first declared they would not yield an inch, in the end military incidents were few, mostly involving cases in which the German army marginally overstepped its allotted line. Considering the speed mandated for the German takeover and the situation of extreme tension created by the prevailing war preparedness, the handover was actually less fraught than feared. But it was a different matter in the anarchic zone between the two armies.[21]

In České Budějovice, the central square 'was packed with a great crowd, wandering about in uneasy, restless silence'. Coulson's hotel was 'surrounded by refugees who were obviously very poor'. 'Here and there in that crowd a woman wept or a man ranted. We seemed to be in a besieged town in which the population of the surrounding countryside had sought refuge.' As to outlying areas: 'In other places guerrilla warfare was going on and there was no authority whatever. Many had been killed and wounded.' There circulated 'reports, rumours, protests, complaints, lamentations of every kind'. A man hurried to Coulson's table: 'Before we could say anything, he began to talk in hurried, nervous undertones. Budweiss, he gabbled, could not be handed over to Germany. It was a Czech town, a purely Czech town. It was absolutely essential to make this quite clear to Berlin. Suddenly he raised his voice with startling abruptness. "We are human beings!" he shouted, striking his chest with his clenched hand. "We are not cattle or furniture, to be handed over to others."' In a sign of things to come, Coulson, who spoke Russian, found that a few words in that language could work wonders to establish a friendly rapport with his Czech counterparts, whether or not they understood him.[22]

Nor could Coulson check on the advancing SS. It was not just the German army that swept in as the Czechs cleared out, it was the full Nazi apparatus, beginning with triumphal visits by Henlein and Hitler himself. Hitler visited the 'liberated' towns of Aš, Františkové lázně, and Cheb on 3–4 October, 'to indescribable rejoicing'. Henlein spoke alongside him in Cheb. 'For five years have we fought for freedom.

Through the actions of the Führer, our struggle has ended in victory. We thank our Führer with brimming hearts,' he beamed.[23] Henlein was the hero of the hour after all. The population posted signs and flags in many places in preparation for the *Wehrmacht*'s arrival. They threw flowers at the soldiers, asked them to sign autographs, and welcomed them to stay at their homes. They organised balls and hung lanterns. It was a matter both of the Sudeten Germans having rid themselves of the 'hated Czechs', in the propaganda catchphrase, and having 'reunited with their German brethren'. The invasion thus ostensibly met with genuine and widespread rejoicing among the Sudeten Germans, though again one must be careful in assessing the depth of pro-Nazi opinion. No doubt Nazism had the momentum of its conquests behind it. A people exposed to years of mendacious propaganda on the merits of the Reich had yet to be exposed to its reality. But celebrations were to some extent mandatory, now that the SdP was again dominant. They may also have reflected relief at the avoidance of war – a war in which the Sudeten Germans would have been particularly exposed. When a Czech officer asked a German woman whether they were happy 'that you are now with Hitler', she replied: 'Yes, we are happy that no war is coming.'[24]

The men of the Gestapo, in any case, lost no time in celebrations. Based on an order of Heydrich dated from July, they had already begun to put together a list of all 'enemies' of Germany, including Jews, in the region. During the Munich negotiations themselves, various Gestapo and *Sicherheitsdienst* units had been taking positions in surrounding locations, such as Dresden and Vienna, for moving into the Sudetenland according to a region-by-region plan of occupation.[25] These operational units moved in with the German army, though under the command of SS officers, with the primary aim of raiding the files of the regional administrative offices and laying their hands on the full details of their targets. They also used *Freikorps* men as auxiliaries and informers, with the effect of swelling their lists further, whether with actual political adversaries or the objects of private vendettas. As early as 16 October, the Gestapo had established regional headquarters in the main Sudetenland towns of Liberec, Carlsbad, and Opava, each with a host of dependent, surrounding local branches. It was a special brand of 'liberty' that Henlein had brought with him.[26]

The arrests numbered in the thousands. By 13 October, a mere three days after the occupation was completed, 971 people had been seized in Cheb and 403 in Liberec alone. Total arrests are estimated to have risen above 12,000 by the end of 1938, of whom a third were deported to concentration camps in Germany. Some were released early, some later, but many never came back or were so broken that they scarcely had much longer to live.[27]

The Gestapo, finally, came to harass Jews in their homes and workplaces, or to force them to sign 'voluntary agreements' for departure. Many fled, further swelling the ranks of the refugees. An estimated 2,000 were immediately deported to Germany. Every day, Jews were detained, beaten, chased in the streets. They suffered the degraded status of the Nuremberg Laws, or rather the lawlessness that was associated with them.

> On 10 October, in the town of Prachatice, the German-Jewish lawyer Dr Heller was lured by orderlies into 'protective' custody, where he was slapped and beaten until he was profusely bleeding. They dressed him in old clothes and pierced shoes and he was forced to clean dirty toilets with his hands and sweep the streets in various surrounding towns. He was fed pickled herring and dark bread. Dr Heller walked through the streets on his hands, and in public gardens the orderlies grabbed his legs and forced him to crawl through mud and water while shouting: 'I am a Jew – a swine!' After a few weeks of such torment, Dr Heller died. His wife went mad with grief.[28]

WHILE THIS WAS GOING ON, the diplomats assembled again, this time in Berlin, to finalise the small print of the treaty. The Munich

Agreement, indeed, is an oddly short and vague text. The main document fits into less than two pages, plus a map. Its handful of clauses, the first one merely stating 'the evacuation will begin on October 1st', contained at least three areas of ambiguity.[29]

The first related to the map itself. The evacuation was to proceed in an initial four zones, in order, from 1 to 7 October. There was in addition a fifth zone, to be occupied between 8 and 10 October, but because its precise delimitation was left to an international commission yet to be formed, this was not marked on the map. Indeed, this became a set piece of Chamberlain's triumph, back in Britain: to both the public and his cabinet colleagues, he brandished the map and pointed out how much less territory was marked out for transfer than under Hitler's Godesberg ultimatum. Much was made of the international commission and its supposed neutrality. At least some of Chamberlain's cabinet opponents were fooled, and even Duff Cooper initially pronounced the difference between Godesberg and Munich to be more than he had expected. Appeasement at its zenith relied on an implicit, perhaps deliberate misrepresentation.[30]

The second ambiguity, compounding the first, related to the procedure for delimiting this fifth and crucial zone. This was defined merely as the 'remaining territory of preponderantly German character', without stating any percentage threshold. It was left to the international commission to decide what that meant in practice. More territory ended up being included in this fifth zone than in the first four zones put together, so that it was actually fundamental to the treaty. Accordingly, it would quickly become the chief preoccupation of the diplomats assembling in Berlin.

The third ambiguity is that there was to be yet another zone composed of areas where the commission would run plebiscites, to be held no later than the end of November. The mystery, indeed, is why plebiscites should be held in any areas not of 'preponderantly German character', since it was unlikely many Czechs would vote to join the Nazi Reich. The plebiscites were eventually dropped by mutual consent and never conducted, but not before they had caused added confusion in borderline areas where families waited to evacuate because they thought the votes would spare them from annexation.

When Hubert Masařík was asked, having just returned from Munich, to go to Berlin to sit on the international commission, he replied that he had 'done enough work as a grave-digger'.[31] It was to his luckless partner Mastný that the task fell, together with another foreign-ministry delegate and a group of military advisers. The commission comprised the secretary of state of the German foreign office, Ernst von Weizsäcker, the British, French, and Italian ambassadors to Germany – Neville Henderson, André François-Poncet, and Bernardo Attolico – plus Mastný. Weizsäcker was of course the presiding officer. Henderson recalls that the proceedings were 'confused and frequently noisy'; another member of the British delegation described it as a 'shouting match'.[32] Three subcommittees worked under this main commission. One was military, since a key concern was to avoid shooting during the speedy and delicate manoeuvre that was the military handover. Another was to deal with the financial and economic settlement. And a third was responsible for frontier-setting, though this was in practice taken over by the main commission.[33]

The Czechoslovak representatives had been given an insultingly short time to get to Berlin. Apprised of the Munich Agreement in the early hours of 30 September, the government had been told its delegates must present themselves at the Wilhelmstrasse by five o'clock the same day. They arrived two hours late at Berlin's Tempelhof Airport, the commission having already begun without them. Negotiations began in earnest on the delimitation of the crucial fifth zone on 3 October, and it continued in five long subcommittee sessions on this and the following day. The talks soon became bogged down, however, with the Germans demanding the Godesberg line, opposed by the British and French. At stake was how to interpret the phrase 'territory of preponderantly German character', and specifically what German percentage of the population to use and what census to base that percentage on.

The Czechoslovaks asked for a 75 per cent threshold and their own 1930 census. The Germans wanted 51 per cent and a census from 1910.

At this point, François-Poncet suggested a compromise, essentially splitting the difference between the two positions. The choice of criteria for zone five made a difference militarily. Because a significant minority of Germans were Jews or non-Nazis, moreover, adopting 51 per cent as a threshold meant giving up areas where a majority had no desire to be absorbed into the Reich. The choice of census was equally significant. It will be remembered that the 1910 census, in addition to being a generation old, had been performed by the Habsburgs on the basis of the *Umgangsprache*, or language of everyday use, a criteria that was heavily skewed towards German. Revanchism against the Versailles Treaty, not self-determination, was the leading criterion for the German position.

Hitler, who was still going through his triumphal tour of the Sudetenland and had just reached Carlsbad, now took charge. On his orders, Ribbentrop woke François-Poncet up in the middle of the night to accuse him of breaching the Munich Agreement and threaten him with occupation up to the Godesberg line if the commission did not comply immediately with German demands. The French ambassador protested, and he and his British counterpart both called home. The responses from Chamberlain and Daladier were that they thought what had been agreed in Munich was 51 per cent and 1918 – not extremely helpful, since 1918 had not been a census year. In any case, Ribbentrop himself summoned all three ambassadors the next day, 5 October, and, in the Czechoslovaks' absence, they simply acceded to the German position, signing a protocol with a map to that effect.

The Czechoslovaks made a last attempt to plead with Weizsäcker, hoping to gain credit from Beneš's resignation that very day. They sent the cabinet minister Hugo Vavrečka in person to Berlin. They appealed to W. J. Carr, the American ambassador, for his counterpart in Berlin to ask the members of the international commission for leniency, and they organised a parallel appeal by Štefan Osuský to Daladier personally. The American government formally declined to help on the same day Ribbentrop issued his diktat. It was all in vain.[34] After another overnight cabinet session in Prague, Mastný was told to accept the new position, and the occupation of the fifth zone started the following day. After the plebiscites were replaced with some minor horse trading at the margins, the border was finally set on 20 November. The Czechoslovaks had lost their entire fortifications, along with much else. There was an almost perfect match with the Godesberg map.

Even the arch-appeaser Henderson was so disgusted with the commission's proceedings that he thought of resigning. He wrote to Halifax that 'it would be as unwise as it would be misleading to encourage the Czechoslovak government to believe that they have much to hope from the International Commission'.[35] Henderson had a point. The difference between Godesberg or Munich and the various other proposals of September was never to be found in the wording. Earlier proposals, including the Anglo–French plan which the Czechoslovaks had accepted, contained no deadline and left them in control while the international commission deliberated. Munich, like Godesberg, allowed immediate German occupation, letting Hitler dictate implementation, and therein lay his victory.

Even this, though, was not all. A brief annex to the Munich Agreement specified that Britain and France guaranteed the borders of the rump Czechoslovak state, to be joined in the future by Italy and Germany in the same commitment. Militarily, of course, this was nonsense. If Britain and France were not prepared to fight for Czechoslovakia when it was armed to the teeth and ensconced in its thick web of fortifications, why should they be expected to do so when it had basically become open territory? The Czechs did not care much for the Franco–British guarantee, though they kept a keen eye on Germany's failure to accede to it as an indicator of its intentions.[36] The annex, however, exceeded the treaty's lacunae in insidiousness. It would prove the prompt for making Czechoslovakia's defeat even more complete. The text specified that Germany and Italy would accede to the joint guarantee 'when the question of the Polish and Hungarian minorities in Czechoslovakia has been settled'. Chamberlain and Daladier had been fooled into endorsing Poland and Hungary's own annexationist claims, something they had avoided doing even at their lowest point in the September crisis.

The Polish government had delivered an ultimatum to Prague on the evening of 30 September for the transfer of the Teschen district, massing troops on the border. The Prague government decided to accept the Polish ultimatum on 1 October, and discussions opened between the two military general staffs directly the same day. An evacuation in phases was agreed with the Poles, beginning on 2 and ending on 11 October.[37]

Central to the cabinet decision to accept Polish demands were military reasons. A war with Poland would have been impossible to explain to the people after no resistance had been offered to Germany. There was the risk that it would draw in the Germans, who had a non-aggression treaty in place with the Poles, had endorsed Polish claims in the Munich Agreement, and, it was rightly assumed, were only looking for an excuse to drive their armies all the way to Prague.[38] As discussed earlier, Polish decision-making was not quite as myopic as outside observers have sometimes assumed. Poland had been aggressive in its demands in September, but it only followed suit on its threats after the ink was dry on the Munich Agreement and the Entente partners themselves had dropped Czechoslovakia. With their southern neighbour out, the Poles turned to their own defence. If the Polish occupation schedule matched almost exactly that of the Sudetenland, this was no coincidence. The concern was that the Germans would themselves annex Teschen, with its coal mines and heavy industry, if Poland did not do so first.[39] Polish motivations thus involved, beyond narrow-minded irredentism, a legitimate loss of faith in French commitments and a desire to fortify the country's strategic position. More questionably, the Polish government would also grab the northern Slovak mountain districts of Spiš and Orava in an adjustment completed on 30 November.

A similar dynamic applied to Hungarian demands, though here the Czechoslovaks held out longer, more territory was at stake, and the situation was complicated by the republic's recent grant of autonomy to Slovakia and Ruthenia, where the territorial adjustment fell. Before Munich, the Hungarians had been more cautious than the Poles. They remained at risk from the Little Entente, and in the event of war they had little wish to find themselves on the wrong side of the French and British. On 22 September, the Hungarians had nevertheless sent a note to Prague asking for the same treatment for the Hungarian minority as for the Sudeten Germans, accompanied by a token military deployment on the border.[40] Negotiations began on 9 October in Komárno, in Slovakia. The Czechoslovak side was represented by Jozef Tiso, minister plenipotentiary for Slovakia but also the head of his own Slovak cabinet in formation, and by Edmond Bacyznyj, his Ruthenian counterpart. Ruthenia, in particular, was at risk of complete elimination because the Poles and Hungarians had grand plans for establishing a joint frontier, though as it turned out this was not to German liking.[41]

The Hungarians upped the pressure in October and called up fresh army classes, infiltrated the coveted territories with bands of 'irredentists' across the border, and played havoc with Ruthenia's already stormy politics by covertly triggering a coup.[42] Eventually, Czechoslovakia and Hungary appealed for joint mediation by Germany and Italy, and a conference assembled in Vienna at the beginning of November. But Ribbentrop and Galeazzo Ciano ended up sitting alone in chambers and issuing another diktat. Though Hungary failed to carve up Ruthenia entirely, the Vienna arbitrage of 2 November was hugely in its favour and it got most of what it had asked for. Lacroix had confirmed in late October that it would be best for Czechoslovakia to fall on German and Italian mercy in the negotiations, and that neither Britain nor France would provide support.[43] The Slovak and Ruthenian negotiators were overconfident, and they hardly knew what they were doing. While the Polish ultimatum came in the context of Czech military retreat and involved circumscribed concessions, nevertheless, the Hungarian settlement was a sign that Czechoslovakia had now entirely fallen into the German orbit.

Czechoslovakia lost 29 per cent of its territory as a result of the German, Polish, and Hungarian annexations. The Czech lands on their own – Bohemia, Moravia, and Czech Silesia – were shorn of 37 per cent of their total area. The population loss for Czechoslovakia was 4.7 million, or about one-third of the country's total. The Czech lands lost 3.6 million people, more if one counts the refugees. Most of this, or 3.4 million, came from the Sudetenland. The Polish annexation of Teschen claimed 175,000 people, of whom 79,000 were identifiable as Poles based on the 1930 census. Slovakia and Ruthenia were hit almost as badly, losing 19 and 26 per cent of their total area respectively and in excess of a million people altogether. A total of 1.2 million Czechs, Slovaks, and Ruthenes were left outside the rump Czechoslovakia's borders. The number of Czechs living in the regions annexed by Germany alone had been in excess of 700,000.[44]

Just as significant was the damage done to the national economy and transport network. The country lost a staggering 70 per cent of its iron and steel production capacity and 80 per cent of its chemical and cement industries. It was stripped of two-thirds of its coal production and close to three-quarters of its electricity generation capacity. This left it dependent on Germany for energy imports, with no available substitutes. A modern industrial state that relies on a single neighbour for its energy supply is not independent.[45] Slovakia lost its main eastern city, Košice, and Ruthenia had to let go of both its capital, Užhorod, and its second-largest town, Mukačevo. Rump Ruthenia even saw its rail link cut with the rest of the state. Nor was it possible to travel by rail from Prague to Brno, the Czech lands' second-largest city and Moravia's administrative centre, without crossing through Germany.

Militarily, the rump state was just as vulnerable. It was not only that the fortifications were gone. Plzeň and its armament works were closely hemmed in by German territory. In Slovakia, the German annexations extended to Petržalka, which is so close to the capital as to be a suburb of Bratislava today. In Bohemia, the border stood just beyond Mělník, a town where it is possible to have dinner and still be back for an early bedtime in Prague. By panzer, it was a breezy morning's ride to the Czech capital.

THE RUMP REPUBLIC ITSELF was at threat of collapse. In Prague, the pressures accumulating on the decision-makers must have felt bewildering, a recipe for panic as well as despair. From the first days of October, the government was faced not just with the problems of border adjustment and the international commission in Berlin, but with Nazi demands for a major slice of its rolling stock and banking reserves. It had to demobilise its troops, reallocate thousands of civil servants, and put in place a new border with its German neighbour. As winter approached, it needed urgently to address energy and food supply issues. It was confronted with the Polish and Hungarian demands, with their own host of diplomatic, military, economic, and humanitarian implications. In the middle of all this, the Slovak and Ruthenian leaders had made demands for autonomy, and a new status had to be arranged, forming a whole new basis for the Czechoslovak state. Finally, there were the tens of thousands of refugees and their needs to deal with, and all this amid fears of popular unrest, rumours of an impending military coup, and the threat that the Germans would not stop at the new border anyway.[46]

Civil society was the first to mobilise on behalf of the refugees. Appeals for donations appeared in the newspapers as early as 3 October, and humanitarian bodies such as the Czechoslovak Red Cross, *Charita*, and *České srdce* ('Czech heart'), as well as a number of local town and county councils, stepped in. People who could tried to move in with relatives, sometimes quite distant, or managed to find accommodation with benevolent but complete foreigners. Many stayed wherever they had landed before they could find a proper place to stay, finding themselves massed in schools, orphanages, inns, warehouses, castles, and

even libraries and disused railway cars. About 60,000 were directed
to temporary camps originally intended for the evacuation of Prague
during the war. Many of these places at first lacked kitchens, shower
rooms, stoves, or bedclothes and blankets, and some refugees needed to
be provided with, in addition to food, basic necessities such as soap or
shoes.[47] Well-to-do farmers were encouraged to take in their destitute
brethren, having lost their equipment and animals but not their skills.
Eventually, government took over from private committees, motivated
partly by epidemiological concerns, and by December an Institute for
the Care of Refugees was ready to take on the coordination of voluntary assistance and official action. Foreign care, especially British,
was also at work, as both the lord mayor of London and the League
of Nations high commissioner for refugees Neill Malcolm moved to
provide funds, material aid, and technical help.[48]

Slovak and Ruthenian autonomy had undergone a long gestation,
and their advent was not solely the result of Munich. The revolution-
aries in exile during the First World War, as they plotted the creation
of Czechoslovakia out of the Habsburg collapse, had already planned
for an undefined Slovak autonomy which the Czechs had been guilty
of reneging on as they had become masters in their own home. The
HSĽS or Slovak People's Party had long campaigned for autonomy,
though it had never attracted more than a minority of Slovak votes.
Its leader, the Catholic priest, banker, and politician Andrej Hlinka,
had inconveniently died in August. Tiso, his successor, lost no time in
taking up the cause. It is important, however, to stress that Tiso was not
an independentist, but a pro-Czechoslovak figure who was an MP and
had even served as a cabinet minister in Prague in 1927–8. The Syrový
emergency government of September had contained three Slovak ministers, including the autonomist Matuš Černák. Discussions, picked up
in the pre-Munich days, resumed at a more intense pace in the early
days of October, in parallel at the governmental level in Prague and at
an all-party conference in Slovakia. On 7 October, Tiso was appointed
minister for Slovakia and empowered to form his own autonomous

government in Bratislava, and a wide-ranging autonomy status was adopted, to be formally passed into law the next month.[49]

The proclamation of Ruthenian autonomy followed a more convoluted process, complicated by the fragmented nature of local politics and Hungarian intervention both open and covert. Slovak motivations mixed longstanding national ambition and the fear of finding themselves chained to the sinking Czech lodestar. Polish and Hungarian demands, indeed, played a major role in forcing the disunited Slovak political parties to the side of the HSĽS. Bratislava was not just exposed geographically to Germany, it also had a large German-speaking population, and it was extremely tempting to the Slovaks to try and save themselves by relying on the Germans rather than their embattled Czech brethren. In the end, the pursuit of their own political path was to be fateful to Czechoslovakia, or as it now became called Czecho-Slovakia, since it was by pushing the Slovaks towards independence in March 1939 that Hitler was able to justify the invasion of the rump Czech lands.[50]

More than Slovak or Ruthenian affairs, though, it was clear in Prague that the dominant influence on the country's fate would be German. The public mood may not have gone through the five phases of grief, but it moved in a mere few days from the panicked appeals mixed with bitterness that had characterised Munich's immediate aftermath to a cold-headed realisation that pacifying Hitler was now the only option. As everyone realised, down to the local burgomaster, 'we must go with Germany'.[51] The leading newspapers on both left and right agreed that, in the words of an anonymous writer in *Lidové noviny*, an organ that had always been close to the Castle, 'if we cannot sing with the angels, we must howl with the wolves'.[52] The nationalist *Národní listy* agreed, and so did the powerful *Venkov*.[53] *Přítomnost* gave voice to two conflicting opinions as to what to do with democratic German refugees, one suggesting that they were in danger and must be integrated, the other warning that they would be an excuse for another Nazi invasion and could not be saved.[54] The mystery contribution in

Lidové noviny, meanwhile, was the most revealing: it was penned by Jan Stránský, the son of Jaroslav Stránský – the socialist MP who had gone to visit Beneš on the day of Munich to urge him to reject its verdict – a pillar of the Czechoslovak Republic and a man of part-Jewish descent to boot. 'We naively believed that a French signature is worth more than the paper and ink used to write it, and we foolishly took at face value passionate words from the English about right and fairness. Fine, we are now the wiser.' The Czechs would have to look after themselves and do what the Germans said.

What this meant in terms of the rump republic's internal political set-up was less clear. The right-wing Agrarians, even though they had participated in or led all of the successive 1930s governments, were now in the ascendant simply as a result of Beneš's discomfiture. *Venkov*, the Agrarian press organ, published a series of opinion pieces arguing for the establishment of an 'authoritarian democracy'. This was to be freed from 'corruption and patronage', must be dedicated to the common good, and, in accents that recalled Polish or Austrian clerical fascism, must renew with the values of land and religion.[55] The Communist Party had already shut itself down and its leaders fled. A number of right and centre parties announced their merger into a Party of National Unity in November, and the remaining left-wing groupings merged to form a National Workers' Party. The new National Unity Party leader and prime minister was Rudolf Beran, the Agrarian Party secretary.

At the same time, an active debate arose as to the causes of the national collapse and the role of party democracy, and it continued to be carried out at least until the great Karel Čapek died on Christmas Day – a death that was probably hastened by Munich and yet saved him from the concentration camps that would have awaited him under German occupation. In the main, it was thought that 'Dictatorship, even if one must recognise its many successes in Europe, does not suit our national character and political maturity.'[56] A two-party space, moreover, resembled the American or the British system more than the dictatorships, and it was ambiguous who was being emulated exactly. A new constitution in preparation never saw the light of day. Even Beran refrained from authoritarian and anti-Semitic measures, though what private persons or the autonomous Slovak government did was another matter.[57] What became known as the 'Second Republic' embarked on its brief life in a shadow world, from the beginning caught between disaster and impending annexation.

If in Britain and France it was still possible, for a few months, to continue in the delusion that a lasting peace had been achieved, it was indeed plain to the Czechs and Slovaks that they had been delivered into the German vice. Goering had already advised Mastný officially, at the beginning of October, that Germany would not tolerate Beneš remaining as head of state. The new foreign minister Chvalkovský visited Hitler twice, in mid-October 1938 and January 1939. Both meetings were disasters. Instead of listening to the minister's plea for leniency on border arrangements and for support in the Polish and Hungarian matters, Hitler warned him against any independence in foreign policy and demanded domestic changes, including banning the Communist Party, reducing army size, ending press freedom, and limiting the role of Jews in public life. On the second visit, the foreign minister was screamed at and almost assaulted, and he came out physically shaking. Unable to make any of the requests he had planned (e.g. about Czech schools), he was given a list of demands that included revoking all foreign alliances, leaving the League of Nations, laying off all Jews and all civil servants unfriendly to Germany, demobilising entirely, handing over part of the national bank's gold reserves, and entering into fresh trade commitments with Germany.[58]

Hitler also asked for compliance with the demands of his minion, Ernst Kundt. Kundt, indeed, having remained behind in Prague, now played a repeat of Henlein's role, this time for the destruction of the rump Czechoslovakia. From being on the run during the September mobilisation days, he had become the de facto leader of the Bohemian German community. He could expound Nazism openly from the parliamentary tribune and was politically and judicially untouchable, on pain of instant annihilation for the whole country. Kundt made it loudly clear that, in his opinion, Munich was not so much a matter of border as of ideological realignment. He began demanding new cultural and administrative privileges for the remaining Germans, now 4 per cent of the population, as well as their complete segregation from Jews.[59]

George Kennan, the American diplomat of future Cold War fame, came into the junior role of secretary of legation in Prague on the very day of the Munich conference, and he ended up being a keen observer of local conditions in its aftermath. The Germans were 'dangling Bohemia over the abyss', wrote Kennan. 'There seem to be very few people here who are convinced that the present situation is permanent and who do not fear that the outcome, sooner or later, will be a German occupation.'[60] The German chargé d'affaires Hencke concurred, writing that 'Not only political circles but the man in the street expresses the view to anyone who would hear it that Germany will not leave Czechoslovakia alone, and that the occupation of the whole country is only a matter of time.'[61] This was hardly surprising. The Reich press had been discussing the liquidation of Czechoslovakia as early as October.[62] In December already, Kundt was proclaiming to his followers that they would finally get all they wanted 'in two or three months'.[63] The saying in the Sudetenland about the rump republic was that 'things will soon change'. The Germans were doing nothing to develop the new boundaries into a permanent frontier, putting up no permanent custom or passport control offices. Osuský would soon warn from Paris that German embassy staff had been asked to take their holidays before March 1939 and reserve officers to place themselves in a state of readiness by February.[64] The pressure to conform to German conditions was irresistible. The government even decided to change the side of the road on which vehicles drove, from left to right, to fit better with the German road system.[65]

For the Sudetenland itself, finally, existence in the Reich was ironically but unsurprisingly not living up to its promise. Henlein took over both as *Reichskommissar*, based in Liberec, and as Nazi Party *Gauleiter* for the same region. But in order to prevent a local identity from taking root, the annexed regions were broken up, with the south-eastern and southern regions joined up with Bavaria and Austria rather than with Henlein's fiefdom. Reich laws and practices were quickly enforced and, even for Germans, the loss of personal liberty was significant. Organisations likely to further cultural specificity, such as the *Turnverband* gymnastics organisation from which Henlein himself had sprung, were dissolved or merged into their Reich equivalents. Naturally, the SdP was absorbed into the Nazi Party.[66] Unemployment fell further, but it had already been low in the last year of the republic. The annexed regions were immediately yoked to the German economic and armament plans, its workers forced into the *Deutscher Arbeitsfront*, and as consumer goods fell in availability or rose in price relative to wages, disillusionment began to bite.[67] Henlein eventually committed suicide in American captivity in 1945. During the war, however, the private rivalries that had divided the SdP, particularly between Nazis and *Kameradschaftsbund* clerical fascists, resurfaced and returned to haunt him, pitting him against Heydrich and the SS and coming close to costing him his position and life.[68] The Czech joke that had been current in the last summer before Munich had perhaps at last come true: 'Hitler told Henlein that the Sudeten Germans can't have autonomy because that's promised to the Czechs.'[69]

A. J. P. TAYLOR, the international historian, once described the Munich Agreement as 'a triumph for British policy' and 'a triumph for all that was best and most enlightened in British life', on the grounds that it was a victory for the right to self-determination.[70] It is tempting merely to sneer at this assessment. Diplomatic historians are prone to forget that there are more than just territorial stakes in the international-relations game, and that real people live in the territories shown on their maps. Yet Munich, beyond the question of appeasement and the strategic dilemma for which it is best known, also holds a mirror to the issues and ambiguities of self-determination. Perhaps the Nazis would have won a plebiscite in the Sudetenland had one been carried out in October 1938. Yet the force of impetus counts in politics, as the ups and downs of SdP fortunes through 1938 attest (the *Anschluss*, the May mobilisation, the failed September coup). Success breeds success, and the flowers thrown at Hitler's troops are no proof of long-held, majority desires to come under Nazi rule. On the contrary, based on the 1935 election results, it is doubtful that the areas annexed to the Reich contained 50 per cent or more Nazi supporters: even if one counts all SdP voters as Nazi, which is a gross approximation, there were enough democratic Germans, Jews, and Czechs in the Sudetenland to make a majority.

A second problem is that self-determination can come at the cost of regional, and indeed global, stability. A third is that self-determination begs the question of minority rights within the territories concerned. Munich offers an extreme example of the trade-offs involved.

Karl Josef Hahn was an 'Aryan' German living in Carlsbad, but his wife, Renata, was a converted Jew. On the evening of 9 October, a group of SA and SS men appeared in his living room asking for her. *Kristallnacht* had begun in the Sudetenland, just as it had begun all over Germany.

Hahn came along as they took his wife away, filing through a gesticulating crowd to a hotel where, together with others who had been beaten and whose faces were bleeding, they were rounded up and put on a lorry. Some were weeping. Renata was three months pregnant. Around midnight they were submitted again to the angry mob and to an anti-Semitic speech. Led by the SS into a waiting room, Hahn was attacked for having helped Jewish immigrants as a lawyer, then hit in the face when he protested that he was actually a German literature teacher. Renata's uncle had been an Austrian officer during the First World War, four times wounded, but he had made an enemy by winning a trial between a butcher and his wife, and this man now saw his chance for revenge. The uncle was tortured. They were all packed into dark cells, to be interrogated again the next day. The questioning, when it resumed, took place on the third floor of the police station, and it was possible to see the picturesque Carlsbad panorama with its hills, woods, and villas through a large window. As Hahn stood before his interrogators, a huge fire became visible outside: the synagogue was burning. We have this testimony because eventually Hahn was able to leave and, by paying bribes and turning over his flat to a *Wehrmacht* officer, to take his wife with him. Many were not so lucky.[71]

Synagogues burned in Most, Teplice, Marienbad, Ústí nad Labem, and elsewhere: forty-four were destroyed, and numerous cemeteries were desecrated.[72] Jewish businesses and homes were attacked in actions that lasted sporadically into 1939. In Carlsbad alone, seventy-one hotels and ninety-three other businesses belonging to Jews were seized.[73] A number of those who could not prove Czechoslovak nationality found themselves stranded in the no-man's-land between the new borders for several weeks, surviving on the kindness of local peasants, in the open country, as winter approached. They were helped on their way out by the activist Marie Schmolková, working from Prague, and with the cooperation of the Czech and the British authorities, who promised to take some of them into Palestine.[74]

According to the 1930 census, there were 29,789 people in the Sudetenland whose religion was Judaism, though by the criteria of the Nuremberg Laws the number was almost certainly higher. They had been joined by refugees from Germany and Austria, perhaps as many as 10–15,000, and the total number of Jews on religious criteria must therefore have been something above 40,000.[75] How many escaped after Munich is not known, due both to the administrative disarray and because some must have sought to flee both the Sudetenland and the rump republic outside legal channels. Estimates of the number of Jews who managed to escape after Munich thus vary between around 20,000 and 27,000.[76]

There was also a scramble to leave the rump Czechoslovakia itself, with a surge in visa applications to the United States. The British government had issued 2,500 certificates, or authorisations to immigrate into Palestine, to be placed mainly at the disposal of Jewish refugees from the Sudetenland.[77] Because the procedure was onerous, however, it is not clear that all or even most of these certificates were ever used. Max Brod, the editor and friend of Franz Kafka and the man without whom his novels would have been lost, was among those who applied. Brod recounts how, in a tale worthy of Kafka himself, Czech chicanery went to work and he was provided with interminable forms to fill and inventories to have verified. The British were no better. Brod and his wife and friends were waiting for a stamp from the British embassy to be pasted in their passports, but the embassy had run out and was waiting for resupply, and in the end they were only able to leave Prague on the very night of the German invasion. Brod found himself sitting in a train compartment at 4 a.m., in Moravská Ostrava on the Polish border, gazing at a German soldier on the platform who, thankfully, remained impassive until the train began to move again and pulled out of the station, the last one to leave the country.[78]

For the German and Austrian political refugees who had not already left, or for anyone who had been active on the side of the democratic Germans, the situation was no better. Just as Jewish organisations attempted to help their own, Sudeten German Social-Democratic committees did their best to obtain visas for the Germans who were most exposed. Among the three most prominent *activists* of Czechoslovakia, Siegfried Taub managed to escape to Stockholm and Wenzel Jaksch to Paris, but Ludwig Czech remained stranded and ended up in Theresienstadt. A British Red Cross worker recounts how he visited a camp where 130 German Social-Democrats were held by the Nazis, after Munich. The inmates' foreman told him: 'We are good Republicans. We gave our blood for this Republic. We wanted to defend our homes and our freedom. We had weapons in our hands; but we were betrayed and sold. We are still good Republicans, we still want our homes and freedom, whether England and France want us to have them or not. Freedom – freedom – freedom! The whole room took up the cry, giving the clenched fist salute and shouting *Freiheit*! *Freiheit*! *Freiheit*!'[79]

The annexed Sudetenland was a less directly threatening environment for Czechs, but it offered ludicrously reduced civil rights compared to what the Germans had enjoyed under the republic. Czech employees were immediately removed from all administrative posts, including municipal. The language of administration became exclusively German. All Czech civic organisations were closed down, as well as many schools, primary and secondary. Czech children were banned from secondary schools anyway, and there was to be no Czech theatre, radio, or cinema. The Czech newspapers of the Sudetenland soon closed, either forcibly or through the indirect effect of censorship, and listening to Czech (or any 'foreign') radio invited punishment.[80] Even having a conversation in Czech in public could be dangerous if it took place in front of the wrong persons.[81] In March 1939, there was another wave of beatings, assaults, arrests, and deportations, with no recourse to justice for those who stayed.

An oft-repeated argument in favour of appeasement was that all this destruction and suffering bought the Allies valuable time to rearm. That may be so, though this book has argued otherwise. One of the numerous tasks the post-Munich Czechoslovak government found itself dealing with was to dispose of its now useless armament stockpiles. It turned first to the British, but also to France, Holland, and Romania. According to Feierabend, who was a minister at the time, this made no headway for lack of a sense of urgency on the other side. Eventually, Germany demanded pre-emptive rights. Upon occupation, the Germans seized more than 400 tanks, 1,000 warplanes, 2,500 artillery pieces, 40,000 machineguns, 100,000 pistols, a million rifles, and in excess of a billion rounds of ammunition. The Škoda armaments complex, part-owned by the French firm Schneider-Creusot until its shares were transferred to a bank consortium in December 1938, ended up in the sphere of the Hermann Göring Werke. The mass of the Czech armaments industry passed to the Reich and remained in service throughout the Second World War. Even the armoured turrets on the fortifications were taken and transferred to the German West

Wall, finally closing up the defensive line that had been wide open in September 1938, when the French and British chose not to fight.[82]

Jan Masaryk in London and Osuský in Paris, in their regular phone conversations with Krofta and Beneš, spoke Czech or Slovak, secure in the notion that they would not be understood in Britain or France. Sometimes, though, they talked in quite blunt, even coarse language. This was in the pre-Munich days still, and Hubert Masařík, who was a member of the foreign minister's cabinet, writes that he warned them to be more careful. It is hard to imagine Beneš indulging in the use of expletives, but Masaryk apparently called Chamberlain 'the old pisser' and regularly garnished his discussions of British policy with quite colourful expressions. Chamberlain, his special adviser Wilson, and Ambassador Henderson came in as 'cretins' and 'Nazi boot-lickers'.

> Masaryk: 'The wicked old pisser is longing to lick Adolf's back-side. His tongue is hanging out.'
> Beneš: 'Stuff it back again! Bring him to his senses.'
> – The old beast hasn't any senses left, except to smell out the Nazi rubbish-heap and hang around it.
> – Then have a talk with Horace Wilson. Ask him to warn the Prime Minister that England is in danger too if we do not all stand firm. Can't he be made to understand this?
> – How can you talk to Wilson? He is nothing but a jackal!

But they forgot that the telephone lines ran through Germany, where they were being tapped. Goering's counter-espionage services passed their content on to a legation councillor in London, who in turn communicated them to Wilson.[83]

This was unlikely to dispose Chamberlain well to the Czechoslovaks, and it may have encouraged him in the delusion that Hitler was a man who could better be trusted. But beyond the unfortunate aspects of this anecdote, what surely comes through is the unfathomable levels of frustration, the sheer, unbearable exasperation the Czechoslovak side must have felt month after month. The tragedy of Munich, indeed, rested ultimately in an inability to communicate the right message, an almost nightmarish powerlessness to get through what the Czechoslovaks knew to be the situation. Sitting on its borders and having welcomed so many of its exiles, they were well aware of the nature of the Nazi regime. Hitler's ultimate ambitions were never a mystery to them. Neither the Czechoslovak public nor the decision-makers in the Castle and Czernin Palace had any illusions as to Henlein's double game. They could never convince either Daladier or Chamberlain of the lucidity of their views.

After he had resigned, Beneš gave a farewell speech on the radio. This was restrained, even dry and dull in some respects. But it is worth quoting a few of his words:

> I don't want to go through the past again, or criticise. Nor should you expect words of recrimination from me about any party. History will judge all that, and it will judge fairly. I will only say what we all painfully feel: that the sacrifices which were asked of us so insistently [here the wording had been changed from 'the sacrifices that were forced upon us'] are incommensurate and they are unjust. The nation will never forget it, even if it bears the situation with the dignity, calm, and confidence that have earned it the respect of all. In this resides the strength and moral grandeur of its sons and daughters.[84]

Both the certainty of the nation's future travails and the confidence that it would come through were contained in that speech. On the eve of the conference, a petition had urged: 'The men who hold the fate of Europe in their hands wish to deny that this fight is but the beginning to more serious problems and a more serious struggle, which can only lead to a world war under worse conditions.'[85] Perhaps these were self-serving words, including the bitter notion that what had happened to Czechoslovakia would happen, in turn, to others. But the Czechs had a sense of the long sweep of events when it came to the struggle with their powerful neighbour, and it was that broader awareness that failed the men who signed the Agreement in Munich over their heads.

František Moravec, the head of the intelligence-gathering services, got advance warning from his moles of the German invasion of March 1939. A few days before it was due, he organised a meeting with a Major H. Gibson from MI6, at the British embassy, to arrange for a speedy transfer of his best men out of the country. He told his superiors he was going on a business trip, and he ordered potentially sensitive material to be burnt. Shortly after five o'clock on the day before the invasion, Moravec and a hand-picked team of his officers boarded a Dakota air-craft, at Ruzyně Airport, on their way to Britain.[86] It was only twelve men and a few files with information about their German agents, but finally the value of Czech cooperation had been recognised and Czech help enlisted in the coming world war.

Chronology of 1938 events

February	20	Hitler vows protection to ten million neighbouring Germans.
March	12–14	Germany invades Austria and performs *Anschluss*.
	23–24	Several Czechoslovak German activist parties merge with SdP.
	28	Henlein visits Hitler in Berlin and is instructed to up his demands.
April	1	Hodža submits First Plan to SdP.
	12	Formation of Daladier government.
	21	Hitler orders Keitel to update Plan Green.
	23–24	SdP party rally. Henlein makes Carlsbad demands.
	28–29	First Anglo–French talks over Czechoslovakia.
May	20	German troop movements in Saxony.
		Czechoslovak government decrees partial mobilisation.
	22–29	First two rounds of municipal elections.

June	12	Last round of municipal elections.
July	3–6	Final ceremonies of *Všesokolský slet*.
	20	Runciman mission launched.
	27	Second Plan circulated.
August	3	Runciman arrives in Czechoslovakia.
	12	Full-scale German mobilisation begins.
	21	France recalls first reservists.
	29	Presentation of Third Plan.
September	2	SdP rejects Third Plan.
	6	Beneš forwards Fourth Plan to SdP.
	7	Moravská Ostrava incident.
		SdP breaks off negotiations with Czechoslovak government.
	12	Hitler closes Nuremberg party rally with fiery speech.
	13	SdP foments uprising in the Sudetenland.
	14	Czechoslovak government imposes martial law.
	15	Chamberlain visit to Berchtesgaden.
		Flight of Henlein and other SdP leaders to Germany.
		'*Heim ins Reich!*' proclamation.
	16	Chamberlain returns to London.
		Nečas mission to Paris.
	18	Second set of Anglo–French talks in London.
	19	Anglo–French plan submitted in Prague.
	20	Czechoslovak government rejects Anglo–French plan.
		Freikorps attack frontier.

21   Anglo–French 'ultimatum'.

Czechoslovak government accepts Anglo–French plan.

Nationwide mass demonstrations.

22   Wave of strikes and marches.

Hodža government resigns. Appointment of government of national concentration headed by Syrový.

Chamberlain meets Hitler in Godesberg.

23   Hitler hands Godesberg memorandum to Chamberlain.

Russia warns Poland not to intervene against Czechoslovakia.

Czechoslovak government decrees general mobilisation.

24   Chamberlain returns from Godesberg.

Czechoslovakia cuts all external communications.

France formally announces partial mobilisation.

25   Third set of Anglo–French meetings in London.

Czechoslovakia formally turns down Godesberg terms.

26   Gamelin makes appearance at Anglo–French talks.

Roosevelt issues appeal for peace.

Hitler issues final ultimatum. *Sportpalast* speech.

	27	Last-minute French and British cabinet meetings.
		Production of Halifax 'timetable'.
	28	Britain mobilises navy and air force.
		Final French and British appeals to Hitler and Mussolini.
		Munich conference proposed.
	29	Munich conference takes place.
	30	Four powers sign Munich Agreement.
		Syrový broadcasts acceptance to Czechoslovak people.
		International commission assembles in Berlin.
		Polish ultimatum for the evacuation of Teschen and other districts.
October	1	Germany begins occupation of Sudetenland.
		Czechoslovakia accedes to Polish demands.
	5	Beneš resigns.
	10	Occupation of Sudetenland effectively completed.
November	2	Arbitration award of Slovak and Ruthenian territory to Hungary.
	9–10	*Kristallnacht* pogroms.
March 1939	15	Germany invades rest of the Czech lands.

Notes

Epigraph

1. František Halas, *Torso naděje* (Prague, 1945), pp. 20–3.

1. In the boa's gaze

1. 'Záznam o hovoru vyslance Masaryka s Lordem Halifaxem v sobotu 12. Března odpoledne', Archiv Ministerstva Zahraničních Věcí [AMZV] / Fond II/6 / Londýn / 1937–39, ff. 2–3.
2. Marcia Davenport, *Too strong for fantasy* (New York, 1967), p. 325.
3. Ibid., pp. 326–33; Pavel Kosatík & Michal Kolář, *Jan Masaryk, Pravdivý příběh* (Prague, 1998), p. 51.
4. Antonín Sum, *Otec a syn, Tomáš Garrigue a Jan Masarykové ve vzpomínkách přátel a pamětníků* (Prague, 2000), p. 9.
5. David Faber, *Munich: the 1938 appeasement crisis* (London, 2009), pp. 32–41.
6. Telford Taylor, *Munich: the price of peace* (London, 1979), pp. 194–5.
7. Alice Teichova, *An economic background to Munich* (Cambridge, 1974), p. 47.
8. Ibid., p. 50.
9. Ibid., pp. 76–86, 206–7, 286–8, 299 & 338–9.
10. Richard Francis Crane, *A French conscience in Prague: Louis Eugène Faucher and the abandonment of Czechoslovakia* (New York, 1996), pp. 4–5 & 70–1.
11. Geoffrey Cox, *Countdown to war: a personal memoir of Europe, 1938–1940* (London; 1988), p. 37.

12. Johann Wolfgang Bruegel, *Czechoslovakia before Munich: the German minority problem and British appeasement* (Cambridge, 1973), pp. 160–1; *Documents on German Foreign Policy, 1918–1945* [DGFP], Series D (13 vols, London, 1949–64), vol. I, p. 36.

13. Sydney Morrell, *I saw the crucifixion* (London, 1939), pp. 25–31.

14. Zdeněk Karník, *České země v éře První republiky* (3 vols, Prague, 2003), vol. III, pp. 110–12 & 134.

15. Derek Sayer, *Prague, capital of the twentieth century: a surrealist history* (Princeton, 2013), pp. 144–8.

16. Karník, *České země v éře První republiky*, vol. III, pp. 191–9.

17. Ibid., vol. I, pp. 327 & 338–9.

18. Kurt Grossmann, *Emigration, Geschichte der Hitler-Flüchtlinge 1933–1945* (Frankfurt, 1969), pp. 25–8.

19. Werner Röder, 'Drehscheibe – Kampfposten – Fluchstation, Deutsche Emigranten in der Tschechoslowakei', in Peter Heumos (ed.), *Drehscheibe Prag: zur deutschen Emigration in der Tschechoslowakei, 1933–1939* (Munich, 1992), p. 21; Vojtěch Blodig, 'Die tschechoslowakischen politischen Parteien und die Unterstützung der deutschen und österreichischen Emigration in den 30er Jahren', in Peter Glotz (ed.), *München 1938: das Ende des alten Europa* (Essen, 1990), p. 259.

20. Brigitte Seebacher-Brandt, 'Die deutsche politische Emigration der Tschechoslowakei', in Glotz, *München 1938*, p. 230; Bohumil Černý, *Most k novému životu: německá emigrace v ČSR v letech 1933–1939* (Prague, 1967), p. 16.

21. Röder, 'Drehscheibe – Kampfposten – Fluchstation', pp. 16–20.

22. Ibid., p. 25; Černý, *Most k novému životu*, pp. 83–8.

23. Černý, *Most k novému životu*, p. 88.

24. Seebacher-Brandt, 'Die deutsche politische Emigration', p. 237; Röder, 'Drehscheibe – Kampfposten – Fluchstation', pp. 24–5.

25. Blodig, 'Die Unterstützung der deutschen und österreichischen Emigration', p. 253.

26. Grossmann, *Emigration*, pp. 29–30.

27. Röder, 'Drehscheibe – Kampfposten – Fluchstation', pp. 23–4.

28. Thomas Kraft, '"Wie geht es euch? Was macht ihr?" Oskar Maria Graf in Prag und Brünn 1934–1938', in Heumos, *Drehscheibe Prag*, p. 123.

29. Kurt Weisskopf, *The agony of Czechoslovakia '38/68* (London, 1968), pp. 86–7.

30. Otto Strasser, *Exil* (Munich, 1958), p. 78.

31. Ibid., pp. 91–3; Černý, *Most k novému životu*, pp. 138–51.

32. Černý, *Most k novému životu*, p. 164.
33. Seebacher-Brandt, 'Die deutsche politische Emigration', p. 230.
34. Grossmann, *Emigration*, pp. 92–3.
35. Ibid., pp. 73–5; Heinz Kühn, *Widerstand und Emigration: die Jahre 1928–1945* (Hamburg, 1980), pp. 145–6.
36. Röder, 'Drehscheibe – Kampfposten – Fluchstation', p. 22.
37. Černý, *Most k novému životu*, pp. 19–20 & 23–7; Kühn, *Widerstand und Emigration*, pp. 131–2.
38. Kühn, *Widerstand und Emigration*, pp. 134–6.
39. Sayer, *Prague, capital of the twentieth century*, pp. 13–18.
40. Robert Kvaček, *Československý rok 1938* (Prague, 1988), p. 9.
41. G. E. R. Gedye, *Fallen bastions* (London, 1939), p. 407.
42. Sayer, *Prague, capital of the twentieth century*, pp. 142–4.
43. Mann lived in Switzerland until then. Magali Laure Nieradka, 'Der Mann von Proseč – Über die Familie Mann und Rudolf Fleischmann', in Brinson Charmian & Marian Malet (eds), *Exiles in and from Czechoslovakia during the 1930s and 1940s* (Amsterdam, 2009), pp. 7–19.
44. Anna Janištinová, 'Deutsche Künstler im Prager Exil 1933–1938', in ibid., pp. 38–9.
45. Ibid., pp. 33–6.
46. Ibid., pp. 29–32.
47. Prokop Drtina, *Československo můj osud* (2 vols, Toronto, 1982); vol. I, p. 45.
48. František Kubka, *Mezi válkami* (Prague, 1969), p. 173.
49. Monica Curtis (ed.), *Documents on international affairs 1938* (2 vols, London, 1943), vol. II, pp. 12–13. Translation in the original.
50. Ralf Gebel, *'Heim ins Reich!': Konrad Henlein und der Reichsgau Sudetenland (1938–1945)* (Munich, 1999), pp. 81–2.
51. Drtina, *Československo můj osud*, pp. 47–8.
52. Karník, *České země v éře První republiky*, vol. I, p. 558.
53. Ibid., vol. II, pp. 135–40; Gebel, *'Heim ins Reich!'*, pp. 29–30.
54. Karník, *České země v éře První republiky*, vol. II, pp. 140–2 & 185–95; Gebel, *'Heim ins Reich!'*, pp. 31–3.
55. Gedye, *Fallen bastions*, p. 393.
56. Gebel, *'Heim ins Reich!'*, p. 43; Bruegel, *Czechoslovakia before Munich*, p. 110.
57. Morrell, *I saw the crucifixion*, pp. 10–11.
58. Karník, *České země v éře První republiky*, vol. II, pp. 498–9.
59. Gebel, *'Heim ins Reich!'*, p. 24.
60. Morrell, *I saw the crucifixion*, p. 13.

61. Gebel, 'Heim ins Reich!', pp. 32–3, 45, 153 & 165; Radomír Luža, *The transfer of the Sudeten Germans* (London, 1964), p. 98; Mark Cornwall, 'Heinrich Rutha and the unraveling of a homosexual in Czechoslovakia', *GLQ*, 8 (2002), pp. 319–47.

62. Drtina, *Československo můj osud*, pp. 95–7.

63. Gebel, 'Heim ins Reich!', pp. 51–2; Bruegel, *Czechoslovakia before Munich*, pp. 116 & 131–2.

64. Bruegel, *Czechoslovakia before Munich*, p. 140.

65. Luža, *The transfer of the Sudeten Germans*, p. 60. Translation in the original.

2. The struggle begins

1. Gedye, *Fallen bastions*, pp. 334–9.

2. Vojtěch Mastný, *Vzpomínky diplomata* (Prague, 1997), pp. 78–9 & 86.

3. Mastný to Prague, 12 March 1938, in Jindřich Dejmek (ed.), *Československá zahraniční politika v roce 1938* (2 vols, Prague, 2000), vol. I, pp. 187–90.

4. Mastný, *Vzpomínky diplomata*, pp. 80–3; Krofta Memorandum, 24 February 1938, and Krofta to Osuský, 13 March 1938, Dejmek, *Československá zahraniční politika*, vol. I, pp. 133–5 & 194.

5. Gedye, *Fallen bastions*, p. 317.

6. See both the untitled editorial and 'Velké Německo', *Přítomnost*, 16 March 1938, pp. 161–7.

7. Karník, *České země v éře První republiky*, vol. I, pp. 169–77.

8. Morrell, *I saw the crucifixion*, pp. 77–81.

9. Zbyněk Zeman, *The life of Edvard Beneš* (Oxford, 1997), pp. 5–15.

10. Edvard Beneš, *Mnichovské dny* (Prague, 1968), pp. 198–9.

11. Cox, *Countdown to war*, p. 38.

12. Ibid.

13. Milan Hodža, *Die neue Situation Europas und die Tschekoslovakei* (Prague, 1938), p. 31.

14. Curtis, *Documents on international affairs*, pp. 117–20.

15. 'Záznam výkladu ministra zahraničních věcí K. Krofty', 3 March 1938, Dejmek, *Československá zahraniční politika*, vol. I, p. 162.

16. R. Laffan, 'The crisis over Czechoslovakia, January to September 1938', *Survey of International Affairs*, 2 (1951), pp. 58–9.

17. Karník, *České země v éře První republiky*, vol. III, p. 504.

18. Ibid., p. 513; Detlef Brandes, *Die Sudetendeutschen im Krisenjahr 1938* (Munich, 2008), pp. 67–8.

19. Růžena Hlušičková (ed.), *Protifašistický a národně osvobozenecký boj českého a slovenského lidu 1938–1945* (7 vols, Prague, 1979), vol. I/1/1, pp. 89–90.

20. Brandes, *Die Sudetendeutschen im Krisenjahr*, pp. 70–1 & 92–4.

21. Ibid., pp. 62–6.

22. *Deutsche Landpost*, 15 March 1938, p. 1 and 17 March 1938, p. 1; *Prager Tagblatt*, 17 March 1938, p. 3.

23. *Deutsche Landpost*, 24 March 1938, p. 1; *Prager Tagblatt*, 22 March 1938, pp. 1–2.

24. 'Bericht Konrad Henleins über seine Audienz beim Führer', March 1938, in Václav Král (ed.), *Die Deutschen in der Tschechoslowakei 1933–1947* (Prague, 1964), p. 163.

25. Bruegel, *Czechoslovakia before Munich*, p. 216. Translation in the original.

26. Beneš, *Mnichovské dny*, p. 40.

27. Paul-Boncour to Corbin, 21 March 1938, *Documents Diplomatiques Français 1932–1939*, [DDF], Second Series (19 vols, Paris, 1963–86), vol. IX, pp. 4–6.

28. *Le Temps*, 13 April 1938, p. 6.

29. Curtis, *Documents on international affairs*, pp. 120–3.

30. Beneš, *Mnichovské dny*, pp. 43–4.

31. 'Record of Anglo–French conversations, held at No. 10 Downing Street, on April 28 and 29, 1938', *Documents on British Foreign Policy, 1919–1939* [DBFP], Third Series (10 vols, London, 1949), vol. I, pp. 212–16.

32. Ibid., pp. 216–19; the French version of the document is at DDF, Second Series, vol. IX, pp. 562–87.

33. 'Record of Anglo–French conversations', DBFP, Third Series, vol. I, pp. 219–22.

34. Ibid., pp. 222–3.

35. Ibid., p. 226.

36. 'Notes by Mr. Strang on conversations with members of His Majesty's Legation at Prague, May 26–7, 1938', 29 May 1938, ibid., p. 405; Masaryk to Prague, 10 March 1938, AMZV / Fond II/6 / Londýn / 1937–39, ff. 1–3.

37. R. H. Haigh, D. S. Morris, & A. R. Peters (eds), *The Guardian book of Munich* (Aldershot, 1988), p. 9.

38. James Barnes & Patience Barnes, *Hitler's Mein Kampf in Britain and America* (Cambridge, 1980), pp. 45–8.

39. Václav Černý, *Křik koruny české, Paměti 1938–1945* (Brno, 1992), p. 28.

40. Seebacher-Brandt, 'Die deutsche politische Emigration', p. 236; Douglas Reed, *Nemesis? The story of Otto Strasser* (London, 1940), p. 189; Wenzel Jaksch, *Europe's road to Potsdam* (London, 1963), pp. 302–3.

41. For example Miloš Vaněk, 'Vydírat postupně', *Právo lidu*, 6 September 1938, p. 1.

42. Krofta to Osuský, 13 March 1938, Dejmek, *Československá zahraniční politka*, vol. I, p. 194.

43. Luža, *The transfer of the Sudeten Germans*, pp. 73–4. Translation in the original.

44. Drtina, *Československo můj osud*, pp. 91–4.

45. Karník, *České země v éře První republiky*, vol. II, p. 188; Kamil Krofta, *Z dob naší první republiky* (Prague, 1939), pp. 179–81.

46. Drtina, *Československo můj osud*, pp. 98–9.

47. The speech was ambiguous and was received with some puzzlement. Beran's preparedness to accommodate the SdP, though, seems attested to by a meeting with the German ambassador Ernst Eisenlohr, in which he mooted the topic: Eisenlohr to Berlin, 27 March 1938, DGFP, Series D, vol. II, pp. 193–6.

48. For the speech, see *Venkov*, 1 January 1938, p. 3. For reactions, see *Český deník*, 5 January, p. 1 or *Literární noviny*, 12 February 1938, pp. 1–2. On the controversy and Agrarian Party rectification, see Drtina, *Československo můj osud*, pp. 52–4 or Krofta, *Z dob naší první republiky*, pp. 243–4.

49. 'Henlein ante portas?', *Literární noviny*, 12 February 1938, pp. 1–2.

50. Newton to Halifax, 20 March 1938, DBFP, Third Series, vol. I., pp. 73–4.

51. Newton to Halifax, 11 April 1938, ibid., pp. 138–40.

52. Halifax to Newton, 23 March 1938, ibid., pp. 90–1.

53. Halifax to Newton, 12 April 1938, ibid., pp. 149–50.

54. Daniel Hucker, *Public opinion and the end of appeasement in Britain and France* (Farnham, 2011), pp. 29, 43 & 48.

55. 16 May 1938, quoted in Haigh et al., *The Guardian book of Munich*, pp. 23–4.

56. Faber, *Munich*, p. 189.

57. Ibid., pp. 191–3.

58. Ibid., pp. 191–2.

59. Kubka, *Mezi válkami*, pp. 157–62.

60. Yvon Lacaze, *L'opinion publique française et la crise de Munich* (Berlin, 1991), pp. 163–7, 360–70 & 383–420.

61. *L'Epoque*, 16 April 1938, p. 5.

62. Rudolf Jaworski, 'Die Tschechoslowakei in der NS-Propaganda des Jahres 1938', in Glotz, *München 1938*, pp. 164–72.

63. Engelbert Schwarzenbeck, *Nationalsozialistische Pressepolitik und die Sudetenkrise 1938* (Munich, 1979), pp. 242–3 & 319–21.

64. Brandes, *Die Sudetendeutschen im Krisenjahr*, pp. 43–4; František Vašek, 'Diverzní a psychologické operace II. Oddělení Abwehru v severovýchodných Čechách a severozápadní Moravě 1936–1939' in Zdeněk Radvanovský (ed.), *Historie okupovaného pohraničí 1938–1945* (12 vols, Ústí nad Labem, 1999), vol. I, p. 42.

65. Masaryk to Prague, 24 February 1938, Dejmek, *Československá zahraniční politka*, vol. I, p. 137.

66. Morrell, *I saw the crucifixion*, pp. 65–6.

67. Beneš, *Mnichovské dny*, p. 34.

68. Beneš to Paris, London, and Berlin, 11 April 1938, ibid., pp. 352–4; Krofta to Paris, London, and Berlin, 12 April 1938, Dejmek, *Československá zahraniční politka*, vol. I, p. 314.

69. Karník, *České země v éře První republiky*, vol. III, p. 512; Beneš, *Mnichovské dny*, p. 34.

70. Bruegel, *Czechoslovakia before Munich*, p. 127; Brandes, *Die Sudetendeutschen im Krisenjahr*, pp. 59–60.

71. Cox, *Countdown to war*, p. 45.

72. Gedye, *Fallen bastions*, p. 406.

73. Morrell, *I saw the crucifixion*, p. 16; Hlušičková, *Protifašistický boj*, vol. I/1/2, p. 9.

74. *L'Epoque*, 16 April 1938, p. 5.

75. Keith Robbins, 'Konrad Henlein, the Sudeten question and British foreign policy', *The Historical Journal*, 12 (1969), pp. 674–97.

76. Ibid., p. 675; Paul Vyšný, *The Runciman mission to Czechoslovakia* (Basingstoke, 2003), p. 8.

77. 'Note of a conversation with Mr. Churchill and Sir Archibald Sinclair', 15 May 1938, DBFP, Third Series, vol. I, pp. 633–5; Harold Nicolson, *Diaries and letters, 1930–39* (London, 1966), pp. 340–1.

78. Robbins, 'Konrad Henlein in British foreign policy', pp. 693–4.

79. Vyšný, *The Runciman mission*, p. 13.

3. Faithful we remain

1. *Český deník*, 26 April 1938, p. 1

2. *Lidové noviny*, 25 April 1938, p. 1.

3. Alexander Henderson, *Eyewitness in Czechoslovakia* (London, 1939), pp. 44–6; Hlušičková, *Protifašistický boj*, vol. I/1/2, pp. 8–10.

4. *Der Lebenswille des Sudetendeutschtums* (Carlsbad, 1938), pp. 20–35.

5. Ibid., pp. 36–54.

6. Ibid., pp. 63–94; see also Curtis, *Documents on international affairs*,
    pp. 130–7.

7. *Lidové noviny*, 27 April 1938, p. 1.

8. 'Co máme dělat?', *Lidové noviny*, 26 April 1938, p. 1.

9. P. V., 'Jasná odpověď na jasnou řeč', *Přítomnost*, 27 April 1938, p. 258.

10. Kvaček, *Československý rok 1938*, pp. 77–9; *Lidové noviny*, 2 May 1938, pp. 1–3.

11. *A-Zet*, 2 May 1938, p. 1; *Národní politika*, 1 May 1938, p. 1.

12. Brandes, *Die Sudetendeutschen im Krisenjahr*, pp. 136–7.

13. Adolf Zeman, *Československá golgota* (Prague, 1947), pp. 41–2.

14. *Mnichov v dokumentech* (2 vols, Prague, 1958), vol. II, p. 82; Hlušičková,
    Protifašistický boj, vol. I/1/1, pp. 174–5 & vol. I/1/2, pp. 18–20.

15. Hlušičková, *Protifašistický boj*, vol. I/1/2, pp. 69–70.

16. Karník, *České země v éře První republiky*, vol. III, pp. 595–6; Kvaček,
    Československý rok 1938, p. 139.

17. Hlušičková, *Protifašistický boj*, vol. I/1/2, pp. 63–6.

18. Brandes, *Die Sudetendeutschen im Krisenjahr*, pp. 132–6 & 173.

19. Newton to Halifax, 8 May 1938, DDFP, Third Series, vol. I, pp. 263–4; Beneš,
    Mnichovské dny, pp. 55–8.

20. Beneš, *Mnichovské dny*, pp. 364–9.

21. Taylor, *Munich: the price of peace*, pp. 390–1.

22. Karník, *České země v éře První republiky*, vol. III, pp. 524–5; Jaroslav
    Kokoska, *Spor o agenta A-54* (Prague, 1994), p. 85.

23. Faber, *Munich*, p. 179.

24. Pavel Šrámek, *Československá armáda v roce 1938* (Brno, 1996), p. 30.

25. Cox, *Countdown to war*, p. 16.

26. Kubka, *Mezi válkami*, p. 166.

27. Karník, *České země v éře První republiky*, vol. II, p. 528.

28. Kvaček, *Československý rok 1938*, pp. 52–3 & 57–8.

29. Yvon Lacaze, *La France et Munich: étude d'un processus décisionnel en matière
    de relations internationales* (Berne, 1992), pp. 133–4.

30. Brandes, *Die Sudetendeutschen im Krisenjahr*, p. 155.

31. Karel Zelený (ed.), *Vyhnání Čechů z pohraničí 1938* (2 vols, Prague, 1996), vol.
    I, p. 162.

32. 'Memorandum on Operation "Green"', 22 April 1938 and 'Directive for
    Operation "Green" from the Führer to the Commanders in Chief', 30 May
    1938, DGFP, Series D, vol. II, pp. 239–40 & 357–62; William Shirer, *The rise
    and fall of the Third Reich* (3rd edn, New York, 1992), p. 496. Translation in
    the original.

33. Morrell, *I saw the crucifixion*, pp. 63–4.

34. Ibid., pp. 62–3; Cox, *Countdown to war*, p. 38.

35. Curtis, *Documents on international affairs*, pp. 151–62; Beneš, *Mnichovské dny*, pp. 111–14.

36. Halifax to Henderson, 4 May 1938, DBFP, Third Series, vol. I, pp. 243–5.

37. Beneš, *Mnichovské dny*, p. 94.

38. Ibid., pp. 91–2.

39. Halifax to Bonnet, 7 July 1938, DBFP, Third Series, vol. I, pp. 545–6.

40. Brandes, *Die Sudetendeutschen im Krisenjahr*, p. 202.

41. Beneš, *Mnichovské dny*, pp. 110–13.

42. Masaryk to Prague, 29 June 1938, Dejmek, *Československá zahraniční politika*, vol. I, p. 586.

43. Osuský to Beneš, 21 September 1938, ibid., vol. II, p. 349.

44. Lacaze, *L'opinion française et Munich*, pp. 96–8; Edvard Beneš *Paměti: od Mnichova k nové válce a k novému vitežstvi* (Prague, 1947), pp. 49 & 56.

45. Curtis, *Documents on international affairs*, pp. 142–4. Translation in the original.

46. Marek Waic, *Sokol v české společností 1862–1938* (Prague, 1996), pp. 12–15 & 103–7.

47. Kvaček, *Československý rok 1938*, pp. 117–23.

48. Jan Uhlíř, 'X. všesokolský slet roku 1938 a podíl sokolstva na zápase obranu republiky', *Historie a vojenství*, 4 (1997), pp. 47–70.

49. Morrell, *I saw the crucifixion*, pp. 73–6.

50. Weisskopf, *The agony of Czechoslovakia*, p. 73.

51. Kvaček, *Československý rok 1938*, pp. 117–23; Morrell, *I saw the crucifixion*, pp. 71–2.

52. Uhlíř, 'X. všesokolský slet', pp. 48–53.

53. Ibid., pp. 53–9.

54. Weisskopf, *The agony of Czechoslovakia*, pp. 74–5.

4. Czechs and Germans

1. Robert Kaplan, *Balkan ghosts: a journey through history* (New York, 1993), p. x.

2. For example, Mary Heimann, *Czechoslovakia: the state that failed* (New Haven, 2009), pp. 77–86.

3. 'Nuremberg and Aussig', *The Times*, 7 September, p. 13; Halifax to Henderson, 4 May 1938, DBFP, vol. I, pp. 243–5; Faber, *Munich*, p. 205.

4. See Marcus Banks, *Ethnicity: anthropological constructions* (London, 1996), pp. 1–2 & 39–48.
5. George De Vos & Lola Romanucci-Ross (eds), *Ethnic identity: creation, conflict, and accommodation* (3rd edn, Walnut Creek, 1995), pp. 13 & 23–4.
6. Walker Connor, 'The nation and its myth', in Anthony D. Smith (ed.), *Ethnicity and nationalism* (Leiden, 1992), p. 50.
7. Charles Ingrao, *The Habsburg monarchy 1618–1815* (Cambridge, 1994), pp. 36–7.
8. Ibid., pp. 99–100.
9. James Van Horn Melton, *Absolutism and the eighteenth-century origins of compulsory schooling in Prussia and Austria* (Cambridge, 1988), p. 225.
10. Jaksch, *Europe's road to Potsdam*, pp. 66–7.
11. K. V. Müller, 'Volksbiologische Beziehung zwischen Tschechen und Deutschen', in Helmut Preidel (ed.), *Die Deutschen in Böhmen und Mähren* (Gräfelfing, 1952), pp. 295–9.
12. The list of names can be found in Konstantin Höss, *Die SdP im Parlament: ein Jahresbericht 1935/6* (Carlsbad, 1937), pp. 35–7.
13. Josef Krejčí, 'Kolik je Němců v Československo?', *Přítomnost*, 25 May 1938, pp. 333–4.
14. Josef Krejčí, 'Ochránci čisté rasy', *Přítomnost*, 4 May 1938, pp. 275–6.
15. Gebel, *'Heim ins Reich!'*, p. 43.
16. Hubert Masařík, *Le dernier témoin de Munich* (Lausanne, 2006), p. 48.
17. Elizabeth Wiskemann, 'Czechs and Germans after Munich', *Foreign Affairs* (October 1938), pp. 291–2.
18. Ibid.
19. Nathan Glazer & Daniel Moynihan (eds), *Ethnicity: theory and experience* (Cambridge, Mass., 1975), p. 19.
20. Luža, *The transfer of the Sudeten Germans*, p. 2.
21. On ethnicity and boundaries, see Fredrik Barth, *Ethnic groups and boundaries* (London, 1969), pp. 9–38.
22. Elizabeth Wiskemann, *Czechs and Germans* (2nd edn, Oxford, 1967), pp. vii–x.
23. Ibid., p. 1.
24. Pavel Doležal, *Tomáš G. Masaryk, Max Brod und das Prager Tagblatt (1918–1938)* (Frankfurt, 2004), pp. 108–13.
25. Vyšný, *The Runciman mission*, p. 142.
26. V. K-ý, 'Kdo potlačuje naše Němce?', *Přítomnost*, 27 July 1938, pp. 468–9.
27. Henderson, *Eyewitness in Czechoslovakia*, p. 85. Translation in the original.

28. Brandes, *Die Sudetendeutschen im Krisenjahr*, pp. 77–82.

29. Bruegel, *Czechoslovakia before Munich*, p. 223.

30. Brandes, *Die Sudetendeutschen im Krisenjahr*, p. 182.

31. Henderson, *Eyewitness in Czechoslovakia*, pp. 95–6.

32. Luža, *The transfer of the Sudeten Germans*, p. 126. Translation in the original.

33. Brandes, *Die Sudetendeutschen im Krisenjahr*, pp. 252–8.

34. Hans Lemberg, 'Tschechen und Deutsche in der ersten Tschechoslowakischen Republik', in Glotz, *München 1938*, p. 49.

35. Brandes, *Die Sudetendeutschen im Krisenjahr*, pp. 32–5 & 120.

36. Ibid., p. 7.

37. Karník, *České země v éře První republiky*, vol. III, pp. 506–7.

38. Weisskopf, *The agony of Czechoslovakia*, pp. 15–18.

39. Karník, *České země v éře První republiky*, vol. III, pp. 506–7.

40. Maurice Hindus, *We shall live again* (London, 1939), pp. 146–7.

41. Bruegel, *Czechoslovakia before Munich*, pp. 83, 144 & 150.

42. Wiskemann, *Czechs and Germans*, pp. 149–53.

43. Bruegel, *Czechoslovakia before Munich*, pp. 149–50; Luža, *The transfer of the Sudeten Germans*, pp. 43–4.

44. Brandes, *Die Sudetendeutschen im Krisenjahr*, pp. 30–5.

45. Emil Adam & Vitězslav Jurásek (eds), *Vzpomínky IV, Soužití čechů a němců na Znojemsku* (Znojmo, 2006), p. 27.

46. Brandes, *Die Sudetendeutschen im Krisenjahr*, pp. 89–91 & 98.

47. Zelený, *Vyhnání Čechů z pohraničí*, p. 102; see also Lubomir Doležel, *Život s literaturou* (Prague, 2013), pp. 26–7.

48. Zelený, *Vyhnání Čechů z pohraničí*, pp. 185–6.

49. Ibid., pp. 31, 39–41 & 111; see also Emil Ovčáček, *Opožděná zvědectví 1938* (Děčín, 1999), pp. 35 & 194.

50. Karník, *České země v éře První republiky*, vol. III, pp. 532–5; Brandes, *Die Sudetendeutschen im Krisenjahr*, pp. 183–6.

51. Karník, *České země v éře První republiky*, vol. II, pp. 498–9; Luža, *The transfer of the Sudeten Germans*, p. 59.

52. Gedye, *Fallen bastions*, p. 434.

53. Beneš, *Mnichovské dny*, pp. 85–6.

54. Ibid., pp. 103–4 & 115.

55. Lacaze, *La France et Munich*, p. 155.

56. Beneš, *Mnichovské dny*, p. 119.

57. Vyšný, *The Runciman mission*, pp. 103–4 & 111–13.

58. Lacaze, *La France et Munich*, pp. 156–9.

NOTES

59. Beneš, *Mnichovské dny*, pp. 147–9.
60. Vyšný, *The Runciman mission*, pp. 80–2.
61. Ibid., pp. 128–33.
62. Ibid., pp. 148–50; Beneš, *Mnichovské dny*, pp. 160–2.
63. Vyšný, *The Runciman mission*, p. 150.
64. Ibid., pp. 152–3.
65. Ibid., pp. 170–1.
66. 'Poslání lorda Runcimana', *Český deník*, 31 July 1938, pp. 1–2.
67. 'Proč anglický poradce?', *Venkov*, 28 July 1938, p. 2.
68. Ferdinand Peroutka, 'Co se děje?', *Přítomnost*, 17 August 1938, pp. 513–14.
69. Camill Hoffmann, *Politisches Tagebuch, 1932–1939* (Klagenfurt, 1995), pp. 212–13.
70. Masařík, *Le dernier témoin de Munich*, pp. 285–6.
71. Weisskopf, *The agony of Czechoslovakia*, pp. 79–81.
72. Bruegel, *Czechoslovakia before Munich*, p. 234.
73. Ibid., pp. 239–40; Vyšný, *The Runciman mission*, p. 175.
74. Taylor, *Munich: the price of peace*, p. 406.
75. Vyšný, *The Runciman mission*, pp. 221–2.
76. Ibid., p. 168.
77. Ibid., pp. 224–6.
78. Ibid., pp. 234–5.
79. Ibid., pp. 243–55.
80. Ibid., pp. 174, 215–16, 245, 275.
81. Ibid., p. 332.
82. Ibid., p. 238.
83. Ibid., pp. 263–4.
84. Ibid., pp. 268–70.
85. Ibid., pp. 271–2; Beneš, *Mnichovské dny*, pp. 218–20.
86. Vyšný, *The Runciman mission*, pp. 313–14.
87. Neville Henderson, *Failure of a mission, Berlin 1937–1939* (London, 1940), p. 130.
88. Vyšný, *The Runciman mission*, p. 312.
89. Hlušičková, *Protifašistický boj*, vol. I/1/3, pp. 18–19.
90. Ibid., vol. I/1/2, pp. 148–9; Kubka, *Mezi válkami*, p. 162.
91. Věra Holá (ed.), *Mnichov vzpomínková kronika* (Prague, 1969), pp. 125–7.
92. *Český deník*, 5 September 1938, p. 1.
93. Hlušičková, *Protifašistický boj*, vol. I/2/1, pp. 20–3.
94. Ibid., pp. 37–41.

95. Brandes, *Die Sudetendeutschen im Krisenjahr*, p. 247.

96. Cox, *Countdown to war*, p. 42.

97. Zdeněk Kalista, *Do proudu života* (2 vols, Brno, 1996), vol. II, p. 430.

98. Mastný, *Vzpomínky diplomata*, p. 117; Mastný to Prague, 6 August 1938, Dejmek, *Československá zahraniční politika*, vol. II, p. 112–13.

99. Curtis, *Documents on international affairs*, p. 189. Translation in the original.

100. Ibid., pp. 191–7.

101. Faber, *Munich*, p. 290.

102. Karník, *České země v éře První republiky*, vol. III, pp. 571–2; Brandes, *Die Sudetendeutschen im Krisenjahr*, pp. 260–1.

103. Brandes, *Die Sudetendeutschen im Krisenjahr*, p. 272.

104. Holá, *Mnichov vzpomínková kronika*, pp. 168–71; Gedye, *Fallen bastions*, pp. 447–8.

105. Brandes, *Die Sudetendeutschen im Krisenjahr*, p. 264; Henderson, *Eyewitness in Czechoslovakia*, p. 184; Hindus, *We shall live again*, p. 225; Joan Griffin & Jonathan Griffin, *Lost liberty? The ordeal of the Czechs and the future of freedom* (London, 1939), pp. 29–33; Morrell, *I saw the crucifixion*, pp. 153–4.

106. Henderson, *Eyewitness in Czechoslovakia*, pp. 179–80; Brandes, *Die Sudetendeutschen im Krisenjahr*, pp. 264–7; Griffin & Griffin, *Lost liberty?*, pp. 23–6.

107. Holá, *Mnichov vzpomínková kronika*, pp. 178–81; Brandes, *Die Sudetendeutschen im Krisenjahr*, p. 273.

108. Laffan, 'The crisis over Czechoslovakia', pp. 311–13.

109. Karník, *České země v éře První republiky*, vol. III, pp. 572–3.

110. Morrell, *I saw the crucifixion*, p. 176.

111. Schwarzenbeck, *Nationalsozialistische Pressepolitik*, pp. 356 & 362.

112. Brandes, *Die Sudetendeutschen im Krisenjahr*, p. 281.

113. Ibid., pp. 260–1; Laffan, 'The crisis over Czechoslovakia', pp. 312–16.

114. Hubert Ripka, *Munich: before and after* (London, 1939), pp. 47–8; Curtis, *Documents on international affairs*, pp. 205–6. Translation in the original.

115. Griffin & Griffin, *Lost liberty?*, pp. 40–1; Josef Hudl & Friedrich Slotty, 'Aufruf der Lehrer und Professoren', *Deutsche Zeitung Bohemia*, 18 September 1938, p. 1.

116. 'Die Situation in der SdP', *Deutsche Zeitung Bohemia*, 17 September 1938, p. 1.

117. Hlušičková, *Protifašistický boj*, vol. I/2/1, p. 107.

118. Gebel, 'Heim ins Reich!', p. 51.

119. Morrell, *I saw the crucifixion*, pp. 208–12 & 217–18. Translation in the original.

120. Gedye, *Fallen bastions*, pp. 408–9.
121. 'Ein Aufruf Henleins den er ganz allein zu verantworten hat', *Deutsche Zeitung Bohemia*, 16 September 1938, p. 1; partly quoted in translation in Griffin & Griffin, *Lost liberty?*, pp. 38–9.
122. Brandes, *Die Sudetendeutschen im Krisenjahr*, pp. 230–2.
123. Griffin & Griffin, *Lost liberty?*, pp. 42–5; Laffan, 'The crisis over Czechoslovakia', pp. 315–16.
124. Weisskopf, *The agony of Czechoslovakia*, pp. 106–8. Translation in the original.
125. Griffin & Griffin, *Lost liberty?*, p. 37; Ripka, *Munich: before and after*, pp. 18–21 & 28–31.

5. In the millions

1. Ripka, *Munich: before and after*, pp. 17–18.
2. 'Nuremberg and Aussig', *The Times*, 7 September 1938, p. 13.
3. Ladislav Feierabend, *Politické vzpomínky* (3 vols, Brno, 1994–6), vol. I, pp. 12–13.
4. Spectator, 'Válka jinými prostředky', *Přítomnost*, 14 September 1938, pp. 581–3.
5. Krofta circular telegram, 13 September 1938, Dejmek, *Československá zahraniční politika*, vol. II, p. 263.
6. Masaryk to Prague, 15 September 1938, ibid., pp. 278–9 and 283.
7. 'Záznam výkladu ministra zahraničních věcí' and Krofta to Paris and London, 16 September 1938, ibid., pp. 291–301 & 304–5.
8. 'Text of the Prime Minister's statement to the press on September 11, 1938', DBFP, vol. II, pp. 680–1.
9. Osuský to Prague, 13 September 1938, Dejmek, *Československá zahraniční politika*, vol. II, pp. 268–70.
10. John E. Dreifort, 'The French role in the least unpleasant solution', in Maya Latynski (ed.), *Reappraising the Munich Pact: continental perspectives* (Washington, D.C., 1992), pp. 38–9; reflections on Daladier's logic and his fear of French isolation are available at 'Munich', Archives Nationales [AN] / 496AP/ 8 / Dr2, ff. 16–18.
11. Lacaze, *La France et Munich*, pp. 181–2 & 189.
12. Lacroix to Bonnet, 17 September 1938, DDF, vol. XI, pp. 275–7; Beneš, *Mnichovské dny*, p. 243.
13. Lacaze, *La France et Munich*, pp. 199–200; Henri Noguères, *Munich, ou la drôle de paix* (Paris, 1963), pp. 138–9; Antoine Marès, 'Dossier J. Nečas',

in 'Munich 1938: mythes et réalités', *Revue des études slaves*, 52 (1979), pp. 135–40; Drtina, *Československo můj osud*, pp. 102–4.

14. Marès, 'Dossier J. Nečas', p. 138; Dejmek, *Československá zahraniční politka*, vol. II, pp. 284–5.

15. Lacaze, *La France et Munich*, pp. 201–2.

16. Osuský to Beneš, 19 September 1938, Dejmek, *Československá zahraniční politka*, vol. II, pp. 328 & 331.

17. Taylor, *Munich: the price of peace*, pp. 737–45; Shirer, *The rise and fall of the Third Reich*, pp. 521–4.

18. Faber, *Munich*, pp. 301–3.

19. 'Record of an Anglo–French conversation held at No. 10 Downing Street on September 18, 1938', DBFP, vol. II, pp. 373–99.

20. Ibid.

21. Ibid.

22. Curtis, *Documents on international affairs*, pp. 213–14.

23. Drtina, *Československo můj osud*, p. 108.

24. Curtis, *Documents on international affairs*, pp. 214–16.

25. Beneš, *Mnichovské dny*, pp. 259–60.

26. Ibid., p. 260.

27. Ibid. Hodža had separately asked Lacroix to explain whether and how the Anglo–French plan was compatible with the maintenance of France's treaty obligations: Lacaze, *La France et Munich*, pp. 211–13; Ripka, *Munich: before and after*, pp. 78–9 & 88–9.

28. Drtina, *Československo můj osud*, p. 114.

29. Ibid., pp. 112–13.

30. Beneš, *Mnichovské dny*, pp. 267–9.

31. Richard Vašek, 'Ve vládě v čase krize. Memoáry Františka Ježka', in Josef Tomeš & Richard Vašek (eds), *Mnichov ve vzpomínkách pamětníků* (Prague, 2012), pp. 52–3.

32. 'Protokol ze schůze ministerské rady', Hlušičková, *Protifašistický boj*, vol. I/2/1, pp. 121–6.

33. Ripka, *Munich: before and after*, p. 103.

34. Drtina, *Československo můj osud*, pp. 114–15.

35. Karník, *České země v éře První republiky*, vol. III, pp. 590–1.

36. Beneš, *Mnichovské dny*, pp. 261–2; Bonnet to Lacroix, 21 September 1938, DDF, Second Series, vol. XI, p. 394.

37. Curtis, *Documents on international affairs*, p. 217.

38. Rudolf Halík, 'Zrazeni ...', *Venkov*, 21 September 1938, p. 1.

39. Quoted in Ripka, *Munich: before and after*, pp. 99–100. Translation in the original.
40. Holá, *Mnichov vzpomínková kronika*, pp. 206–9.
41. Ibid.
42. http://www.ujdeto.cz/lyrics/jan-werich/proti-vetru-cz/, last consulted 5 December 2017.
43. Hlušičková, *Protifašistický boj*, vol. I/2/1, pp. 129–30.
44. Gedye, *Fallen bastions*, p. 466.
45. Karník, *České země v éře První republiky*, vol. III, pp. 592–3.
46. Ibid., pp. 582–3.
47. Henderson, *Eyewitness in Czechoslovakia*, p. 11.
48. Cox, *Countdown to war*, pp. 69–70.
49. Morrell, *I saw the crucifixion*, p. 195.
50. Cox, *Countdown to war*, p. 70; Henderson, *Eyewitness in Czechoslovakia*, p. 207; Černý, *Křik koruny české*, p. 58.
51. Feierabend, *Politické vzpomínky*, p. 17.
52. Drtina's account is at Drtina, *Československo můj osud*, pp. 117–29.
53. Morrell, *I saw the crucifixion*, p. 201.
54. Ripka, *Munich: before and after*, pp. 108–9. Translation in the original.
55. Ibid., pp. 106–8. Translation in the original.
56. *Český deník*, 22 September 1938, p. 1; *Právo lidu*, 22 September 1938, p. 1; see also Hindus, *We shall live again*, pp. 268 & 306.
57. 'Zkouška nervů a diplomatického umění', *Český deník*, 18 September 1938, p. 1.
58. *České slovo*, 22 September 1938, pp. 1 & 2.
59. Milena Jesenská, 'Průřez tří dnů', *Přítomnost*, 28 September 1938, pp. 613–15.
60. Hlušičková, *Protifašistický boj*, vol. I/2/2, pp. 4–10 & 24.
61. Holá, *Mnichov vzpomínková kronika*, p. 224.
62. Ripka, *Munich: before and after*, p. 142. Translation in the original.
63. Griffin & Griffin, *Lost liberty?*, pp. 75–6.
64. Kalista, *Do proudu života*, p. 432.
65. This account of the Godesberg talks is based on Shirer, *The rise and fall of the Third Reich*, pp. 530–5 and Taylor, *Munich: the price of peace*, pp. 805–19.
66. Shirer, *The rise and fall of the Third Reich*, pp. 534–5.
67. Brandes, *Die Sudetendeutschen im Krisenjahr*, p. 288.
68. Quoted in Griffin & Griffin, *Lost liberty?*, p. 95. Translation in the original.
69. Ibid., pp. 95–6.
70. Ibid., p. 98.

71. Brandes, *Die Sudetendeutschen im Krisenjahr*, p. 293.
72. Ibid., pp. 301–3.
73. Ibid., p. 309.
74. Drtina, *Československo můj osud*, pp. 137–9.
75. Cox, *Countdown to war*, pp. 70–1.
76. Ripka, *Munich: before and after*, p. 111.
77. Ibid., pp. 112–13; Beneš, *Mnichovské dny*, pp. 279–80.
78. Ripka, *Munich: before and after*, p. 105.
79. Beneš, *Mnichovské dny*, pp. 292–3.
80. Ibid.
81. Drtina, *Československo můj osud*, pp. 143–5.
82. Šrámek, *Československá armáda*, pp. 35–6.
83. Drtina, *Československo můj osud*, p. 149.

6. Preparing for war

1. Beneš, *Mnichovské dny*, pp. 301–2. For more information on this chapter, see P. E. Caquet, 'The balance of forces on the eve of Munich', *International History Review*, 40 (2018), pp. 20–40, online at www.tandfonline.com/10.108 0/07075332.2017.1309559.
2. H. C. T. Stronge, 'The Czechoslovak army and the Munich crisis: a personal memorandum', *War and society: a yearbook of military history*, 1 (1975), pp. 162–77, at p. 168; Milan Hauner, 'La Tchécoslovaquie en tant que facteur militaire', in Antoine Marès (ed.), 'Munich 1938: mythes et réalités', *Revue des études slaves*, 52 (1979), p. 187.
3. Šrámek, *Československá armáda*, pp. 14–16.
4. On military cooperation, see 'Etude de stratégie combinée', 1936, Service Historique de la Défense [SHD] / GR 7 N / 3110.
5. Lacaze, *La France et Munich*, pp. 361–2.
6. Bilateral talks and a conference in Bled, Yugoslavia, produced a set of agreements between the Little Entente and Hungary in August: Dejmek, *Československá zahraniční politka*, vol. I, pp. 196–7 & 238–9 & vol. II, pp. 162–70.
7. Ripka, *Munich: before and after*, p. 145.
8. Drtina, *Československo můj osud*, p. 154.
9. Williamson Murray, 'Munich, 1938: the military confrontation', *Journal of Strategic Studies*, 2 (1979), pp. 282–302, at p. 294.
10. Lacaze, *La France et Munich*, pp. 315–16.
11. Beneš, *Mnichovské dny*, pp. 303–7.

12. Lacaze, *La France et Munich*, pp. 324–6.
13. Quoted in Ripka, *Munich: before and after*, pp. 114–15. Translation in the original.
14. Anna Cienciala, 'The view from Warsaw', in Latynski, *Reappraising the Munich Pact*, pp. 90–2.
15. Faber, *Munich*, p. 315.
16. Hugh Ragsdale, *The Soviets, the Munich crisis, and the coming of World War II* (Cambridge, 2004), pp. 112–26.
17. Ibid., pp. 113–15 & 118.
18. Ibid., pp. 51–2; Curtis, *Documents on international affairs*, p. 139.
19. Curtis, *Documents on international affairs*, p. 109.
20. Ibid., pp. 224–5.
21. Williamson Murray, *The change in the European balance of power 1938–1939* (Princeton, 1984), p. 126; Miloslav John, *Září 1938: role a postoje spojenců ČSR* (Brno, 2000), pp. 246–7.
22. Lacaze, *La France et Munich*, p. 366; Ragsdale, *The Soviets, the Munich crisis, and the coming of World War II*, pp. 59–60. Ragsdale writes that evidence Romania did grant formal authorisation is fabricated, pp. 149–51.
23. Ragsdale, *The Soviets, the Munich crisis, and the coming of World War II*, pp. 89 & 140.
24. John, *Září 1938: role a postoje spojenců*, p. 262.
25. Ibid., pp. 263–6.
26. For studies of an eastern thrust through the Black Forest in the direction of Bohemia, see SHD / GR 7 N / 3715 & 3450.
27. Taylor, *Munich: the price of peace*, p. 709.
28. Jon Kimche, *The unfought battle* (London, 1968), p. 94; Mueller-Hillebrand, *Das Heer 1933–1945* (3 vols, Darmstadt, 1954), vol. I, pp. 38 & 42.
29. 'Directives pour l'offensive entre Rhin et Luxembourg', 9 June 1938, including maps and annexes, SHD / GR 7 N / 3715; preliminary studies at SHD / GR 7 N / 3450.
30. 'Instruction personnelle et secrète pour le commandant du groupe d'armées en vue des opérations initiales à conduire éventuellement entre Rhin et Moselle', 24 July 1939, SHD / GR 1 N / 48.
31. Lacaze, *La France et Munich*, pp. 466–7.
32. Sources: SHD / GR 7 N / 2325; GR 7 N / 3714 ; GR 7 N / 3603; GR 7 N / 3434; Mueller-Hillebrand, *Das Heer*, pp. 25–6, 59–61 & 75–9; Murray, 'Munich, 1938: the military confrontation', pp. 283–4; Šrámek, *Československá armáda*, pp. 66–7; František Nesvadba, *Proč nezahřměla děla* (Prague, 1986),

pp. 380–4; Zdeněk Procházka (ed.), *Vojenské dějiny Československa 1918–1939* (5 vols, Prague, 1985–9), vol. III, pp. 382–3, 477 & 513–16; and Miloslav John, *Září 1938* (2 vols, Brno, 1997), vol. II, pp. 34–44 & 208–9. Numbers exclude less combat-worthy territorial or *Landwehr* divisions.

33. The story of German rearmament and the obstacles it faced is told in full in Mueller-Hillebrand, *Das Heer*.

34. John, *Září 1938*, vol. II, pp. 165–7.

35. Winston S. Churchill, *The Second World War* (6 vols, Boston, 1948–53), vol. I, pp. 301–2.

36. Robert Jacomet, *L'armement de la France 1936–1939* (Paris, 1945), pp. 16, 87 & 289.

37. Henry Dutailly, *Les problèmes de l'armée de terre française, 1935–1939* (Paris, 1980), pp. 401–2.

38. Procházka, *Vojenské dějiny Československa 1918–1939*, p. 518; John, *Září 1938*, vol. II, pp. 129–30; Mueller-Hillebrand, *Das Heer*, pp. 72 & 133.

39. Hauner, 'La Tchécoslovaquie en tant que facteur militaire', p. 184; Ian Grimwood, *Hoping for the best but preparing for the worst: the aftermath of Munich* (London, 1998), p. 202.

40. Kenneth Macksey, *Guderian panzer general* (London, 1975), pp. 65–6; Kimche, *The unfought battle*, pp. 139–40; John, *Září 1938*, vol. I pp. 73–5 & vol. II, pp. 129–30.

41. Maurice Gustave Gamelin, *Servir* (3 vols, Paris, 1946–7), vol. III, p. 65.

42. John, *Září 1938*, vol. II, pp. 85–7.

43. Williamson Murray, 'German air power and the Munich crisis', *War and society: a yearbook of military history*, 2 (1977), pp. 107–18, at p. 115; Greg Baughen, *The rise of the bomber: RAF–Army planning, 1919 to Munich 1938* (Stroud, 2016), pp. 220–4; Grimwood, *Hoping for the best*, pp. 32–3; Taylor, *Munich: the price of peace*, p. 865.

44. Murray, 'German air power', p. 111.

45. Air Ministry, *The rise and fall of the German air force* (Kew, 1948), pp. 19–20; Edward Homze, *Arming the Luftwaffe* (Lincoln, 1976), pp. 240–1; 'The growth of fighter command, July 1936–June 1940', The National Archives [TNA] / AIR 41/14, f. 69; 'Note pour Monsieur le Président du Conseil sur la situation des effectifs et des approvisionnements de l'armée de l'air', 22 November 1938, SHD / AI / 2B1; Procházka, *Vojenské dějiny Československa 1918–1939*, p. 518; and Nesvadba, *Proč nezahřměla děla*, pp. 138–40.

46. 'Rapport au conseil supérieur de l'air', 15 March 1938, SHD / AI / 1B5.

47. Air Ministry, *The rise and fall of the German air force*, pp. 19–20; Homze, *Arming the Luftwaffe*, pp. 240–1.

48. 'Establishment and strength of metropolitan force and overseas squadrons as at 30th September 1938', TNA / AIR 8/218; 'Note pour Monsieur le Président du Conseil', SHD / AI / 2B1; Procházka, *Vojenské dějiny Československa 1918–1939*, p. 518; Nesvadba, *Proč nezahřměla děla*, pp. 138–40.

49. 'Rapport au conseil supérieur de l'air', SHD / AI / 1B5.

50. Murray, 'German air power', pp. 111–12.

51. Baughen, *The rise of the bomber*, p. 227.

52. Murray, 'German air power', p. 115.

53. Ibid., pp. 111–17; Air Ministry, *The rise and fall of the German air force*, pp. 19–20.

54. Churchill, *The Second World War*, pp. 297 & 304.

55. 'Ansprache des Oberbefehlshaber des Heeres an die höhere Generalität des Heercs', July 1938, in Klaus-Jürgen Müller, *General Ludwig Beck, Studien und Dokumente zur politisch-militärischen Vorstellungswelt und Tätigkeit des Generalstabschefs des deutschen Heeres 1933–1938* (Boppard am Rhein, 1980), pp 563 4.

56. Hauner, 'La Tchécoslovaquie en tant que facteur militaire', pp. 188–9.

57. Rudolf Sander, 'Válečná československá armáda v září 1938', *Historie a vojenství*, 1 (1996), pp. 38–64, at pp. 53–4.

58. See prior tables plus Taylor, *Munich: the price of peace*, pp. 706–9; Murray, *The change in the European balance of power*, pp. 221–9.

59. Ludvík Svoboda, *Cestami života* (2 vols, Prague, 1971), vol. I, pp. 148–9; Weisskopf, *The agony of Czechoslovakia*, pp. 127–8.

60. Doc. 388-PS, 18 September 1938, *Nazi conspiracy and aggression* (11 vols, Washington, 1946–7), vol. III, pp. 345–6; Marian Zgorniak, 'Forces armées allemandes et tchécoslovaques en 1938', *Revue d'histoire de la deuxième guerre mondiale*, 122 (1981), pp. 61–72, at pp. 64–5; Murray, *The change in the European balance of power*, p. 230.

61. Jonathan Zorach, 'Czechoslovakia's fortifications', *Militärgeschichtliche Mitteilungen* (1976), pp. 81–94, at p. 85; Taylor, *Munich: the price of peace*, p. 399. There were also a few works in Slovakia.

62. Zorach, 'Czechoslovakia's fortifications', p. 85.

63. John, *Září 1938*, vol. II, p. 385.

64. Taylor, *Munich: the price of peace*, p. 713; John, *Září 1938*, vol. I, pp. 194–5 & vol. II, pp. 387–8.

65. Zorach, 'Czechoslovakia's fortifications', pp. 88–9.

66. Zgorniak, 'Forces armées allemandes et tchécoslovaques en 1938', pp. 69–70; Nesvadba, *Proč nezahřměla děla*, pp. 380–4.

67. 'Denkschrift über die Erfolgsaussichten einer kriegerischen Aktion gegen die Tschechoslowakei', 3 June 1938, in Müller, *General Ludwig Beck*, p. 531; Mueller-Hillebrand, *Das Heer*, p. 63.

68. 'Notes by Hitler's Adjutant (Schmundt) on Conference on Operation "Green"', 3 September 1938, and 'Manuscript Notes by Hitler's Adjutant (Schmundt) on Conference at Nuremberg', 9–10 September, DGFP, Series D, vol. II, pp. 686–7 & 727–30. Translation in the original.

69. This is sometimes labelled Plan VIII. See Zgorniak, 'Forces armées allemandes et tchécoslovaques en 1938', pp. 70–1 and maps in Nesvadba, *Proč nezahřměla děla*, p. 385 and Šrámek, *Československá armáda*, p. 70.

70. 'Ansprache des Oberbefehlshaber des Heeres an die höhere Generalität des Heeres', July 1938, in Müller, *General Ludwig Beck*, pp. 563–4.

71. Rundstedt had a mere three *Landwehr* divisions guarding his rear: Zgorniak, 'Forces armées allemandes et tchécoslovaques en 1938', p. 64.

72. 'Denkschrift über die Erfolgsaussichten einer kriegerischen Aktion gegen die Tschechoslowakei', 3 June 1938, in Müller, *General Ludwig Beck*, pp. 528–36.

73. Churchill, *The Second World War*, pp. 280–1.

74. M. Messerschmidt et al., '*Tableau de la situation stratégique chez les dirigeants allemands en 1938*', in René Girault (ed.), *La puissance en Europe 1938–1940* (Paris, 1984), p. 109.

75. Murray, *The change in the European balance of power*, pp. 220–1.

76. Ibid., pp. 7–9; Pierre Le Goyet, *Munich, un traquenard?* (Paris, 1988), pp. 382–3.

77. Murray, *The change in the European balance of power*, pp. 243–4.

78. Churchill, *The Second World War*, vol. I, pp. 281–2.

79. Masařík, *Le dernier témoin de Munich*, pp. 292–3.

80. Lacaze, *La France et Munich*, p. 163.

81. Shirer, *The rise and fall of the Third Reich*, pp. 515–18.

82. Ibid., p. 540.

83. Taylor, *Munich: the price of peace*, p. 701.

84. Mueller-Hillebrand, *Das Heer*, p. 63.

85. Taylor, *Munich: the price of peace*, pp. 524–5; Mesures prises au cours de la nuit du 23 au 24 septembre 1938', 24 September 1938 and 'Réunion des officiers du 1er Bureau, des EM des régions', 17 October 1938, SHD / GR7N / 2461 / 2.

7. Last orders

1. Vilém Sacher, *Pod rozstříleným praporem* (Prague, 1991), p. 11.
2. H. C. T. Stronge, 'The Czechoslovak army and the Munich crisis', p. 170.
3. Karník, *České země v éře První republiky*, vol. III, p. 612.
4. Cox, *Countdown to war*, pp. 71–2.
5. Ripka, *Munich: before and after*, p. 139. Translation in the original.
6. Ibid., p. 137.
7. Hlušičková, *Protifašistický boj*, vol. I/2/2, pp. 33–4.
8. Holá, *Mnichov vzpomínková kronika*, p. 279.
9. Morrell, *I saw the crucifixion*, p. 227.
10. Ibid., pp. 228–30.
11. Karník, *České země v éře První republiky*, vol. III, p. 613; Sander, 'Válečná československá armáda', p. 53.
12. Murray, *The change in the European balance of power*, p. 234.
13. Svoboda, *Cestami života*, pp. 121–5.
14. *Mnichov v dokumentech*, vol. II, p. 251.
15. Henderson, *Eyewitness in Czechoslovakia*, p. 218. Translation in the original.
16. Faber, *Munich*, p. 346.
17. Ibid., pp. 347–51.
18. Masaryk to Prague, 24 September 1938, Dejmek, *Československá zahraniční politka*, vol. II, p. 387.
19. Lacroix to Bonnet, 25 September 1938, DDF, Second Series, vol. XI, pp. 528–9.
20. Ripka, *Munich: before and after*, p. 120. Translation in the original.
21. 'Record of an Anglo–French conversation held at No. 10 Downing Street on September 25, 1938, 9.25 p.m.', DBFP, Third Series, vol. II, pp. 520–35.
22. Ibid.
23. 'Statement made by the prime minister to the cabinet on Monday, 26th September as to information conveyed to him that morning by General Gamelin', TNA / CAB 23/95/9, ff. 258–9. See also 'Conversation du général Gamelin avec M. Neville Chamberlain du 26 Septembre 1938', 27 September 1938, DDF, Second Series, vol. XI, pp. 612–13.
24. 'Compte rendu des conversations techniques du général Gamelin au cabinet office, 26 Septembre 1938', DDF, Second Series, vol. XI, pp. 571–5.
25. Curtis, *Documents on international affairs*, pp. 235–6.
26. Hucker, *Public opinion and the end of appeasement*, p. 254.
27. Ibid., pp. 66–7.
28. Ibid., p. 67.

29. Taylor, *Munich: the price of peace*, p. 832.
30. Lacaze, *L'opinion française et Munich*, pp. 67–8.
31. Taylor, *Munich: the price of peace*, pp. 772–5.
32. Lacaze, *L'opinion française et Munich*, pp. 611–12.
33. *Literární noviny*, 20 July 1938, pp. 1–2.
34. Ibid.
35. Černý, *Křik koruny české*, pp. 33–4.
36. *Mnichov v dokumentech*, vol. II, p. 292.
37. Černý, *Křik koruny české*, pp. 34–5.
38. *Mnichov v dokumentech*, vol. II, p. 293.
39. Ibid., pp. 296–9.
40. Ripka, *Munich: before and after*, p. 144.
41. *Mnichov v dokumentech*, vol. II, pp. 299–300.
42. Thomas Mann, *This peace* (New York, 1938), pp. 26–7.
43. Ripka, *Munich: before and after*, pp. 156–7; 'These men condemn Chamberlain', *Daily Herald*, 22 September 1938, p. 2.
44. Curtis, *Documents on international affairs*, pp. 270–1.
45. Griffin & Griffin, *Lost liberty?*, p. 119; Drtina, *Československo můj osud*, p. 175.
46. *Národní politika*, 30 September 1938, p. 2.
47. Kubka, *Mezi válkami*, p. 180.
48. Curtis, *Documents on international affairs*, pp. 249–60. Translation in the original.
49. Lacaze, *La France et Munich*, p. 223; 'Mesures prises au cours de la nuit du 23 au 24 septembre 1938', 24 September 1938 and 'Réunion des officiers du 1er Bureau, des EM des régions', 17 October 1938, SHD / GR7N / 2461 / 2.
50. Dreifort, 'The French role in the least unpleasant solution', p. 21.
51. Faber, *Munich*, pp. 357–9.
52. Curtis, *Documents on international affairs*, p. 261.
53. 'Letter from Mr. Chamberlain to Herr Hitler', 26 September 1938, DBFP, Third Series, vol. II, pp. 541–2.
54. 'Note of a conversation between Sir Horace Wilson and Herr Hitler at Berlin on September 26, 1938, 5pm', ibid., pp. 554–8.
55. Faber, *Munich*, pp. 377–8.
56. Taylor, *Munich: the price of peace*, pp. 881–8.
57. François-Poncet to Bonnet, 27 September 1938, DDF, Second Series, vol. XI, p. 589.
58. Lacaze, *La France et Munich*, pp. 238–9.

59. 'Note du ministre', 27 September 1938, DDF, Second Series, vol. XI, pp. 605–6.

60. Bonnet to François-Poncet, 28 September 1938, ibid., pp. 630–1.

61. Karník, *České země v éře První republiky*, vol. III, p. 612; Henderson, *Eyewitness in Czechoslovakia*, pp. 216–19.

62. Gedye, *Fallen bastions*, p. 453.

63. Milena Jesenská, 'Průřez tří dnů', *Přítomnost*, 28 September 1938, pp. 613–15.

64. Ibid.

65. Karník, *České země v éře První republiky*, vol. III, p. 614.

66. Cox, *Countdown to war*, p. 68.

67. 'Budeme se bránit', *Lidové noviny*, 26 September 1938, p. 1.

68. 'Národ je jednotný a nadšení', *Venkov*, 24 September 1938, p. 1.

69. 'Anglie rozhodnutá i pro válku', *Lidové noviny*, 28 September 1938, p. 1.

70. *Český deník*, 28 September 1938, p. 1.

71. *Právo lidu*, 24 September 1938, p. 1.

72. Griffin & Griffin, *Lost liberty?*, pp. 108–9.

73. Henderson, *Eyewitness in Czechoslovakia*, p. 220.

74. Brandes, *Die Sudetendeutschen im Krisenjahr*, p. 305.

75. Drtina, *Československo můj osud*, pp. 167–70.

76. Faber, *Munich*, p. 379.

77. Ripka, *Munich: before and after*, p. 198.

78. Beneš, *Mnichovské dny*, pp. 337–9; Aide-mémoire, 28 September 1938, Dejmek, *Československá zahraniční politka*, vol. II, pp. 436–8.

79. Kubka, *Mezi válkami*, p. 189.

80. Beneš, *Mnichovské dny*, pp. 332–4; Drtina, *Československo můj osud*, pp. 163–5.

81. Curtis, *Documents on international affairs*, p. 262.

82. Ragsdale, *The Soviets, the Munich crisis, and the coming of World War II*, p. 170.

83. Curtis, *Documents on international affairs*, pp. 262–7.

84. François-Poncet to Bonnet, 28 September 1938, DDF, Second Series, vol. XI, pp. 646–9.

85. Curtis, *Documents on international affairs*, p. 272.

86. Taylor, *Munich: the price of peace*, pp. 890–1.

87. Ibid., pp. 890–5; Faber, *Munich*, pp. 384–9.

8. An unbearable choice

1. Ripka, *Munich: before and after*, pp. 216–17.

2. Drtina, *Československo můj osud*, p. 178.

3. Masařík, *Le dernier témoin de Munich*, pp. 303–4 & 308.

4. Ibid., p. 304.

5. Ibid., pp. 304–5. Masařík's complete report, on which this account is based, is to be found in Masařík, *Le dernier témoin de Munich*, pp. 304–10, in French translation and in Hubert Masařík, *V proměnách Evropy: paměti československého diplomata* (Prague, 2002), pp. 241–4, in the Czech original.

6. Masařík, *Le dernier témoin de Munich*, p. 305.

7. Ibid., p. 306.

8. Faber, *Munich*, pp. 405–7.

9. Ibid., pp. 408–10; 'Munich, par Edouard Daladier', AN / 496AP/ 8 / Dr3, ff. 124–6.

10. Faber, *Munich*, p. 411.

11. Ibid., p. 412.

12. There is some confusion as to whether the Czechs were introduced into the *Führerbau* conference room itself or into rooms at the Hotel Regina. Taylor, after some verification, asserts that it was at the hotel: Taylor, *Munich: the price of peace*, p. 49. Daladier, in an interview given years later, assigned it to the *Führerbau* conference room: Le Goyet, *Munich, un traquenard?*, p. 361, while the text by Masařík is ambiguous. The Hotel Regina nevertheless appears to have been the most likely location.

13. Masařík, *Le dernier témoin de Munich*, pp. 308–9.

14. Ibid., pp. 306–7 & 309.

15. Le Goyet, *Munich, un traquenard?*, pp. 365–6; Noguères, *Munich, ou la drôle de paix*, p. 314.

16. André François-Poncet, *Souvenirs d'une ambassade à Berlin, Septembre 1831–Octobre 1938* (Paris, 1946), p. 333.

17. Masařík, *Le dernier témoin de Munich*, p. 307.

18. Milan Kundera, *The unbearable lightness of being* (London, 2000), p. 217.

19. Ripka, *Munich: before and after*, p. 229; Beneš, *Mnichovské dny*, p. 346.

20. Drtina, *Československo můj osud*, p. 180.

21. Ibid.; Vašek, 'Ve vládě v čase krize', pp. 54–5.

22. Hlušičková, *Protifašistický boj*, vol. I/2/2, pp. 102–3.

23. Drtina, *Československo můj osud*, pp. 180–2.

24. 'Protokol', Hlušičková, *Protifašistický boj*, vol. I/2/2, pp. 99–102.

25. Ibid.

26. Ibid.

27. Beneš, *Mnichovské dny*, pp. 340–1; Drtina, *Československo můj osud*, pp. 180–3.

28. Beneš, *Mnichovské dny*, pp. 341–2.

29. 'Protokol', Hlušičková, *Protifašistický boj*, vol. I/2/2, pp. 102–3.

30. Theodor Procházka, *The second republic* (New York, 1981), pp. 11–12.

31. Sirius, 'Kterou cestou?', *Venkov*, 30 September 1938, p. 1.

32. George Kennan, *From Prague after Munich: diplomatic papers, 1938–1940* (Princeton, 1968), p. v.

33. Holá, *Mnichov vzpomínková kronika*, pp. 309–10.

34. Morrell, *I saw the crucifixion*, pp. 287–9.

35. Feierabend, *Politické vzpomínky*, pp. 21–2.

36. Henderson, *Eyewitness in Czechoslovakia*, p. 230.

37. Holá, *Mnichov vzpomínková kronika*, pp. 319–20; Henderson, *Eyewitness in Czechoslovakia*, p. 231; Ripka, *Munich: before and after*, p. 235.

38. Gedye, *Fallen bastions*, pp. 487–8.

39. 'Ustoupili jsme přesile', *Lidové noviny*, 1 October 1938, p. 1.

40. 'Mnichovský diktát přijat s protestem k celému světu', *České slovo*, 1 October 1938, p. 1

41. 'Lide náš, zemědělci českoslovenští!', *Venkov*, 2 October 1938, p. 1.

42. Noguères, *Munich, ou la drôle de paix*, pp. 312–13.

43. Taylor, *Munich: the price of peace*, pp. 65–6.

44. François-Poncet, *Souvenirs d'une ambassade à Berlin*, p. 334.

45. Faber, *Munich*, p. 1.

46. Taylor, *Munich: the price of peace*, p. 65.

47. Hindus, *We shall live again*, p. 349.

48. *České slovo*, 1 October 1938, p. 2.

49. Hindus, *We shall live again*, p. 337.

50. Ripka, *Munich: before and after*, p. 231.

51. 'Záznam Kanceláře prezidenta republiky o návštěvě poslanců', Hlušičková, *Protifašistický boj*, vol. I/2/2, pp. 106–8; Holá, *Mnichov vzpomínková kronika*, pp. 348–57.

52. Ibid.

53. *Mnichov v dokumentech*, vol. II, p. 374.

54. *Lidové noviny*, 3 October 1938, p. 2.

55. Hlušičková, *Protifašistický boj*, vol. I/2/2, pp. 90–1 & 104–6.

56. Karník, *České země v éře První republiky*, vol. III, p. 618.

57. Ibid., pp. 619–20; Holá, *Mnichov vzpomínková kronika*, pp. 368–71; Drtina, *Československo můj osud*, pp. 188–90.

58. 'Předseda vlády arm. gen. Syrový mluví k občanstvu', *Venkov*, 1 October 1938, p. 1; Henderson, *Eyewitness in Czechoslovakia*, pp. 229–30.

9. After Munich

1. Feierabend, *Politické vzpomínky*, p. 55; Dušan Tomášek, *Deník druhé republiky* (Prague, 1988), p. 86; 'Coiffeur a tailor', Karel Blažek, *Lidové noviny*, 19 November 1938, p. 1.

2. Procházka, *The second republic*, p. 71.

3. Hlušičková, *Protifašistický boj*, vol. I/3/2, p. 50; Henderson, *Eyewitness in Czechoslovakia*, p. 200.

4. Tomášek, *Deník druhé republiky*, p. 27; Cox, *Countdown to war,* pp. 77–8.

5. Jan Gebhart & Jan Kuklík, *Druhá republika 1938–1939* (Prague, 2004), p. 33; Kvaček, *Československý rok 1938*, p. 251.

6. Zelený, *Vyhnání Čechů z pohraničí*, pp. 98, 104, 148 & 150.

7. Hlušičková, *Protifašistický boj*, vol. I/3/1, pp. 191–2; reports on the German occupation of Břeclav and German violence in Nýřansko, Moravská Ostrava, and Háje in *Mnichov v dokumentech*, vol. II, pp. 314–20 & 326–30; and Zelený, *Vyhnání Čechů z pohraničí*, pp. 26–7, 46–7, 50–3, 57–8, 95–6 & 172–3.

8. Zelený, *Vyhnání Čechů z pohraničí*, p. 98.

9. Ibid., pp. 38 & 104.

10. Radvanovský, *Historie okupovaného pohraničí*, vol. I, pp. 7–8.

11. Zelený, *Vyhnání Čechů z pohraničí*, pp. 34–5, 44–5 & 188–9.

12. Hlušičková, *Protifašistický boj*, vol. I/3/2, pp. 67–9 & 79–85; and for testimonials Zelený, *Vyhnání Čechů z pohraničí*, pp. 33–4 & 45–6.

13. Zelený, *Vyhnání Čechů z pohraničí*, pp. 37, 65 & 94.

14. Ibid., pp. 52–3.

15. Holá, *Mnichov vzpomínková kronika*, pp. 420–1.

16. Max Brod, *Une vie combative* (Paris, 1964), pp. 354–5; Henderson, *Eyewitness in Czechoslovakia*, p. 243.

17. Hlušičková, *Protifašistický boj*, vol. I/3/2, p. 100; Holá, *Mnichov vzpomínková kronika*, p. 410; Zelený, *Vyhnání Čechů z pohraničí*, p. 66.

18. Zelený, *Vyhnání Čechů z pohraničí*, p. 99.

19. Cox, *Countdown to war*, pp. 77–8.

20. R. G. Coulson, 'Czechoslovakian adventure', *Quarterly Review* (January 1939), pp. 138–9; Zelený, *Vyhnání Čechů z pohraničí*, pp. 163–4.

21. Coulson, 'Czechoslovakian adventure', pp. 130–1.

22. Ibid., pp. 132–3 & 137.

23. Gebel, *'Heim ins Reich!'*, p. 66.

24. Ibid., pp. 64–7.

25. Oldřich Sládek, *Zločinná role gestapa: nacistická bezpečnostní policie v českých zemích 1938–1945* (Prague, 1986), pp. 33–8.

26. Ibid., pp. 40–3.

27. Ibid., pp. 41 & 49.

28. Helena Krejčová, 'Židovská komunita v Sudetech a její osudy po Mnichovu – 1938', in Helena Krejčová (ed.), *Židé v Sudetech* (Prague, 2000), p. 133.

29. The treaty is in Curtis, *Documents on international affairs*, pp. 289–90.

30. Taylor, *Munich: the price of peace*, pp. 899–900.

31. Ibid., p. 56.

32. Procházka, *The second republic*, p. 18.

33. The proceedings are described in Procházka, *The second republic*, pp. 15–26 and in fuller detail in Karel Straka, *Vojáci, politici a diplomaté* (Prague, 2008).

34. Hlušičková, *Protifašistický boj*, vol. I/3/1, pp. 33, 40 & 53–4.

35. Procházka, *The second republic*, p. 29; Henderson, *Failure of a mission*, pp. 170–1.

36. Hencke to Berlin, 18 November 1938, in *Mnichov v dokumentech*, vol. II, pp. 348–51; Feierabend, *Politické vzpomínky*, pp. 37–8; Rudolf Procházka, 'O novou zahraniční politiku', *Národní listy*, 22 October 1938, p. 1.

37. Gebhart & Kuklík, *Druhá republika*, pp. 24–6; Procházka, *The second republic*, pp. 45–51.

38. Hlušičková, *Protifašistický boj*, vol. I/3/1, pp. 4–8.

39. Cienciala, 'The view from Warsaw', p. 93.

40. Lacaze, *La France et Munich*, pp. 361–2.

41. Procházka, *The second republic*, pp. 33–5; Feierabend, *Politické vzpomínky*, p. 40.

42. Feierabend, *Politické vzpomínky*, pp. 43–4; Gebhart & Kuklík, *Druhá republika*, pp. 153–4; Procházka, *The second republic*, pp. 35–40; Kennan, *From Prague after Munich*, pp. 58–74.

43. Feierabend, *Politické vzpomínky*, pp. 48–9.

44. Karník, *České země v éře První republiky*, vol. III, pp. 625–6; Gebhart & Kuklík, *Druhá republika*, pp. 26 & 153–5; Procházka, *The second republic*, p. 28.

45. Karník, *České země v éře První republiky*, vol. III, pp. 626–7; Feierabend, *Politické vzpomínky*, p. 51; Procházka, *The second republic*, pp. 41–2; and Gebhart & Kuklík, *Druhá republika*, pp. 163–4. For similar estimates produced by the Germans themselves, see Shirer, *The rise and fall of the Third Reich*, p. 569.

46. Hlušičková, *Protifašistický boj*, vol. I/3/1, pp. 6–7 & 39–40 and vol. I/3/2, pp. 107–9; Feierabend, *Politické vzpomínky*, pp. 35–6.

47. 'Nezapomeňte na hraničáře', *Lidové noviny*, 3 October 1938, p. 3; Francis Dostál Raška, 'Úprchlické tábory v Čechách a na Moravě po mnichovském diktátu', *Soudobé dějiny*, 8 (2001), pp. 732–45, at pp. 733–9; Tomášek, *Deník druhé republiky*, pp. 58 & 63; Jaroslav Macek, 'Uprchlíci z pohraničí v roce 1938', in Petr Prouza (ed.), *Češi a Němci historická tabu* (Prague, 1995), p. 135.

48. Feierabend, *Politické vzpomínky*, p. 83; Kvaček, *Československý rok 1938*, pp. 249–50; Raška, 'Úprchlické tábory', pp. 740–3.

49. Procházka, *The second republic*, pp. 60–1; Gebhart & Kuklík, *Druhá republika*, pp. 74–81.

50. Gebhart & Kuklík, *Druhá republika*, pp. 78–9 & 83–4; on Slovakia see also Kennan, *From Prague after Munich*, pp. 15–18.

51. Coulson, 'Czechoslovakian adventure', p. 141.

52. Petr Bílý, 'Nová Evropa', *Lidové noviny*, 4 October 1938, p. 1; quoted in Tomášek, *Deník druhé republiky*, p. 29.

53. *Národní listy*, 2 October 1938, p. 1; Rudolf Halík, 'Lidu pravdu!', *Venkov*, 4 October 1938, p. 1.

54. 'Co s německými uprchlíky?', *Přítomnost*, 12 October 1938, pp. 655–6.

55. Leaders by Rudolf Halík, *Venkov*, 22 & 23 October 1938, both p. 1.

56. *Venkov*, 12 November 1938, p. 1.

57. Gebhart & Kuklík, *Druhá republika*, pp. 45–7 & 50–73.

58. Procházka, *The second republic*, pp. 13–14; Gebhart & Kuklík, *Druhá republika*, pp. 152–8; Feierabend, *Politické vzpomínky*, pp. 102–3.

59. Gebhart & Kuklík, *Druhá republika*, pp. 146–7; Feierabend, *Politické vzpomínky*, pp. 104–5.

60. Kennan, *From Prague after Munich*, pp. 10–11 & 39.

61. Hencke to Berlin, 18 November 1938, in *Mnichov v dokumentech*, vol. II, pp. 348–51.

62. Zdeněk Smetáček, 'Mnichovská politika', *Lidové noviny*, 23 October 1938, p. 1.

63. Tomášek, *Deník druhé republiky*, p. 113.

64. Ibid., p. 123; Kennan, *From Prague after Munich*, pp. 39–40.

65. 'Bude se jezdit vpravo', *Český deník*, 12 November 1938, p. 3.

66. Gebhart & Kuklík, *Druhá republika*, p. 31; Gebel, *'Heim ins Reich!'*, pp. 101–35.

67. Gebel, *'Heim ins Reich!'*, pp. 239–43 & 263–7.

68. Ibid., pp. 146–56 & 164–76.

69. Henderson, *Eyewitness in Czechoslovakia*, p. 301. Translation in the original.

70. A. J. P. Taylor, *The origins of the Second World War* (London, 1961), p. 189.

71. Karl Josef Hahn, *Kristallnacht in Karlsbad* (Prague, 1998), pp. 70–87.

72. Gebhart & Kuklík, *Druhá republika*, p. 33.

73. Gebel, *'Heim ins Reich!'*, p. 78.

74. Livie Rothkirchenova, *Osud židů v protektorátu, 1939–1945* (Prague, 1991), pp. 19–22; Milena Jesenská, 'V zemi nikoho', *Přítomnost*, 29 December 1938, pp. 827–9.

75. Krejčová, 'Židovská komunita v Sudetech', pp. 129–30; Rothkirchenova, *Osud židů v protektorátu*, pp. 21–2.

76. Stanislav Biman, 'Nacionální proud v německé společnosti a jeho vztah k židům', in Krejčová, *Židé v Sudetech*, p. 113; Krejčová, 'Židovská komunita v Sudetech', p. 137; Zdeněk Radvanovský, 'K otázce uprchlíků z pohraničí českých zemí po Mnichovu 1938', in Radvanovský, *Historie okupovaného pohraničí*, vol. II, p. 44.

77. Rothkirchenova, *Osud židů v protektorátu*, p. 25.

78. Bohumil Černý, 'Emigrace židů z českých zemí v letech 1938–1941', in Ivan Pfaff (ed.), *Češi a svět* (Prague, 2000), p. 183; Brod, *Une vie combative*, pp. 346–8.

79. Seebacher-Brandt, 'Die deutsche politische Emigration der Tschechoslowakei', pp. 243–4; Bruegel, *Czechoslovakia before Munich*, pp. 301–2. Translation in the original.

80. Gebhart & Kuklík, *Druhá republika*, pp. 34–5; Procházka, *The second republic*, p. 32; Zelený, *Vyhnání Čechů z pohraničí*, pp. 19, 90–3 & 121.

81. 'Po záboru', *Lidové noviny*, 11 November 1938, p. 1.

82. Feierabend, *Politické vzpomínky*, pp. 79–80; Procházka, *The second republic*, pp. 75, 146 & 222; Straka, *Vojáci, politíci a diplomaté*, pp. 69–70.

83. Masařík, *Le dernier témoin de Munich*, pp. 233–5; Leonard Mosley, *On borrowed time* (London, 1969), pp. 23–4.

84. Hlušičková, *Protifašistický boj*, vol. I/3/1, pp. 51–3.

85. Ibid., vol. I/2/2, pp. 90–1.

86. Jiří Šolc, *Po boku prezidenta: generál František Moravec a jeho zpravodajská služba ve světle archivních dokumentů* (Prague, 2007), pp. 62–3.

Bibliography

Archives

London   The National Archives
Paris   Archives Nationales
             Service Historique de la Défense
Prague   Archiv Ministerstva Zahraničních Věcí
             Národní Archiv

Published archival collections

Dejmek, Jindřich (ed.), *Československá zahraniční politika v roce 1938*, 2 vols, Prague: Nakladatelství Karolinum, 2000.

Documents Diplomatiques Français, 1932–1939, Second Series, 19 vols, Paris: Imprimerie nationale, 1963–86.

Documents on British Foreign Policy, 1919–1939, Second and Third Series, 65 vols, London: HM Stationery Office, 1946.

Documents on German Foreign Policy, 1918–1945, Series D, 13 vols, London: HM Stationery Office, 1949–64.

Hlušičková, Růžena (ed.), *Protifašistický a národně osvobozenecký boj českého a slovenského lidu 1938–1945*, 7 vols, Prague: Státní ústřední archiv, 1979.

Král, Václav (ed.), *Die Deutschen in der Tschechoslowakei 1933–1947*, Prague: Nakladatelství ČSAV, 1964.

Mnichov v dokumentech, 2 vols, Prague: Státní nakladatelství politické literatury, 1958.

Nazi Conspiracy and Aggression, 11 vols, Washington: US GPO, 1946–7.

Printed sources

Der Lebenswille des Sudetendeutschtums, Carlsbad: Karl H. Frank, 1938.

Adam, Emil & Jurásek, Vitězslav (eds), *Vzpomínky IV, Soužití čechů a němců na Znojemsku*, Znojmo: Kruh občanů České republiky vyhnaných v r. 1938 z pohraničí, 2006.

Beneš, Edvard, *Paměti: od Mnichova k nové válce a k novému vitežstvi*, Prague: Orbis, 1947.

Beneš, Edvard, *Mníchovské dny*, Prague: Svoboda, 1968.

Brod, Max, *Une vie combative*, Paris: Gallimard, 1964.

Bruegel, Johann Wolfgang, *Czechoslovakia before Munich: the German minority problem and British appeasement*, Cambridge: Cambridge University Press, 1973.

Černý, Václav, *Křik koruny české, Paměti 1938–1945*, Brno: Atlantis, 1992.

Churchill, Winston S., *The Second World War*, 6 vols, Boston: Houghton Mifflin, 1948–53.

Coulson, R. G., 'Czechoslovakian adventure', *Quarterly Review* (January 1939).

Cox, Geoffrey, *Countdown to war: a personal memoir of Europe, 1938–1940*, London: W. Kimber, 1988.

Curtis, Monica (ed.), *Documents on international affairs 1938*, 2 vols, London: Oxford University Press, 1943.

Davenport, Marcia, *Too strong for fantasy*, New York: Charles Scribner's Sons, 1967.

Doležel, Lubomir, *Život s literaturou*, Prague: Academia, 2013.

Drtina, Prokop, *Československo můj osud*, 2 vols, Toronto: Sixty-eight Publishers, 1982.

Feierabend, Ladislav, *Politické vzpomínky*, 3 vols, Brno: Atlantis, 1994–6.

François-Poncet, André, *Souvenirs d'une ambassade à Berlin, Septembre 1831–Octobre 1938*, Paris: Flammarion, 1946.

Gamelin, Maurice Gustave, *Servir*, 3 vols, Paris: Plon, 1946–7.

Gedye, G. E. R., *Fallen bastions*, London: Gollancz, 1939.

Griffin, Joan & Griffin, Jonathan, *Lost liberty? The ordeal of the Czechs and the future of freedom*, London: Chatto & Windus, 1939.

Grossmann, Kurt, *Emigration, Geschichte der Hitler-Flüchtlinge 1933–1945*, Frankfurt: Europäische Verlagsanst, 1969.

Hahn, Karl Josef, *Kristallnacht in Karlsbad*, Prague: Vitalis, 1998.

Haigh, R. H., Morris, D. S. & Peters, A. R. (eds), *The Guardian book of Munich*, Aldershot: Wildwood House, 1988.

Halas, František, *Torso naděje*, Prague: Fr. Borový, 1945.

Henderson, Alexander, *Eyewitness in Czechoslovakia*, London: Harrap & Co., 1939.

Henderson, Neville, *Failure of a mission, Berlin 1937–1939*, London: Hodder & Stoughton, 1940.

Hindus, Maurice, *We shall live again*, London: Collins, 1939.

Hodža, Milan, *Die neue Situation Europas und die Tschekoslovakei*, Prague: Orbis, 1938.

Hoffmann, Camill, *Politisches Tagebuch, 1932–1939*, Klagenfurt: Alekto, 1995.

Holá, Věra (ed.), *Mnichov Vzpomínková kronika*, Prague: Svoboda, 1969.

Höss, Konstantin, *Die SdP im Parlament: ein Jahresbericht 1935/6*, Carlsbad: Karl Frank, 1937.

Jaksch, Wenzel, *Europe's road to Potsdam*, London: Thames & Hudson, 1963.

Janaček, Oldřich, *Z počátků odboje 1938–1941*, Prague: NV, 1969.

Kalista, Zdeněk, *Do proudu života*, 2 vols, Brno: Atlantis, 1996.

Kennan, George, *From Prague after Munich: diplomatic papers, 1938–1940*, Princeton: Princeton University Press, 1968.

Krofta, Kamil, *Z dob naší první republiky*, Prague: Laichter, 1939.

Kubka, František, *Mezi válkami*, Prague: Svoboda, 1969.

Kühn, Heinz, *Widerstand und Emigration: die Jahre 1928–1945*, Hamburg: Hoffmann und Campe, 1980.

Kundera, Milan, *The unbearable lightness of being*, London: Faber & Faber, 2000.

Mann, Thomas, *This peace*, New York: Alfred A. Knopf, 1938.

Masařík, Hubert, *Le dernier témoin de Munich*, Lausanne: Noir sur blanc, 2006.

Masařík, Hubert, *V proměnách Evropy: paměti československého diplomata*, Prague: Paseka, 2002.

Mastný, Vojtěch, *Vzpomínky diplomata*, Prague: Karolinum, 1997.

Morrell, Sydney, *I saw the crucifixion*, London: P. Davies, 1939.

Müller, Klaus-Jürgen, *General Ludwig Beck, Studien und Dokumente zur politisch-militärischen Vorstellungswelt und Tätigkeit des Generalstabschefs des deutschen Heeres 1933–1938*, Boppard am Rhein: Harald Boldt, 1980.

Nicolson, Harold, *Diaries and letters, 1930–39*, London: Collins, 1966.

Ovčáček, Emil, *Opožděná zvědectví 1938*, Děčín: Lev, 1999.

Reed, Douglas, *Nemesis? The story of Otto Strasser*, London: J. Cape, 1940.

Ripka, Hubert, *Munich: before and after*, London: Gollancz, 1939.

Sacher, Vilém, *Pod rozstříleným praporem*, Prague: NV, 1991.

Strasser, Otto, *Exil*, Munich: Strasser, 1958.

Stronge, H. C. T., 'The Czechoslovak army and the Munich crisis: a personal memorandum', *War and society: a yearbook of military history*, 1 (1975).

Svoboda, Ludvík, *Cestami života*, 2 vols, Prague: Naše vojsko, 1971.

Tomeš, Josef & Vašek, Richard (eds), *Mnichov ve vzpomínkách pamětníků*, Prague: Masarykův ústav, 2012.

Weisskopf, Kurt, *The agony of Czechoslovakia '38/68*, London: Elek, 1968.

Wiskemann, Elizabeth, *Czechs and Germans*, 2nd edn, Oxford: Oxford University Press, 1967.

Zelený, Karel (ed.), *Vyhnání Čechů z pohraničí 1938*, 2 vols, Prague: Ústav mezinárodních vztahů, 1996.

Zeman, Adolf, *Československá golgota*, Prague: Josef R. Vilímek, 1947.

Press

A-Zet	*Foreign Affairs*	*Národní politika*
České slovo	*L'Epoque*	*Prager Tagblatt*
Český deník	*Le Temps*	*Právo lidu*
Daily Herald	*Lidové noviny*	*Přítomnost*
Deutsche Landpost	*Literární noviny*	*Venkov*
Deutsche Zeitung Bohemia	*Národní listy*	

Secondary literature

Air Ministry, *The rise and fall of the German air force*, Kew: Public Record Office, 1948.

Banks, Marcus, *Ethnicity: anthropological constructions*, London: Routledge, 1996.

Barnes, James & Barnes, Patience, *Hitler's Mein Kampf in Britain and America*, Cambridge: Cambridge University Press, 1980.

Barth, Fredrik, *Ethnic groups and boundaries*, London: Allen & Unwin, 1969.

Baughen, Greg, *The rise of the bomber: RAF–Army planning, 1919 to Munich 1938*, Stroud: Fonthill Media, 2016.

Brandes, Detlef, *Die Sudetendeutschen im Krisenjahr 1938*, Munich: Oldenbourg, 2008.

Caquet, P. E. 'The balance of forces on the eve of Munich', *International History Review*, 40 (2018), pp. 20–40.

Černý, Bohumil, *Most k novému životu: německá emigrace v ČSR v letech 1933–1939*, Prague: Lidová demokracie, 1967.

Černý, Bohumil, 'Emigrace židů z českých zemí v letech 1938–1941', in Ivan Pfaff (ed.), *Češi a svět*, Prague: Euroslavica, 2000.

Charmian, Brinson & Malet, Marian, *Exiles in and from Czechoslovakia during the 1930s and 1940s*, Amsterdam: Rodopi, 2009.

Connor, Walker, 'The nation and its myth', in Anthony D. Smith (ed.), *Ethnicity and nationalism*, Leiden: E. J. Brill, 1992.

Cornwall, Mark, 'Heinrich Rutha and the unraveling of a homosexual in Czechoslovakia', *GLQ*, 8 (2002).

Crane, Richard Francis, *A French conscience in Prague: Louis Eugène Faucher and the abandonment of Czechoslovakia*, New York: Columbia University Press, 1996.

De Vos, George & Romanucci-Ross, Lola (eds), *Ethnic identity: creation, conflict, and accommodation*, 3rd edn, Walnut Creek: Altamira, 1995.

Doležal, Pavel, *Tomáš G. Masaryk, Max Brod und das Prager Tagblatt (1918–1938)*, Frankfurt: P. Lang, 2004.

Dutailly, Henry, *Les problèmes de l'armée de terre française, 1935–1939*, Paris: Imprimerie nationale, 1980.

Faber, David, *Munich: the 1938 appeasement crisis*, London: Pocket Books, 2009.

Gebel, Ralf, *'Heim ins Reich!': Konrad Henlein und der Reichsgau Sudetenland (1938–1945)*, Munich: R. Oldenbourg, 1999.

Gebhart, Jan & Kuklík, Jan, *Druhá republika 1938–1939*, Prague: Paseka, 2004.

Girault, René (ed.), *La puissance en Europe 1938–1940*, Paris: Sorbonne, 1984.

Glazer, Nathan & Moynihan, Daniel (eds), *Ethnicity: theory and experience*, Cambridge, Mass.: Harvard University Press, 1975.

Glotz, Peter (ed.), *München 1938: das Ende des alten Europa*, Essen: Hobbing, 1990.

Grimwood, Ian, *Hoping for the best but preparing for the worst: the aftermath of Munich*, London: Minerva Press, 1998.

Heimann, Mary, *Czechoslovakia: the state that failed*, New Haven: Yale University Press, 2009.

Heumos, Peter, *Drehscheibe Prag: zur deutschen Emigration in der Tschechoslowakei, 1933–1939*, Munich: Oldenbourg, 1992.

Homze, Edward, *Arming the Luftwaffe*, Lincoln: University of Nebraska Press, 1976.

Hucker, Daniel, *Public opinion and the end of appeasement in Britain and France*, Farnham: Ashgate, 2011.

Ingrao, Charles, *The Habsburg monarchy 1618–1815*, Cambridge: Cambridge University Press, 1994.

Jacomet, Robert, *L'armement de la France 1936–1939*, Paris: Lajeunesse, 1945.

John, Miloslav, *Září 1938*, 2 vols, Brno: Bonus A, 1997.

John, Miloslav, *Září 1938: role a postoje spojenců ČSR*, Brno: Votobia, 2000.

Kaplan, Robert, *Balkan ghosts: a journey through history*, New York: Picador, 1993.

Karník, Zdeněk, *České země v éře První republiky*, 3 vols, Prague: Libri, 2003.

Kimche, Jon, *The unfought battle*, London: Weidenfeld and Nicolson, 1968.

Kokoska, Jaroslav, *Spor o agenta A-54*, Prague: Naše Vojsko, 1994.

Kosatík, Pavel & Kolář, Michal, *Jan Masaryk, Pravdivý příběh*, Prague: Mladá fronta, 1998.

Krejčová, Helena (ed.), *Židé v Sudetech*, Prague: Česká křesťanská akademie, 2000.

Kvaček, Robert, *Československý rok 1938*, Prague: Panorama, 1988.

Lacaze, Yvon, *L'opinion publique française et la crise de Munich*, Berne: Peter Lang, 1991.

Lacaze, Yvon, *La France et Munich: étude d'un processus décisionnel en matière de relations internationales*, Berne: Peter Lang, 1992.

Laffan, R., 'The crisis over Czechoslovakia, January to September 1938', *Survey of International Affairs*, 2 (1951).

Latynski, Maya (ed.), *Reappraising the Munich Pact: continental perspectives*, Washington, D.C.: Woodrow Wilson Center, 1992.

Le Goyet, Pierre, *Munich, un traquenard?* Paris: France-Empire, 1988.

Luža, Radomír, *The transfer of the Sudeten Germans*, London: Routledge, 1964.

Macksey, Kenneth, *Guderian panzer general*, London: Macdonald and Lane's, 1975.

Marès, Antoine, 'Munich 1938: mythes et réalités', *Revue des études slaves*, 52 (1979).

Mosley, Leonard, *On borrowed time*, London: Weidenfeld & Nicolson, 1969.

Mueller-Hillebrand, Burkhart, *Das Heer 1933–1945*, 3 vols, Darmstadt: E. S. Mittler & Sohn, 1954.

Müller, K. V., 'Volksbiologische Beziehung zwischen Tschechen und Deutschen', in Helmut Preidel (ed.), *Die Deutschen in Böhmen und Mähren*, Gräfelfing: Edmund Gans, 1952.

Murray, Williamson, 'German air power and the Munich crisis', *War and society: a yearbook of military history*, 2 (1977).

Murray, Williamson, 'Munich, 1938: the military confrontation', *Journal of Strategic Studies*, 2 (1979).

Murray, Williamson, *The change in the European balance of power 1938–1939*, Princeton: Princeton University Press, 1984.

Nesvadba, František, *Proč nezahřměla děla*, Prague: Naše vojsko, 1986.

Noguères, Henri, *Munich, ou la drôle de paix*, Paris: Laffont, 1963.

Procházka, Theodor, *The second republic*, New York: Columbia University Press, 1981.

Procházka, Zdeněk (ed.), *Vojenské dějiny Československa 1918–1939*, 5 vols, Prague: Naše vojsko, 1985–9.

Prouza, Petr (ed.), *Češi a Němci historická tabu*, Prague: nadace Bernarda Bolzana, 1995.

Radvanovský, Zdeněk (ed.), *Historie okupovaného pohraničí 1938–1945*, 12 vols, Ústí nad Labem: Univerzita Jana Evangelisty Purkyně, 1999.

Ragsdale, Hugh, *The Soviets, the Munich crisis, and the coming of World War II*, Cambridge: Cambridge University Press, 2004.

Raška, Francis Dostál, 'Úprchlické tábory v Čechách a na Moravě po mnichovském diktátu', *Soudobé dějiny*, 8 (2001).

Robbins, Keith, 'Konrad Henlein, the Sudeten question and British foreign policy', *The Historical Journal*, 12 (1969).

Rothkirchenova, Livie, *Osud židů v protektorátu, 1939–1945*, Prague: Trizonia, 1991.

Sander, Rudolf, 'Válečná československá armáda v září 1938', *Historie a vojenství*, 6 (1995) & 1 (1996).

Sayer, Derek, *Prague, capital of the twentieth century: a surrealist history*, Princeton: Princeton University Press, 2013.

Schwarzenbeck, Engelbert, *Nationalsozialistische Pressepolitik und die Sudetenkrise 1938*, Munich: Minerva, 1979.

Shirer, William, *The rise and fall of the Third Reich*, 3rd edn, New York: Fawcett Crest, 1992.

Sládek, Oldřich, *Zločinná role gestapa: nacistická bezpečnostní policie v českých zemích 1938–1945*, Prague: Naše vojsko, 1986.

Šolc, Jiří, *Po boku prezidenta: generál František Moravec a jeho zpravodajská služba ve světle archivních dokumentů*, Prague: Naše vojsko, 2007.

Šrámek, Pavel, *Československá armáda v roce 1938*, Brno: Společnost přátel československého opevnění, 1996.

Straka, Karel, *Vojáci, politici a diplomaté*, Prague: Avis, 2008.

Sum, Antonín, *Otec a syn, Tomáš Garrigue a Jan Masarykové ve vzpomínkách přátel a pamětníků*, Prague: Pragma, 2000.

Taylor, A. J. P., *The origins of the Second World War*, London: Hamish Hamilton, 1961.

Taylor, Telford, *Munich: the price of peace*, London: Hodder and Stoughton, 1979.

Teichova, Alice, *An economic background to Munich*, Cambridge: Cambridge University Press, 1974.

Tomášek, Dušan, *Deník druhé republiky*, Prague: Naše vojsko, 1988.

Uhlíř, Jan, 'X. všesokolský slet roku 1938 a podíl sokolstva na zápase obranu republiky', *Historie a vojenství*, 4 (1997).

Van Horn Melton, James, *Absolutism and the eighteenth-century origins of compulsory schooling in Prussia and Austria*, Cambridge: Cambridge University Press, 1988.

Vyšný, Paul, *The Runciman mission to Czechoslovakia*, Basingstoke: Palgrave, 2003.

Waic, Marek, *Sokol v české společností 1862–1938*, Prague: Univerzita Karlova, 1996.

Zeman, Zbyňek, *The life of Edvard Beneš*, Oxford: Clarendon Press, 1997.

Zgorniak, Marian, 'Forces armécs allemandes et tchécoslovaques en 1938', *Revue d'histoire de la deuxième guerre mondiale*, 122 (1981).

Zorach, Jonathan 'Czechoslovakia's fortifications', *Militärgeschichtliche Mitteilungen* (1976).

Index

INDEX